STUFF MATTERS

HARRY BINGHAM

Stuff Matters

Genius, Risk and
the Secret of Capitalism

FOURTH ESTATE • *London*

First published in Great Britain in 2010 by
Fourth Estate
An imprint of HarperCollins*Publishers*
77–85 Fulham Palace Road
London W6 8JB
www.4thestate.co.uk

1

A catalogue record for this book is
available from the British Library

ISBN 978-0-00-726017-1

Typeset in Minion by G&M Designs Limited,
Raunds, Northamptonshire

Printed and bound in Great Britain
by Clays Ltd, St Ives plc

For N

'See how the true gift never leaves the giver:
returned and redelivered, it rolled on
until the smile poured through us like a river.'

CONTENTS

INTRODUCTION

This is a story which begins with a 7-year-old girl, a broken cooking pot, and a financial crisis.

The 7-year-old, Kat, is the daughter of some good friends of ours and not long ago she spent the weekend with my wife and me. Although we'd lined up a full programme of entertainment, the thing that Kat enjoyed most was our house, a picture perfect thatched cottage. She liked the huge old fireplaces, the chambers once used for smoking meat, the brick ovens used for baking bread. She loved scrambling up into the loft, where you can still see the original thatch poking through the original 350-year-old roof battens.

More than that, Kat was awestruck that the battens had simply been cut from the hedge outside the window, the thatching straw from the field just beyond. In Kat's world, things come from shops, or on trucks, or by order over the internet. Houses certainly aren't hand-built by their owners, using only materials to be found in the surrounding fields and hedgerows. In her eyes, the house was something from a fairy tale, a place that stood half a step from reality.

She was also peculiarly interested in an old metal cooking pot that stands on the hearth, and which we use to store newspaper, firelighters and other bits and pieces for the fire. Kat had somehow got it into her head that the cooking pot too was 350 years old and it fascinated her that this object had (as she thought) once been handled by someone old enough to be her eighteen-times-great grandmother. I didn't have the heart to put her straight for two reasons. First, because the pot certainly looks battered enough to have seen off a century or two, and second, because I knew that a widow once living in this house did own an iron cooking pot. I know that because a neighbour had lent me a volume of local history which happened to record the old lady's will, a document that bequeathed her terribly few possessions to different family members: a stool to one, some farming implements to another, a 'cooking pot with a broken lid' to a third and so on. Though she had almost nothing to leave, she nevertheless cared about the little she had. Back then, stuff *mattered*. Kat somehow sensed that. She understood that this fairy-tale world played by rules different from her own.

We had a lovely weekend with Kat, and when she left, the cooking pot reverted to its previous, non-magical status as Place to Store Firelighters. Quite likely, I'd have thought no more about it, except for the last ingredient of this tale: a financial crisis. Because all this took place the week after Fannie Mae and Freddie Mac imploded. The week when Lehman Brothers went spectacularly bust. The week when the Federal Reserve made an $85 billion loan to bail out the collapsed insurer AIG. The week when Merrill Lynch, a giant investment bank, was sold to Bank of America. The week when the speculative attacks on HBOS, a massive British bank, grew so intense that it too lost its independence.

Next to all of these calamities, the previous victims of the credit crunch hardly seemed to matter. Northern Rock? Phooey! What's £25 billion between friends? Prior to that week, the biggest American victim of the credit crunch had been Bear Stearns, an investment bank forced to sell out for a derisory $2.2 billion. This week, no one was deriding any sale, no matter how small the consideration. You almost got the feeling that if you'd walked down Wall Street in possession of $10 and a bagful of doughnuts, you could have purchased any bank you wanted. 'The doughnuts too, sir? You're too kind.'

In these giddy conditions, a quotation came into my head, one that I couldn't immediately place but which lingered anyway: 'All that is solid melts into air, all that is holy is profaned.' The rhythms were wrong, but the phrase possessed an almost Shakespearean intensity. Sensing that there was more to the fragment than I was remembering, I looked it up:

> All that is solid melts into air, all that is holy is profaned ...
>
> Modern bourgeois society ... a society that has conjured up such gigantic means of production and of exchange, is like the sorcerer who is no longer able to control the powers of the nether world whom he has called up by his spells ... It appears as if a famine, a universal war of devastation, had cut off the supply of every means of subsistence; industry and commerce seem to be destroyed. And why? Because there is too much civilization, too much means of subsistence, too much industry, too much commerce.
>
> – KARL MARX and FRIEDRICH ENGELS, *The Communist Manifesto*

Marx and Engels were writing 160 years ago, yet their description fits the 2008/9 financial crisis almost perfectly. All that is solid *has* melted into air – or, to be more precise, has melted into the hands of a number of very surprised governments and furious taxpayers, the Wall Street sorcerer no longer in control of his spells.

Now, it's probably best to say straight away that I'm no communist. I got a degree in economics from Oxford University, then went straight into the City, where I spent a couple of years working for J.P. Morgan, the same fine bank that went on to buy Bear Stearns for those $2.2 billion.

After two years, I quit. I was an idealistic soul and thought that my talents, such as they were, might be better directed for the Good of Humanity. I'd originally intended to use my training at J.P. Morgan to talk my way into the World Bank, but this was 1989. The Berlin Wall was being torn down. The decrepit Soviet empire was breaking up. The old socialist model had failed, but there was an immense amount of work to be done before the capitalist model could get going properly. In short, Eastern Europe needed help. It needed *me*. So I took a temporary post offering economic advice to the newly democratic government in Poland (it folded shortly afterwards), then found a full-time post at EBRD, a development bank set up to rebuild the East.

I spent the next eighteen months zooming round Eastern Europe, seeking to invest in the promising private enterprises which were springing up everywhere. It was a time of extraordinarily rapid change and, for those of us lucky enough to be in the right place at the right time, responsibility too. But I became disenchanted. Not with the Easterners, who were turning their countries round with extraordinary speed, but with the EBRD itself. The EBRD was owned by a consortium of several dozen governments from East and West, who encumbered it with a hopelessly top-heavy and bureaucractic approvals process. The longer I spent in Eastern Europe, the more I noticed that it was those greedy so-and-sos from the private sector who were doing all the really amazing work – pouring in money, people, skills, energy and know-how. We poor saps in the Good of Humanity sector were coming a distant and unbeloved second.

So I quit my job again. I interviewed with a number of banks, but ended up back where I'd started at J.P. Morgan, where I spent several happy years as a banker in the mergers and acquisitions department. I made money. I worked with some very nice and able people. I enjoyed huge levels of responsibility and expectation. I might have gone on merging and acquiring for many more years to come but, at the end of the 1990s, my wife, Nuala, became ill, bed-bound, edge-of-life-and-death, terrifyingly ill.

So I moved on once more, from the City to the bedside. I cared for Nuala and wrote my first novel. I got an agent. I got a publisher. I found myself stumbling backwards into a new career, making the move from one of the best paid, most widely loathed occupations in existence to one of the worst paying, but most highly regarded ones.

People often ask me if I miss investment banking. I certainly enjoyed my time there, but enjoyment isn't the deepest kind of satisfaction there is. Banking always felt like work – enjoyable, demanding, varied, responsible work, to be sure – but nevertheless something that nobody of sound mind would ever do for fun. Writing has never felt like that. For the last ten years or so, I've put in plenty of hours at the keyboard, and almost none of those hours have felt like work. I feel as though I've found some important part of my essence as a writer. That's the good part. The bad part is that, for all but a very few authors, writing doesn't provide enough income to live on. Most authors supplement their income in other ways and, as soon as Nuala was strong enough for me to give up my role as full-time carer and part-time author, I too rooted around for other ways to make a buck. In 2005, I set up a company called the Writers' Workshop. The idea was that we'd offer editorial advice to first-time writers. To begin with there were just two of us, me and a friend, also a professional author. We built a website, advertised our services, and waited for manuscripts to start rolling in.

And roll they did. To my continuing astonishment, the venture's been a success. Not the sort that buys a private jet and my own holiday island in the Caribbean but, in its own humble way, a success.

My reason for telling you all this is that my own eccentric personal journey through life connects back to that cooking pot. Over the last 350 years, some weird alchemy has taken place, which has utterly transformed the world and our expectations of being human. The Oxfordshire widow who lived in what is now my house seems poor to us today. Her few recorded possessions seem shockingly scanty. No books. No form of entertainment. No form of transport. Nothing mechanical. No complex method of lighting or heating. No soft furnishings. No decorative items that we know of. Nothing to bathe in. No form of time-keeping. No holidays. No health care worth the name. Rudimentary education at best. She'd have had salt, but no sugar, no spices, no tea, no coffee, not much meat. Particularly in winter and spring, her diet would have afforded terribly little variety. Some years, she'd have gone hungry too. She had a few tools for working the land, a few household items, and a minimal amount of furniture. That was all. When Kat encountered a tiny slice of that woman's life, she instantly recognized it as being utterly, astonishingly different from her own.

Yet that widow wasn't unusually poor. In 1674, the average Briton subsisted on somewhat less than $4 per day. Just to be perfectly clear, that number, the $4 a day, has been adjusted to give a figure directly comparable with today's money. The average Zimbabwean today is about as well off as that widow and her peers. They don't throw away broken cooking pots in Zimbabwe now, and they didn't throw them out in seventeenth-century Britain.

If you think that sounds awful, bear in mind that Britain was then the second richest country in the history of world (the Netherlands was somewhat richer). Viewed over the entire span of humanity's existence, seventeenth-century Britain was a place of extraordinary affluence, long lives, comfortable homes, educational and vocational opportunity. The Britain of that cooking pot represented close to the best that humanity had managed in its 199,650 years of existence. In the fifteen centuries following the birth of Christ, the average human lived on the equivalent of about $1.25 a day, an amount now regarded by economists as marking absolute poverty of the most pernicious sort. The kind of poverty that kills and starves, deprives and restricts.

These comparisons are worth hammering home because it's so easy to lose sight of the miracle that has happened over the last 250 years or so, and which Kat called attention to by her fascinated reaction to that vanished world. Some extraordinary alchemy has transformed the human lot from being one of almost universal, grinding poverty to one of very widespread affluence. For sure the world still has far too many poor people in it, but it has a darn sight more rich ones than ever it used to. The miracle of wealth creation is now so well established, so taken for granted, that we start demanding more of it. Make Asia rich! Make Africa rich! Eliminate poverty! Eliminate infectious disease! Free health care for all! Put humans on Mars! Make me live to be a hundred! Low cost air fares, cheap motoring, *and* no climate change, please!

I'm not against those kinds of ambition. On the contrary, I'm entirely in favour of demanding a lot of ourselves, but what's stunning is that we can voice these kinds of aspirations without sounding crazed. Human history can, if you like, be divided in two phases. The first phase lasted for approximately 199,750 years, and represents mankind's existence in a world marked by generalized, extreme, brutish poverty, by horribly compromised life expectancy, by illiteracy and innumeracy, by men and women almost universally failing to achieve their potential.

The second phase, which has lasted 250 years so far, represents mankind's experience of extremely rapid self-enrichment. The world we live in now is one where things are made in China, ordered by laptop, and delivered in an eyeblink; a place of iPods and cornflakes, hedge funds and research labs; a place where roofing materials are no longer cut from hedges and scythed from fields. This world – Kat's world and ours – is mystifyingly complex, but somewhere in that complexity lies the philosopher's stone which turns lead into gold.

Alchemy, however, has its dark side and on the weekend of Kat's visit, that dark side was alive, well and destroying a bank near you. As London and New York convulsed in panic, I realized something shocking. I was a financially literate chap. I'd been an economist, a banker, and (in a very small way) an entrepreneur. Yet there was a respect in which I understood nothing at all about how the world works. I could sketch out supply and demand curves and explain the laws of comparative advantage. I could even have told you what an Asset Backed Security was and how Credit Default Swaps worked and how Lehman Brothers went bankrupt.

But all this was an understanding of the intellect, an understanding that left the rest of me entirely blank. The fact that I understood my own tiny niche in the capitalist system had blinded me to my massive ignorance about everything else. I hadn't generally felt that ignorance, because my background had enabled me to sketch demand curves and blather about different types of security. Nevertheless, the extent of my unknowing was profound. It was though I'd read a million books about Italy without ever having been there.

In the weeks after Kat left us, as governments and central bankers started to mop up after the hurricane, I realized that I wanted to write a guidebook about the world of money. I wanted to understand, and not just at an intellectual level, the magic of the alchemy that has plucked the human race from extreme poverty to its current position of ever-expanding riches. I wanted to understand the storms that blow up out of nowhere, seeming to threaten every assumption which we once took for granted. I wanted to meet the people who make that world turn: multimillionaire entrepreneurs and Indian shift-workers, small-time manufacturers and big company CEOs. I wanted to get to the heart of the miracle, the miracle that has transformed a poor and brutish world into an ever richer and more liberated one. And I wanted to explore the culture of this world, the deep rhythms that make it tick. Above all, I wanted to come to know it the way that a traveller might, with time, come to know Italy.

This book is the outcome of that exploration. The businessmen and women I've spoken to have led companies collectively worth hundreds of billions of dollars. The bankers I've spoken to have handled well over a trillion dollars' worth of mergers and acquisitions transactions and have invested uncountably huge sums on the world markets. But I've also met some of the little guys; the ordinary people doing ordinary jobs who nevertheless play their own crucial part in keeping this precarious alchemy afloat. In short, I wanted to find out about everything an economics degree does not cover, that ten years in the City never gets close to.

I still don't know how to refine oil, smelt metals, extrude plastic, etch silicon, write program codes, or do any other of those fine things that makes Kat's world the rich and prosperous world it is. But I do now have an almost bodily sense of how the whole thing hangs together. I've learned how extraordinarily commonplace financial crises are and how the miracle of capitalism goes on happening nevertheless.

And my journey, unexpectedly, has gone further than that. It's all very well going places and meeting people, but I came to see that the alchemy of wealth happens inside each of us as well. We have strong feelings about money. We are alternately avaricious and ostentatious, greedy and generous, fearful and optimistic. My journey to the land of money wouldn't have been complete unless it stepped inside our own hearts and minds, our own hubbub of powerful emotions.

This book offers an account of my travels. It's given me a sense of the alchemy that turned our world from what it was to what it is, a man-made miracle of creation. It's also taken me to the heart of the paradox that lies at the heart of capitalism, a paradox by which money is both the most important thing there is and something that doesn't matter an iota. I came to see that economics, as taught at university and as reiterated by any number of economics bestsellers, is a fraud, a subject that purports to explain everything but doesn't even understand the thing that lies at its very heart: the human relationship to money.

But those things lie ahead of us, at the journey's end, not at its start. Because this is a trip that starts the only place it can: in the mind and instinct of the entrepreneur.

PART ONE

The Entrepreneur

ONE

Risk

> Men wanted for hazardous journey, small wages, bitter cold, long months of complete darkness, constant dangers, safe return doubtful. Honour and recognition in case of success.
>
> – Advertisement placed by ERNEST SHACKLETON in 1914

It begins with character. Character and a moment of risk.

The risk takes no single form. Perhaps to most of us the moment comes and goes without our even noticing. A conversation overheard; a difficult client with a wild-eyed plan; a death; an idea; a throat irritation.

Most of us, and I include me, look for the life more comfortable. Great wealth would be nice, of course, but we've learned by now that wealth doesn't make home visits. It's an animal to be hunted, not a guest to be entertained. Our desire for comfort – the regular pay cheque, hearth and home, keeping our capital somewhere safe – may not be an overwhelming compulsion. We may be ocean-sailors at the weekend, even if we're wage-slaves during the week. But it's there, the need for security. The poet Philip Larkin called it a Toad, 'its hunkers ... heavy as hard luck, and cold as snow', a Toad that squats there asking us how we'd feel with our capital committed and our income gone. How we'd feel, talking in the pub with our mates, them with their steady jobs and their career progression, and we with a scheme that looked so smart once and so insanely optimistic now.

Accordingly, the moment comes and the moment goes and because we're not on the lookout for it, we don't so much as notice its passing.

Most people aren't like that. One in a hundred? One in a thousand? It's not that they overcome their Toad, that they wrestle the beast into submission, it's that they don't have the Toad at all. William Knox D'Arcy was born to a well-to-do English family in 1849. He was educated at Westminster School, an elite public school located in the rambling embrace of Westminster Abbey, where every British monarch since 1066 has been crowned and the final resting place for seventeen of their kingly souls. In 1866, when their father went bust, the family emigrated to Australia to start all over again. They ended up settling in Rockhampton in Central Queensland, which isn't exactly a big place now, but back then it must have seemed a million miles distant from the Abbey bells.

The young D'Arcy followed his father into law and joined the family firm. A lifetime of prosperous colonial Toad-following seemed to beckon. Then one sunny day in 1882, three brothers entered D'Arcy's office. They were rough men, miners, and they had been sent down the road from the local bank. They brought two things, a story and a lump of rock. The story was quickly told. The three men, Frederick, Edwin and Thomas Morgan, had been prospecting for silver in the Dee valley. They had found no silver and, as we now know, there's no silver there to be found. According to one version of the story, while on the journey back to town, Edwin had felt the call of nature. He walked a little distance from camp and urinated. As he did so, he couldn't help noticing a peculiar black boulder that had clearly rolled into the valley floor from the slopes above. Being a man and a miner, he idly swung his pick at the stone, thinking no more than that stones were there to be hit and picks had been made to do the hitting. He struck the stone. A chipping flew off and glinted. The rock was – or seemed to be – loaded with gold.

The Morgan brothers believed they had almost literally stumbled on a mountain of money, but they knew they needed help. Legal help, to stake a robust claim. Financial help, to bring capital to bear in exploiting the find. Technical help, to extract rock from the mountain and gold from the rock. Commercial help, to sort out hiring and transport and markets and sales. Their first stop had been the bank, the second stop D'Arcy's office. (And perhaps it's worth noting here that there are various different versions of the story in circulation, though the gist of them all is the same.)

Now for just a moment, stop there. Had you been sitting at D'Arcy's desk that day, gazing out at a dusty street, hearing a commotion outside in the anteroom, seeing these three unconventional clients enter your office, listening to their tale and fingering a tiny chipping of black and gold stone – what would you have done? What would you have said? How would you have proceeded?

Let's be realistic. At a very minimum, you'd have noticed that you had the scope to charge your services at premium rate. There weren't so many lawyers in Rockhampton and these three clients were in no position to haggle. If the ore in the rock was gold, then these clients would pay you, and pay you royally, for your legal expertise. That kind of reasoning, however, is amply consistent with being slave to the Toad. No one will pass up a little extra cash, if they don't have to put anything at risk. So you charge your time at a premium rate, but what else? Do you commit significant time and energy to the project, unsure of whether you'll receive a penny in exchange? Do you put some of your own money into it and if so, how much?

To answer the question accurately, you need to be careful about details. You are not wealthy. You have a young wife to support. Your start in life accustomed you to a high standard of living and in Rockhampton, Queensland, cash is hard to acquire and easy to lose. I suggest you would do roughly what I would do. Be interested, but evasive. Seek out as many facts as I could, knowing that time is always ticking by and that my main advantage lies in having been just the fifth person in the world to see and handle that little black stone. I'd talk with my wife. Discuss our own capital position, how much we need for the baby, how much we need for our security. Identify a sum that we can afford to gamble. Find a balance between maintaining a regular weekly income and investing time in a scheme that might be hare-brained or might be the best thing we ever did.

I'd speculate, but sensibly.

That's not how D'Arcy did it. He went in big. Huge. Together with two Queensland entrepreneurs, Thomas Hall and William Pattison, and the miners themselves, he formed a syndicate. The Morgan brothers contributed their mineral rights; the other three would provide a crushing mill for the extraction of the gold. D'Arcy didn't have huge funds at this point, but he threw his all at the project. He gambled. His future. His wife's future. Their baby's future. Everything.

We know this story for one reason and one reason only. The bet paid off. The hill from which that black boulder had tumbled – Morgan Mountain, as it became – was truly a mountain of gold. The entire six man syndicate made a fortune, but D'Arcy made himself richest of all. He returned to England one of the richest men in the world. At its peak, and in present day terms, his wealth ran to several billion pounds. He bought a grand home in town and a magnificent country estate. After his first wife separated from him and then died, he married again and entertained on a prodigious scale.

Character and a moment of risk. Three rough men and a wild story. The spin of a geological wheel. A dazzling outcome.

But perhaps you're not convinced. You're there in that Rockhampton office, gazing out at that dusty street. Perhaps you would have gone in big. Perhaps anyone would. Perhaps it's got nothing to do with character, just a question of being in the right place at the right time. A matter of luck, not temperament.

You might think so, but I haven't played quite straight with you. There's more to tell. D'Arcy was a gambler. A provincial solicitor in back of beyond Queensland doesn't generally have much cash at his disposal. That D'Arcy had enough to make the investment possible at all was because he had already speculated, heavily and successfully, in land. He only possessed the means to bet on Mount Morgan because his appetite for such bets was already strongly evident.

Move the clock forward to the young man's triumphant return to London. He had no financial need to stake anything on anything. He could have bought art, wined and dined, moved in society, held balls, indulged whims – done whatever he wanted. Yet horses and the racetrack still fascinated him. There were only two private boxes at Epsom race course. He owned one and the Queen owned the other. The thunder of horses' hooves did what the clatter of a miner's pick had once done. He needed risk to feel alive.

And one last thing. The main thing. The reason why D'Arcy is an important name and not merely a colonial chancer who came good. In 1900, an emissary from Persia came searching for 'a capitalist of the highest order' to invest money in the hunt for Persian oil. The geology was favourable. The oil business had already made fortunes for Rockefeller in the United States and for Marcus Samuel of Shell in Britain. The idea wasn't crazy and D'Arcy was interested.

Twice already, he had spun the wheel. In land first, then in gold. The horse racing in Britain fed a compulsion but hardly offered stakes large enough to satisfy a gambler's spirit and Persia offered the largest stakes of them all. A businessman, a real one, the kind used to managing complex corporations and large capital investments, might have looked harder before leaping. D'Arcy certainly made a show of thinking hard. He enquired after the geology, he ordered maps and took advice; but the badness of the advice he was given suggests that there was only one answer he'd ever have accepted.

From the Shah of Persia, he purchased a sixty-year concession to search for oil. The cost was £20,000 up front and a further £20,000 worth of shares in the venture. The cost of the bribes spent to gain the Shah's agreement was more again. Even the eunuch who brought the Shah his morning coffee got his baksheesh. The cost of drilling two exploratory wells was estimated at £10,000. Real money, even for a prodigiously wealthy man.

His advisers, however, did not spend much time discussing the cultural complexities of the region: the Shiite hatred for political authority, for Christian interlopers, for foreigners. They did not pause to take account of certain technical challenges: the entire country boasted only a few hundred miles of road; the territories which looked most promising for oil lay across wild and mountainous countryside; and the local labour possessed so few technical skills that few of them had even seen a hammer. They did not allow much of a contingency reserve for the mounted tribesmen who would sweep down from the mountains demanding gold to protect the incomers from bandits – that is to say, from themselves. They did not make full allowance for the fact that Persia was so far away from anywhere with anything that the nearest dentist was to be found in Karachi.

When D'Arcy's men came to drill, the cost of those first two wells was more like £200,000 than the £10,000 predicted. The venture bled money. Drilling started in 1902. In extremely challenging conditions, the equipment continually broke down. As early as 1903, D'Arcy's overdraft stood at £177,000, or a few tens of millions of pounds in today's money.* His bankers had demanded shares in the Mount Morgan mine by way of collateral and, to make matters worse, those shares had fallen to about one eighth of their peak value. Tough times on Easy Street.

Then, in 1904, relief. The drilling team struck oil. The would-be oilman used the news to scour Europe and the United States for new investors, but the well, that had started so promisingly, ran dry. He was advised to shift the exploration effort miles to the southwest. His overdraft grew still further. His bank started to demand the concession itself as collateral. Everything seemed lost.

As things turned out, D'Arcy did succeed in finding an investor, Burmah Oil, whose support enabled the troubled little venture to go on burning cash. By early 1908, however, even Burmah had had enough. It asked D'Arcy to put up more funds or close the whole operation down. He complained, 'Of course I cannot find £20,000 or anything', but stubbornly ignored the deadline. He just allowed it to pass without action or comment. The gambler refused to leave the casino.

Burmah, in turn, ignored their partner's refusal to cooperate and on 14 May 1908 sent a letter to the drilling team in Persia informing them that they should close up shop, sell everything saleable, and come home. The letter took weeks to travel from Glasgow to Persia. And after it was sent but before it arrived, the drilling team struck oil. They hit a gusher so big that the spout

* I'm being a bit vague because there's no clear way to convert one sum to another. In 1903, the retail price index was dominated by food and other very basic items, which played a minor part in the D'Arcy household economy. A better way to make the conversion is probably by using an index of earnings. The discrepancy between the two is very wide, however. One hundred and seventy-seven thousand pounds inflated at consumer prices would be worth about £14 million now. The same sum inflated with average earnings would be worth over £70 million today. Feel free to take your pick.

of oil jetted fifty feet higher than the steepling drilling rig itself. Shortly afterwards, the second exploration well struck oil too, and also on a prodigious scale. When George Reynolds, the tough, single-minded genius of the drilling team, received Burmah's communication, he wrote back sarcastically, '[Your] instructions … may be modified by the fact that oil has been struck', and refused to act on them. The age of Middle Eastern oil had begun. D'Arcy recovered the funds he'd sunk into the sands of Persia and received shares worth some £895,000 to boot. The company that emerged went through several name changes since those early days, but is still alive and well today. The company is now known as BP and is worth approximately $175 billion.

I've told this story at length because it's dramatic and because it makes a point. A moment of risk, of opportunity is not enough. Given the right opportunity, any of us may succeed to a certain extent, but the world has not been shaped by those whose ambitions run 'to a certain extent'. D'Arcy's ambitions were large when he speculated on land, larger when he speculated on gold, and almost boundless when he speculated on oil. You or I would have needed to conquer our aversion to risk to have done even one-tenth of what he managed. He, however, conquered nothing. He wasn't averse to risk, he needed it. When he had all the wealth anyone could ever want, he put himself through almost a decade of financial loss and heartache simply to feel the thrill of that spinning roulette wheel one more time.

The need for risk isn't unique to entrepreneurs, but it's the mark of the breed, all the same. When speaking to entrepreneurs in the course of writing this book, I've asked how much of their capital they put at risk in that first crucial investment, the one that launched them. They all answered the same way: they invested everything they had and in many cases borrowed heavily too. If their business had gone bad, they'd have been wiped out, walked away owning nothing more than fresh air and sunshine. That's the answer I'm given, but in almost every case I've noticed a tiny pause before it comes, one of those micro-habits which supposedly reveal a truth beyond mere words.

What is that hesitation, that nanosecond of delay? I think it comes down to translation. To you and me, who'd much rather not be wiped out, the question about that first investment has many possible answers. For entrepreneurs, that's not the case. There's only one first investment you can make, which is as much as you have. That answer is so instinctive, it takes a moment for them to remember that not everyone thinks the same way. They have to translate their answer from Risk-Think into regular Human-Think, and the pause for translation accounts for that micro-delay.

Allied to risk, and inseparable from it, is restlessness. For most humans, comfort is defined in static terms. The log fire. The hot drink. It's a pastoral ideal, the ideal of a people who will sleep tonight where they slept last night, do tomorrow what they did today. No doubt entrepreneurs like log fires too, but their instincts aren't remotely pastoral. Modern science has discovered a type of neuro-receptor (called the 7R variant of the DRD4) which seems highly linked to Attention Deficit Disorder, as well as novelty-seeking and food- and drug-cravings. In the modern Western world, this receptor isn't one you'd want your kids to have. It's not the sort that promises wonderful educational outcomes or stable career prospects.

People who have this kind of brain receptor, though, aren't ill. The genes responsible for it are doing their job just as nature intended. Since nature has a tidy habit of ensuring that poorly adapted genes are competed into oblivion, then those genes must once have been doing something useful. The question is what.

Enter the Ariaal – not a misspelled font style, but a tribe of semi-pastoral nomads in Africa. Some Ariaal continue to be true nomads, wandering the arid plains of northern Kenya, herding camels, cows, sheep and goats. Some of their brethren, however, have settled down and become farmers. The two groups are genetically identical; it's just the lifestyles that have diverged. Scientists have studied the two groups and found that nomads who had the 'novelty-seeking' receptor were stronger, healthier, better nourished than nomads who lacked it. Among farmers, however, it was the other way around. The novelty-seekers were worse nourished and less well adapted. In short, if you have a wanderer's genes, you'll do well as a wanderer but struggle if asked to settle down.

As far as I know, no one has ever taken cheek swabs from billionaires to conduct the same study, but they've come close. Twin study analysis conducted jointly by St Thomas's Hospital and Imperial College in London and by Case Western Reserve University in Cleveland, suggests that around half somebody's propensity to become self-employed is attributable to their genes – perhaps a rather lower score than you might expect. (Intelligence, for example, is about 75 per cent genetic.) On the other hand, it's not clear that twin study tests such as these are methodologically accurate. Nearly all identical twins share an upbringing, so it's hard to tease out genetic from environmental factors. In a world well set up for such experiments, there would be a plethora of identical twins forcibly separated at birth to make the data analysis easier, but alas such twins are far too rare to generate statistically meaningful results.

What's more, self-employment is not entrepreneurship. Indeed, much entrepreneurship isn't really entrepreneurship. A plumber, for example, or a lawyer, or an accountant may be self-employed, and may choose to house their occupation in a wholly owned, legally incorporated company. But neither self-employment nor corporate status is the test. The test is ambition. It's all very well to start a business in your garage, but unless you start it dreaming of the corporate skyscraper you'll move into one day, you are not an entrepreneur. (And this, by the way, is the real secret of American enterprise. The United States does create a lot of entrepreneurs, but so do some other countries. Almost nowhere, though, do entrepreneurs dream on a bigger scale, as measured by the employment growth expected by an entrepreneur over the first few years of the business's life. Those outsize dreams have a lot to do with what makes the United States what it is.)

Other scientific studies have perhaps got closer to the mark. A very intriguing study conducted by Cambridge University studied the brains of 17 ordinary corporate managers and sixteen entrepreneurs, each of whom had started at least two high-tech companies and who therefore passed any reasonable test of entrepreneurship. Asked to make a series of routine decisions, the managers and entrepreneurs scored about the same. These were sensible people, analysing problems in a sensible way. As soon as they were asked to make decisions involving considerable risk, however, the entrepreneurs were consistently bolder. Knox D'Arcy would, no doubt, have been off the scale.

Bold, please note, is not the same as intelligent. Indeed, it's a commonplace in the venture capital industry that founder-CEOs should be gently eased out of the hot-seat as soon as possible. Noam Wasserman of Harvard Business School quotes one venture capital type as saying:

> Upfront, I ask founders to level with me. If they are interested in working with me on the basis of [their] being a big shareholder, then I am interested. If they are interested in working with me because they have to run the company, then it's probably not going to make sense for us to work together.

This attitude, a common one in the industry, would make no sense if that entrepreneurial boldness was the same thing as profit-maximizing genius. It isn't. It's gambling, linked (as

Wasserman also points out on the basis of careful study) to the tendency among entrepreneurs to be markedly more optimistic about outcomes than their peers.

The trouble is that any attempt to measure optimism in laboratory conditions founders on a basic difference between entrepreneurs and the rest of us. It may, indeed, look to us as though entrepreneurs are 'too' optimistic, yet that's to make the mistake of looking at their world through our eyes. To *us*, failure matters. To *them*, failure doesn't really matter an iota. The failure of a particular venture is not the desired outcome, obviously, but it's not a bad one. The only bad outcome would have been if they hadn't had the nerve to go for it in the first place. Our 'do nothing' default option is their worst case scenario. That's the one they truly can't envisage. Equally, our worst case scenario ('invest up to your neck, then see the whole thing go pear-shaped') is no big deal for them. It's an 'Aw shucks!' outcome, one that just makes them want to go back and try again with something else.

Even the way we respond to success is different. For us, success probably means a new home, a nice car and perhaps (depending on the level of our success) a yacht, a private jet, a football club, or a private island. For them, success means all those things for sure, but it means something else even better: that their 'baby' has flourished, that their act of creation has been rewarded by something that has matured into a confident, independent adulthood. These feelings mean that the risks and rewards we face are quite different from the ones that entrepreneurs face, even if we were both to compute the odds in the exact same way. Little wonder that we end up behaving in sharply different ways.

	How we feel	**How entrepreneurs feel**
Do nothing	Fine. This is our default choice.	Bored. Frustrated. No way.
Try and fail	Oh my God! What do I live on?	At least I gave it a go.
Try and succeed	Jackpot – got the house, got the yacht.	Immense satisfaction – I created something.

Knox D'Arcy is the perfect exemplar of all these things: the optimism, the gambling – and the irresponsibility which (to our pastoral, anti-nomadic minds) is the inevitable result. D'Arcy's judgement about the Mount Morgan mine proved reasonable, but he refused to sell down his investment in it, even after the stock hit absurdly unsustainable heights. His judgement about Persian oil was simply awful. True enough, even that bet came good in the end, but any competent business manager would have made a much better fist of assessing risks and benefits before making any financial commitment – and would, at the very least, have come up with a much more sober estimate of the probable costs and the scale of financing needed.

Yet there's nothing unique about his mindset. I've spoken to upwards of two dozen self-made multimillionaires. (And my threshold level for 'multimillionaire' was high. The median net worth of those I spoke to was well into the tens of millions of pounds.) Almost all of these entrepreneurs used the same kind of language to describe themselves. They're 'restless', have a 'very low boredom threshold', need 'decisions to happen quickly', need 'high energy' and 'passion' from those they work with, couldn't stand the 'slowness' of large corporations.

Some of them did have high educational achievement, but plenty didn't. Typical was one entrepreneur who crammed his three-year law course into an eighteen-month workathon. After getting his degree, he started in corporate finance. He became bored working for others, so set up on his own instead. When he wearied of funding other people's companies, he bought his own. Work was never the challenge, dullness was. With people like that, I almost got the feeling that if they were forced to sit in a classroom or given a pedestrian middle-management job in a dull but worthy company somewhere, they'd end up chewing carpet tiles or jabbing forks into electrical sockets. These were folk who needed stuff to happen and happen fast.

Although entrepreneurs are often described as rule-breakers, it would perhaps be more accurate to say that they're typically not rule-minded. It's not particularly that they seek to break rules, more that they don't really see the rules that are so clear to the rest of us. That's why those 7R-DRD4 variant nomads find it so easy to travel beyond the far horizon. They haven't felt the tug of any prohibition against doing so. It's perhaps also why immigrants are so over-represented in entrepreneurship – around a quarter of all US start-ups are founded by immigrants, for example. Those who are born and brought up in a place feel its rules and mores in their bones. Those who have already left kin and country behind are much less tuned in to those rules in the first place.

These issues may even lie at the heart of one of the oddest results to come out of the torrent of research into entrepreneurship: namely that while only 1 per cent of corporate managers are dyslexic an astonishing 20–35 per cent of entrepreneurs are (the two figures are for UK and US entrepreneurs respectively; the researcher was Julie Logan of the Cass Business School in London). There's no settled interpretation of this research finding, but here's mine. Dyslexics have gone through their school life noticing that the rules which work for others don't seem to hold for them. A is for Apple, B is for Bird, C is for Cat, D is for Dog. That worked for me. If you're non-dyslexic, then it presumably worked for you. For dyslexics, however, even those most basic of all rules seem to make no sense. So what do you – as a bemused child, anxiously seeking the approval of your teachers and parents – do in such a situation? You surely get creative. You develop your own techniques and trust those in preference to the seemingly unreliable ones offered by your teacher. You've learned to invent your own way around problems. You've learned that the rules of Planet Normal just aren't going to work for you – indeed, they don't even make sense. And as soon as you start to think like this, though you may not know it yet, you're an entrepreneur.

If wealth creation is alchemy, then its orginating spark is here. The restlessness of people who can't bear to be still; the risk-taking of those who can't bear to be safe; the decisiveness of those who know that if they want a thing done, they'll need to do it themselves. And from the spark – fire. From the Mount Morgan mine to Middle Eastern oil and the birth of one of the world's largest oil companies.* The ultimate reason why the world today is different from the world 250 years ago is because of the extraordinary creative energy of that entrepreneurial spark. It's that spark which has wrested gold, iron, coal and oil from the earth; which has hewn lumber, bashed metal, invented gadgets, launched ships – and done all those other things which make our world what it is today.

When as non-physicists we read about the Big Bang, it's almost impossible for us to get our heads round the idea that something can come from nothing. In historical terms, though, that's precisely what has happened over the last 250 years. In 1750, the Earth had plenty of gold in her belly, iron in her veins, lumber in her forests. Indeed, she had more of all those things then than now and yet it was a largely useless sort of fertility because it was one that sat alongside almost universal poverty,

* One of the world's largest private sector oil companies, that is. The biggest oil companies in the world are all state owned. The National Iranian Oil Company – the company which sits on all that lovely Persian oil now – has oil reserves about twenty-five times larger than those of BP.

illiteracy and high mortality. Out of that void was created the extraordinary affluence of our modern Western world; something from nothing on a colossal scale and achieved in the space of three or four human lifetimes.

As entrepreneurs go, William Knox D'Arcy isn't the best possible exemplar. He didn't bring the world any extraordinary new vision. He invented no new technology. He was neither manager nor organizer. He wasn't even a particularly astute investor, holding onto his Mount Morgan shares when they touched £17 and watching them fall back all the way to £2. But more than almost anyone else D'Arcy exemplifies the willingness – the compulsion – to gamble his all on a vision of the future. Character and a moment of risk. The start of everything.

TWO

Will

If you start to take Vienna – take Vienna.

– NAPOLEON BONAPARTE

In 1927, Paul Getty had a problem. One of his companies owned a patch of land in Santa Fe Springs, just outside Los Angeles. The land was potentially oil rich and Getty had a rig set up and a drilling team working it. They'd spudded the well in and were 'making hole' at a good rate when the drill bit sheared off and got stuck. Getty doesn't report the precise details, but wells of the era generally ran 3,000 or 4,000 feet deep, so if the bit twisted at around the halfway stage, then it laid maybe 1,500 or 2,000 feet underground. The drill bit was a large chunk of metal that was impossible to drill through. The drilling shaft was perhaps a couple of hand breadths wide.

Fortunately a solution existed to the problem. You could lower a so-called fishing tool down the shaft to fish for the bit and bring it to the surface. The work was delicate, skilled and chancy. After a couple of weeks' work, Getty's men had still not retrieved the bit. The problem was annoying but far from calamitous. 'Twist-offs' were a familiar irritation and any experienced drilling crew would have seen and dealt with plenty in their time.

All the same, two weeks wasted were two weeks wasted. Wages had to be paid and the capital costs of the rig and the lease were not yielding any return. Worse still, competing drilling crews on neighbouring leases would get to the oil sooner. Since neighbouring rigs generally tapped the same pool of oil, every barrel extracted by the guys next door meant one less barrel for you. Getty was already a millionaire by this point and hardly needed to fret about problems of this sort, but then again he was a millionaire precisely because he *did* fret about problems of this sort. On one occasion, he'd owned a lease too small for an oil rig, plus an access route too narrow to take a truck. Most owners would have turned their attention to other things, but not Getty. He commissioned and built a miniature derrick and brought the steelwork to site on a specially built miniature railway. The derrick struck oil and the well made money.

So, faced with this new problem – a jammed drill bit and a halted well – what did he do? You have all the details you need: a drilling shaft 1,500 feet deep and perhaps twelve inches wide; a heavy steel drill bit twisted off and jammed somewhere close to the bottom. You need to find a way to resume drilling as fast and as cheaply as you can.

I won't give you the answer yet – you'll have to wait till the end of the chapter for that – but I will tell you this. Getty was not an inventor. He had no more mechanical ingenuity than you do. Certainly there were countless people drilling for oil in the 1920s who had more drilling experience, a better knowledge of rigs and fishing tools, greater mechanical and technical dexterity. Yet back in 1927, it was not those people who solved the problem, it was Paul Getty.

For now, though, we'll jump forwards in time and across the globe. It's 1975. Bob Dylan has returned to form with *Blood on the Tracks*. Pink Floyd Wishing You Were Here. Bruce Springsteen is *Born to Run*. If your musical tastes are a little more Meryl Streep than that, then you'll be remembering 1975 as the year of Abba's 'I Do, I Do, I Do, I Do, I Do', the least lyrically inventive song title in the history of lyrically uninventive song titles.

But those artists and their concerns are a long way from here, a collection of rice paddies in Surabaya, East Java, Indonesia. What's more the young man looking out at those rice paddies is probably not wishing he was here. But that young man – who was there on a $250 cut-price holiday – has a decision to make. His name is Lakshmi Niwas Mittal and he has been asked by his father to sell those paddy fields. His father was originally from Rajasthan and was not, to start with, by any means a wealthy man. Lakshmi himself had grown up with twenty others in a house with rope beds, no electricity and the only water coming from the hand pump in the yard outside. It wouldn't be quite accurate to say that Mittal's was a poor family. In India, especially then, poor means poor, and the Mittals were middle class by the standards of their place and time.

In due course, Mittal's family moved to an unremarkable house in a poorish district of Calcutta. Young Lakshmi went to school then accountancy college. In the meantime, Lakshmi's father had become partner in a company called the British India Rolling Mill. I'm not sure quite how the company had managed to stagger through a decade or two without noticing that the British had left India in 1947, but presumably its clients loved it anyway. Lakshmi's uncles were involved in steel trading and, in 1963, the family won an important licence to build a steel rolling mill in southern India. Things, unquestionably, were on the up.

It was as part of this ferment of activity that Mittal's father had come by those Indonesian paddy fields. His intent was to build a steel mill there, producing for the local market. Further investigation, however, proved that a small mountain of bureaucracy lay in the way. Paperwork, licences, permits, hassle. Mohan Lal Mittal decided this was too much. A hugely experienced, ambitious, and capable entrepreneur, he gave the challenge his careful consideration, and refused it. He asked his son to extract the family from the mess with as little financial damage as possible.

Here, you should for a moment put yourself into the young Mittal's shoes. You are not a complete novice. You have taken a keen interest in your family's steel operation and have been working in it now for a number of years. For what it's worth, when you left St Xavier's College in Calcutta, you did so with a BCom. and the highest marks ever achieved by a St Xavier's student in accountancy and commercial mathematics. But you have no money of your own. You do not speak Indonesian. You do not possess influential connections in a country with an authoritarian and corrupt government. You have a young wife and are a very long way away from home. And it's 1975, let's remember, when the world seemed a lot larger than it does today, and when India marched with very much less swagger on the global stage.

How would you personally have proceeded if placed in this situation? For you, of course, these questions are purely theoretical, but for the young Mittal in 1975 they were nothing of the sort.

And we already know the answers. Most of us would have sold those paddy fields, probably getting ripped off in the process, then gone home to a comfortable future in Indian steelmaking. We'd have done well, congratulated ourselves for our wisdom and prudence. We'd never even have noticed the size of the opportunity that we had allowed to go by.

Lakshmi Mittal, however, didn't sell the paddy fields. He decided to build a steel mill on them himself. No money? No problem! Back then the Indian government offered export loans equal to 85 per cent of the cost of the equipment and materials being exported. Mittal put together a deal where Indian export loans, plus some shares in the family company, plus some cash from a local partner, plus some more loans from an Indian bank in Singapore were somehow enough to make the whole thing float. He hadn't quite separated himself from his family, but by starting out in an entirely different country, he was making the firmest possible statement of his independence.

He used the funds to build a mini-mill, a term which rather understates the scale of the enterprise involved. A modern *integrated* steel mill handles everything. It takes raw iron ore, melts it down in a blast furnace, extracts the now liquid iron, then starts to adjust the chemistry: removing impurities, controlling the carbon, adding alloying materials as required. Only then can the molten steel be formed into blooms, ingots, slabs and sheet. The scale of enterprise required to manage these things efficiently is colossal. A 'small' integrated mill will produce two million tonnes a year. A large one can produce as many as fifteen million.

Only when judged against these gargantuan standards is there anything 'mini' about a mini-mill, which are typically around one-tenth the size of their integrated cousins. The heart of the mini-mill's method is to cut the raw iron ore out of the process altogether. Instead of the whole cumbersome process of melting metal out of rock, the mini-mill relies on the steel industry's version of the ready-meal: a mixture of scrap metal and direct-reduced iron (a form of the metal which is about 90 per cent pure).

In mid-1970s Indonesia, this technology made perfect sense. Mittal couldn't afford – and the market couldn't sustain – a five million tonne monster plant. What's more, at the time, the Indonesian market was dominated by Japanese companies importing steel from overseas. There was no domestic production at all and when Mittal did his sums, he realized that he could achieve a cost advantage of as much as 50 per cent.

Building the mill took two years. In its first year of operation, the plant made 26,000 tonnes of steel, which brought in revenues of $10 million. The plant made $1 million in profit. But profit and riches is not the same thing. Banks had to be paid. Further capital investment was scheduled. Mittal – by now a father – was paying himself just $250 a month. His car was second-hand and he worked all hours of the clock. But he had his steel plant and it was doing well. By the end of the 1980s, production had grown to 330,000 tonnes. Lakshmi Mittal was 39.

Again, life brought to the still young Mittal another tantalizing moment of opportunity, a sweet intersection of character and risk. It was a moment that you or I would probably not have noticed. If you've built one successful steel plant – and let's face it, most of us haven't – then the temptation would surely be to do the same again, and then again, and then maybe again. If Mittal had been in the business of talking to life coaches that presumably would have been the life-plan he'd have evolved. Mittal could've looked forward to a prospect of extraordinary success. He'd create and operate multiple plants as well as being the first Indian ever to have manufactured steel overseas. He'd be a hero.

However, Mittal didn't want it. As he saw it, building steel plants from scratch was *slow*. Why build them, when you could buy them? The trouble was, in the world of steel, Mittal was still a very small player. His funds were meagre. He had no government or major institution backing him. He had no technological edge, no breakthrough invention, no special access to raw materials. But if you've already done the impossible once, you're not that daunted by the idea of doing it again.

In the West Indies, the state-owned Iron and Steel Co. of Trinidad and Tobago (ISCOTT) was going bust and Mittal reckoned he could fix it. He promised the government that he would turn losses of $10 million a month into profits of the same amount. There was only one condition: if he did as he promised, then he'd win the right to buy the company.

The government agreed. Mittal fired the team of sixty German managers who had been running the plant, and brought in sixty Indians instead, thereby cutting the wage bill by almost $20 million a year. He slashed other costs and ramped up production. In just four years, by 1993, production had more than doubled and Mittal bought the company.

Which was his *second*, not first, major purchase, because in 1991 Mittal had gone to see a government-owned steel plant in Mexico. A plant running at 25 per cent capacity and losing $1 million a day. A year later, in 1992, he bought it.

In 1994, he bought Canada's Sidbec-Dosco.

In 1995, he gobbled up Hamburger Stahlwerke and created a shipping company to handle the group's increasingly global transport logistics.

In the same year, he also bought the Karmet Steel Mill in Temirtau ('Iron Mountain'), Kazakhstan. This was a massive plant, one of the world's biggest. Built by forced labour and prisoners of war in the evil old days of the Soviet Union, the plant was on an almost inconceivable scale. It boasted 1.5 billion tonnes of coal in its own reserves, 1.7 billion tonnes of its own iron ore and its own 435 megawatt power station. It was also, needless to say, a financial basketcase in a country whose economy faced massive issues of its own.

It's hard to overstate how extraordinary all this is. The speed of it. The total lack of concern for geographical or political boundary. The confidence of it: the willingness to take on a Mexican business that was losing a million dollars a *day*. The willingness to acquire a huge, crumbling, loss-making empire in Kazakhstan, certain that the thing is fixable and that you're the right person to fix it.

In this welter of extraordinaries, a few particular points are worth picking out.

First, the extraordinarily successful execution. The Kazakh plant in particular constituted an utterly unprecedented scale of industrial challenge. Take, for example, what is usually a fairly routine aspect of a company's business: paying the workers.

When Mittal bought the plant, he had promised to pay salary arrears in full, averaging about six months' pay per worker. No problem. The funds were there to do it. But few of the workers had bank accounts, so they needed to be paid in cash. No problem. Mittal started to convert hard currency into local cash … until he got a call from the Central Bank. Whoops, sorry, Lakshmi, but if you bring that much hard currency into the country all at once, we're going to have an inflationary problem on our hands. Would you mind stopping, please? So Mittal obliged. He continued to bring in hard currency, albeit in much smaller amounts, but meantime hired a plane to fly in suitcases of cash from the capital city Almaty.

Or take power. Not power for the plant, but for the town itself. It's probably fair to say that there aren't so many enterprises in the West where CEOs need to worry about how their workers are going to keep their homes warm through winter. But up in Temirtau, the temperature can fall to –40°C and the power company, like most things in Kazakhstan, was falling apart. So Mittal bought the power company too, and fixed it. And the local tram services. And the railway. And the TV station. And a few mines while he was at it.

This was Mittal. He didn't simply solve these problems; he solved them in extraordinary fashion. Within a year, this appalling, decaying business was profitable again. Along the way, steel production had doubled. The Kazakh plant now produced in a month what Mittal's first steel mill would have taken ten years to produce at its first year's rate of output.

Given the sheer scale of the problems, it was extraordinary that Mittal managed it at all – but remember that he did it while also owning, managing and turning around steel companies all across the globe, *and* did it with an extremely young and self-created organization.

Secondly, Mittal was an outsider. He came from the wrong place. When you read, for example, about Mark Zuckerberg's amazing success in creating Facebook, you can't help but feel that his success *has* been amazing, but also a little predictable. Social networking was clearly going to take off at some point. It was always more likely to take off in America than anywhere. Mark Zuckerberg was a Harvard student who had been programming computers since he was at middle school. Facebook itself started purely as a Harvard thing, and spread from there.

Please don't misunderstand my point. I'm not knocking the guy. There were loads of other equally privileged, equally well-educated students at Harvard and elsewhere who did not do what Zuckerberg did. But Mittal grew up without electricity. Without running water. With rope beds and twenty in a house. In a country whose economy was not only backward, but self-isolating from the global mainstream. If, in 1950, you were asked to pick the future king of steel, you'd never have come close to picking Mittal. He was in the wrong continent, the wrong country, the wrong part of the wrong country. All he really had going for him was an able and ambitious family that would educate him superbly and (in due course and through their own entrepreneurial efforts) supply the funds to get him going.

To take the point a step further, consider how many other companies could have done what Mittal did. British Steel was a badly run state-owned firm when Thatcher privatized it. The company soon became efficient, profitable and with funds to invest. In 1989, as Mittal was wondering what to do next, British Steel might just as well have been asking itself the same thing. Or the big German producers. Or those in France, Spain, or Italy. Or those in America or Japan or Australia. The list of companies better placed – financially, managerially, technologically, politically – to succeed to pre-eminence was a long and formidable one. And none of them did.

Thirdly, Mittal retained ownership. A slightly more complex point this, but a crucial one. In theory, it's not all that hard to grow fast and aggressively. You go to the stock market or private investors. You raise money. You acquire assets. You grow bigger and you raise more money. You keep going. Needless to say, it's not quite so simple – you need a track record strong enough to persuade investors to trust you with their money – but it's still a much, much easier route to success than funding your growth very largely from your own pocket, as Mittal did.

What's more, steel is a business which involves a lot of *stuff*. Iron mines. Coal mines. Transport. Blast furnaces. Rolling mills. Mini-mills. Power plants. TV stations and railway lines. Tangible kit with a tangible price tag. The reason why most of the billionaires that you're familiar with are involved in software (Bill Gates, Larry Page, Sergey Brin, Larry Ellison, and Mark Zuckerberg, for starters) is a simple one. If you've got a decent computer program, you have most of what you need to succeed. There is not a huge list of physical assets that need to be bought out of cashflow. Steel is the precise reverse of that. There, the assets are everything – and managing to fund an extraordinary amount of growth from cashflow is all the more remarkable as a consequence.

If you're not yet persuaded, then wait till you've heard the end of the story.

Mittal went on buying. He tried to buy a Venezualan producer, but somebody was bugging his phones and the deal went elsewhere. He compensated by buying an iconic Chicago-based steelmaker, Inland Steel.

It was the wrong time. His company was by now loaded with debt. The Asian currency crisis and the post-millennial dot.com slowdown caused a slump in steel prices. The (fairly small) portion of Mittal company shares which were freely traded on the stock market slumped from their opening price of $28.50 per share to less than $2. To the outside world, this looked like a crisis. To an entrepreneur, it was a moment of risk.

For the Mittals – Lakshmi had now been joined at the family firm by his son, Aditya – the first years of the Noughties were the best possible ones. A global slump in the price of steel meant that there was also a global slump in the price of steel mills. Mittal acquired plants in Algeria, Poland, Romania, Macedonia, the Czech Republic, South Africa and France. The economics of these purchases was alluring. Because of the huge fixed costs involved in steel production, there is probably no industry more prone to huge cycles of boom and bust.* That means that the assets you pick up for a song in times of dearth stand to make huge amounts of money in times of plenty. And the Mittals were the only players willing to stack all their chips on red, and wait for the turn of the wheel.

Eventually, the buying spree reached its natural end. In 2006, Lakshmi Mittal made a formal offer for Arcelor SA, the world's largest steelmaker by revenue. The company could boast world-class technology, a century of steelmaking experience, and had achieved its success in the heart of Europe, one of the world's most sophisticated steel markets. (The company was headquartered in Luxembourg, but had recently been formed from a merger involving French and Spanish steel companies as well.)

The bid was one of the most keenly contested in financial history. On the Arcelor side, there was a tangible sense of who do these people think they are? This wasn't the way the world order was meant to work. European flagship companies weren't simply sitting in a shop window, waiting to snapped up by the first emerging market billionaire to take a fancy to them. There was no evidence of racism, as such, in Arcelor's outraged defence, but – well – there *was* outrage. Arcelor had the history. It had the technology. It was the industry's biggest name. It was European. Indeed, it was practically *French*! And the company was about to vanish because it had been out-thought and out-manouevred by the nobody-from-nowhere, Lakshmi Mittal.

---

* Except possibly airlines, which have a similarly scary cost structure and suffer regularly because of it.

Mittal won. The resultant company – ArcelorMittal – is the world's largest steelmaker by any ranking at all. The industry that gave birth to the Industrial Revolution itself had finally been consolidated by a kid from Rajasthan, whose family continues to own slightly more than two-fifths of the resultant behemoth.

This story is astonishing and little known. When the British press talk about Mittal, it is largely in the context of his very large fortune, which has been as high as some $26 billion (and is, of course, down again in the midst of the current slump).

But who cares? Counting Mittal's money misses the point almost as comprehensively as it would be to obsess over Napoleon's medals or to count Einstein's honorary doctorates. Those things – the money, the medals, the doctorates – come with the territory but they are, ultimately, inconsequential.

What matters for the purposes of our investigation into the heart of the capitalist Big Bang itself is what Mittal's story exemplifies to a quite exceptional degree.* And the most striking thing about it is precisely its Napoleonic quality. Its speed. Its surprise. Its boldness and decisiveness. Few entrepreneurs have this quality to the degree that Mittal has it, but they all have it. You can't create a business of any scale without it. If an appetite for risk is the fuse that ignites the entrepreneurial bang, it's the Napoleonic appetite for conquest that propels it forward.

This might, in fact, be a good point to remind you of the millionaire mindset challenge with which I started the chapter. I left you with a drill bit stuck 1,500 feet down a drilling well and an oil crew hanging around with no oil to pump because

---

* I'd say Rockefeller's creation of Standard Oil in the last three decades of the nineteenth century ranks as the greatest industrial achievement of all time. Other players to rate high on any list of great industrialists would be Andrew Carnegie, Henry Ford, and John Wilkinson (the central figure in the Industrial Revolution-era iron industry). I personally would place Mittal alongside that company. No one alive today occupies a higher place.

they can't get the drill bit out. You want to get restarted as soon as possible and you won't make money until you do. Getty's answer, the billionaire's answer, requires Napoleonic thinking. Decision, speed, surprise – and force.

Getty wasn't an oilrigger, he wasn't a mechanic and he wasn't an inventor. But he liked to get things done. So he commissioned a monumental mason – the sort of guy who normally carves tombstones for graveyards – to make him a granite spike. Six feet high, as wide as the drilling shaft, and pointed. Once he had his spike, he transported it over to the hole and dropped it in. Getty didn't know what would happen when a six-foot granite spike fell 1,500 feet onto a jammed drill bit, but he knew that *something* would. And it did. The spike smashed the drill bit. The riggers got drilling again without delay. The device was known as a Paul Getty Special and it became widely used in the oilfields of the day. In the unlikely event that the entrepreneurs of the world come to form a trade union, then I'd suggest that they adopt the Paul Getty Special as their emblem. It might not be subtle, but by God you know when it hits.

And one last thing. A thing that lies at the heart of this book.

It's all very well to call attention to the Napoleonic drive and will of entrepreneurs, but the comparison suffers in one enormous respect. Napoleon's wars devastated a continent. They put back the industrialization of continental Europe by as much as fifty years. They left a legacy of illegimate rulers, aggrieved populations, and entire armies of the dead. Back then, Napoleonic drive had Napoleonic consequences.

These days, the reverse is true. Entrepreneurs are creators. They turn the unproductive into the highly productive. They take advanced technologies and make them available all over the globe.

Needless to say, you can't do these things and make everyone happy. Mittal's career has had its share of controversy. When he bought into Kazakhstan, he worked with some intermediaries of doubtful rectitude. When he buys up steel plants, redundancies often follow. In his coal mines and iron mines, there have been accidents which have cost miners their lives.

Call me heartless, if you wish, but my response to this kind of carping is more baffled than anything else. What on earth do you expect? You can't buy the biggest industrial enterprise in Kazakhstan and not work with people who know the territory, and the business ethics of those people is bound not to be the same as you'd expect in London or New York. Likewise you can't restore an ailing plant to health and not address its cost structure. In almost every case, that will involve redundancies. You can't operate mines in Kazakhstan and not expect accidents that would be inconceivable in more developed countries. Kazakhstan is not Sweden. It is a place where even paying your workers constitutes a challenge, a place where you need to buy, mend, and operate a power plant if your workers are to enjoy any heating.

This isn't to clear Mittal of these charges altogether. It's possible – I just wouldn't know – that Mittal should have put more effort into mine safety earlier and more extensively than he did. I'm quite certain that no one has ever built a global business on Mittal's scale and done it without any errors or regrets along the way. Yet to focus unduly on any errors is to miss the point. Mittal did what no one else was prepared to do. He was prepared to buy one of the least attractive assets in one of the least commercially attractive countries in the world, and make a go of it. He took a bad thing and made it good. He did it in Kazakhstan, in Mexico, in the West Indies, and countless other places besides.

What Mittal did in these places represents the very essence of capitalist energy. It's the energy that took the world of 1770 – poor, backward, illiterate, hungry, unproductive – and turned it into the world of today. It's the energy that turns a rice field into a steel mill, a broken enterprise into a thriving one. It's the energy that lies at the heart of every good thing about capitalism.

But the energy itself is an amoral one. It can be used for good; it can be used for ill. And the next chapter takes us into some morally ambiguous territory indeed, for it's time to consider the art of selling.

THREE

Persuasion

'Ah, Maggie, in the world of advertising, there's no such thing as a lie. There's only expedient exaggeration.'

– ROGER THORNHILL (Cary Grant) in Hitchcock's *North by Northwest*

In the mid-nineteenth century, European scientists led by Louis Pasteur in France and Robert Koch in Germany developed and proved the germ theory of medicine, which swept away centuries of myth and superstition. From new theories new practices. Joseph Lister in Britain was quick to see that if germs caused infection, then surgery was almost an open invitation to gangrene. Since wounds couldn't be heated or filtered – two of the standard ways of eliminating germs in the laboratory – that left only chemical compounds. Lister knew that sewage was successfully deodorised with carbolic acid and began to spray a solution of it on open wounds and surgical instruments – and forced surgeons to wash their hands in a mild carbolic solution before operating. The incidence of gangrene among his patients declined precipitously. By 1870, his innovations had been enthusiastically adopted and improved upon, first in Germany, then further afield. Countless lives were saved. A medical revolution was born.

Needless to say, revolutions breed innovation. In the last three decades of the nineteenth century, a scramble was on to develop ever more effective chemical compounds to play the role of sterilizing agents. One such formulation was developed by a couple of American researchers for use in surgical situations. A couple of decades later, the same product, but heavily diluted, was sold to dentists for use in oral care. Two decades later still, the same product was sold as a mouthwash to America's burgeoning middle class. In honour of the great Joseph Lister, the mouthwash was christened Listerine. It was a nice touch, but almost nobody bought the mouthwash.

Then the young Gerard B. Lambert took over management of the family firm. He had a revolutionary idea of his own. He'd *advertise* the product, something that the company had never done in its history. For a year, nothing happened. The copy was awkward, old-fashioned, uncertain. It didn't work. The firm's profit (which included income from items other than the mouthwash) remained stuck at its historic levels of about $100,000 a year. But then Lambert and his two ad-men, Milton Feasley and Gordon Seagrove, hit gold. Their new ad depicted a gorgeous young woman, alongside copy which told the affecting tale of a handsome young businessman finding himself rejected after a single romantic date. The ad's headline commented darkly, 'He Never Knew Why'.

The answer, said Messrs Lambert, Feasley and Seagrove, was halitosis, a term so obscure that very few doctors would have recognized it and most dictionaries of the age ignored it. All the same, the term had a pleasingly classical ring to it and it *sounded* scientific. As Roland Marchand comments in his *Advertising the American Dream*, 'the ads took the form of quick-tempo sociodramas in which readers were invited to identify with temporary victims in tragedies of social shame. Now the protagonist was not the product but the potential consumer, suffering vicariously a loss of love, happiness, and success.' Consumers responded to the ad in their droves. By

1927, the profits of Lambert Pharmaceutical had increased from $100,000 to more than $4 million. The advertising budget for Listerine saw a fiftyfold increase over a similar time-period.

Naturally enough, if you do something once and it succeeds magnificently, you're under an almost overwhelming temptation to do the same all over again. It was a temptation that Lambert made no effort to resist. No sooner had his halitosis campaign started to take off, than he started to wonder what other ailments might not also be curable by this miracle mouthwash. The answer was quite a few. Listerine, it seemed, was an excellent after-shave tonic. It could cure colds. It would take care of sore throats. It was an excellent astringent, and who could possibly resist its effectiveness as a deodorant?

Listerine might very well have turned out to be the cure for all sorts of other things besides – ingrowing hairs, rough skin, violent conflict, old age – except that success breeds competition, and all kinds of other brands sought to muscle in on Listerine's turf. Laundry starches became beauty baths (for 'Fastidious Women', naturally). New diseases were invented by the score. Do you, for example, suffer from 'acidosis' (sour stomach)? No? Then perhaps you worry about 'bromodosis' or 'homotosis'? (Sweaty foot odours and a lack of attractive home furnishings, respectively.) If you have survived those afflictions, then do you perhaps need to consult a doctor about accelerator toe, ashtray breath or office hips? The world of the 1920s American consumer was strewn with new perils, new cures.

In all of this, it was almost easy to lose sight of one, rather central question. Did Listerine actually do anything for bad breath? The answer, then and now, is that its contribution is decidedly modest. Any liquid, whether a glassful of tapwater or a mouthwash named in honour of the father of antiseptic surgery, will coat the mouth, wash away surplus food particles, and mildly reduce the build-up of dental plaque. Listerine may be somewhat better than pure water in doing just that, but it is certainly a lesser part of good dental hygiene than either brushing or flossing. Indeed, the alcohol content of many mouthwashes may dry the back of the tongue and thereby encourage the growth of the bacteria which are largely responsible for bad breath. If you really want to deal with bad breath then brush your teeth, floss, and, if you really must, gently scrape the back of your tongue with the edge of a teaspoon. Despite fifty years of advertising to the contrary, Listerine does nothing at all to help with colds or sore throats. No data has ever been produced to demonstrate that Listerine has helped the guy get the girl or the girl get her guy.

Lambert's story is the perfect way to introduce the topic of salesmanship. It's a tale which begins with Pasteur, Koch and Lister – a group of scientists responsible for one of the most important set of medical discoveries ever. Their work was rigorous and scientific. It has been of vast and continuing benefit to mankind. By contrast, the story of Listerine mouthwash begins with an invention: a pseudo-medical term, a phoney disease, and unjustifiable medical claims. The product created to honour Lister was founded on a fraud.

Listerine may not have done much to endear itself to medical science, but in the annals of consumer marketing, Gerry Lambert can claim an honoured place. Consumer brands had only been around for some thirty or forty years, when Listerine took off. The first British company to register a trademark was Bass, the brewing company, whose red triangle logo was registered in 1876 and is still in use today. Yet a trademark and a brand are rather different. A trademark as boring as Bass's triangle does nothing to encode a more complex identity in the consumer's mind. If Bass's was the first British trademark, then Lyle's Golden Syrup with its green and gold can and its wonderfully weird illustration* has some claim to be the world's first and longest enduring consumer brand.

America proved to be even more fertile ground for consumer marketing. The challenge for the first marketers of mass-produced consumer goods was to convince buyers that their products were as good as those offered by better known local suppliers. In densely settled Europe, with its long-established communities, those local bonds were often slower to break down. In America, with its vast landmass, unsettled population, and new communities, there was often little or no local bond to conquer. In 1882, Quaker Oats launched a national ad campaign around its logo of a 'man in Quaker garb'. Coca-Cola's famous cursive logo arrived in 1885, though the bottle wouldn't follow for a further thirty years. The year 1900 saw the arrival of Campbell soup served up in a tin looking much the same as it does today.

Important as these innovations were, they remained tentative. In 1900, J. Walter Thompson started to pitch the idea of trademark advertising – that is, the notion of building a family of associations around a familiar logo or product – but it would take the heated, urbanized atmosphere of the Roaring Twenties for Thompson's vision to be fully realized. Gerry Lambert and his reckless talent for invention was one of marketing's first and greatest stars. Lambert was no longer selling a mouthwash; he was selling an aspiration, a lifestyle, a fantasy, a dream.

That's the positive spin. The negative one is that he was also creating a fear that had never existed before – the fear of 'halito-

* The illustration may look like a sleeping lion with flies buzzing around, but it's a whole lot weirder than that. It's actually a reference to the Old Testament's Book of Judges, in which Samson finds that a swarm of bees has nested in the rotting carcass of a lion and produced a honeycomb – 'out of the strong came forth sweetness'. The entire branding seems to associate Lyle's Golden Syrup with exotic roadkill and meat rotting under a desert sun. Not a classic marketing ploy, to put it mildly.

sis' – and answering it with a collection of half-truths and lies. As consumers ourselves, we suspect all salespeople of the same willingness to say anything at all to close the deal. The issue is at its most intense when it comes to branded consumer goods, but all industries need to market their wares. Entrepreneurs need to take risks and show drive to succeed, but they also need to sell, they need to persuade ... and, the worry persists, if they need to lie, then lie they will.

My quest to understand capitalism from the inside required me to understand the selling impulse too. I needed to meet the modern day Gerry Lamberts and understand what made them tick. But I had a problem. When I met senior CEOs and entrepreneurs, I could hardly ask them, 'Would you be prepared to lie outright to gain a sale?' When I did broach the question of salesmanship, I got the kind of answers you might expect. A man who had chaired a major British consumer goods company told me solemnly, 'It's about laying out the advantages and values of your product ... You can't fool the consumer. In the end, it's all about communication.' And I believed him – that is, I believed that he had come to believe that. I suspect that most senior marketers at most blue chip companies believe something very similar.

But Gerry Lambert did set out to fool the consumer. It wasn't that he *wanted* to lie; it was that he didn't much care whether he did or whether he didn't. The modern day advertiser has to live with a host of protective consumer regulations, the scrutiny of advertising watchdogs, a media waiting to pounce, and a globalized market where a scandal in one territory can quickly create havoc in another. One advertiser told me candidly that he welcomed all these advertising regulations, 'however boring and stupid' they might sometimes be, 'because the nature of what we do always pushes us to the max. It makes my job more manageable – more *ethically* manageable – if I know that I just can't lie, however much I might feel pushed to do so.'

In short, the carefully managed world of the modern marketer has become a bad hunting ground for the true salesman. If I wanted to find the unvarnished truth about the sales impulse – Essence of Salesmanship, free of any careful PR overlay, free of any government-imposed restriction – I needed someone whose need for good PR had long since vanished. I needed someone who didn't care what others thought. I needed someone who was a salesman through and through and who wanted to tell me how it worked.

And that was how come I came to be in a bar outside Liverpool Street station in London with a man that I'll simply call Tom. Tom grew up in Essex. He had wide estuary vowels, no fancy schooling, and no Oxbridge polish. In US terms, this was a kid from the wrong bit of New Jersey, not the right bit of Martha's Vineyard. He drifted into the City of London, working in the back office of a major investment bank. Tom knew he could sell stuff. Stocks, bonds, derivatives, he didn't care. He just knew he could sell. But the major investment bank wasn't set up to give Essex kids without much formal education the chance to prove themselves. The major investment bank wanted Oxbridge types speaking to clients and Essex types settling the trades. Tom got bored.

He dabbled in the markets during the dot.com boom and got dot.com busted when the markets crashed. He lost his own savings and his family's savings too. Then a chance conversation in a pub told him about a job opportunity in Madrid. He didn't know much about it, except that the job involved selling shares. He made a call, got offered a job, was on a plane to Spain the following week.

What he encountered there was madness. He found six salesmen yelling into phones. He found a place that had a tape recording of a busy trading room on permanent playback, as a way of making clients feel that they were dealing with a huge organization. He found a place where the chief salesman had a notice above his computer that read, 'You're Steve Fox. You're a broker. Be a cunt.' Tom received five minutes of training – essentially a guy telling him to 'flog shit' – and he was put to work.

That work involved calling punters in the UK – ordinary individuals with some money to invest, very few of them expert in finance – and getting them to buy stock in US companies. Unlike outright criminal enterprises (so-called 'boiler rooms') that stock was always delivered, but the salesmen didn't know or care whether the stock itself was sound, or whether the investment in question made sense for the individuals they were talking to. Their job was selling. Nothing else mattered. It wasn't about stock selection, financial know-how, customer care, or even the bare minimum of business ethics. It was selling, pure and simple.

To cut a long story short, Tom was very good at his job. He quickly became the most successful salesman in the company he joined then quit to set up a super-successful company of his own. The whole thing folded when his business empire was raided by the police, though an attempted prosecution fell lamentably short of proving criminality. He's written an account of his time on the dark side and is looking to turn his talents to more positive ends.

When I met him, I asked him what made a salesman. What was the secret of successful selling? To start with, his answer puzzled me. He said, 'You've got to be a chameleon … You've got to be a really good listener.' Those might sound like plausible answers when written down, but seemed thinner than smoke when spoken in person. There was, on first sight, nothing of the chameleon about Tom. He was dressed in an expensive black open-necked shirt and black trousers. If he'd had less style about him, he'd have had a heavy gold signet ring and, in another era, perhaps a medallion too. He didn't look like a chameleon, he looked like a salesman. You'd have guessed his profession from across the room.

Likewise with the listening. On the whole, when someone claims to be a good listener we think of a therapist, or perhaps the sort of close friend to whom we can pour our heart out, confident of a sympathetic ear and a glass of wine. Tom, on the other hand, would be a terrible therapist, having neither the subtlety nor the patience. Perhaps more accurately, he wouldn't be interested enough to do it. He simply wouldn't have cared about someone's feelings about their mother's inability to cuddle or their partner's lack of sensitivity.

And yet, for all that, he was right. Talking to Tom and reading his book is an eye-opening introduction to how selling works. A salesman's version of 'good listening' is simply about identifying the route into their wallet. For some people, it was letting them think there was a bargain to be had. For one rather lonely old woman, it was simply talking to her about anything at all and making her feel befriended and cared for. For someone else, it was talking to them about Schubert, their favourite composer. For someone else, it was simply about shouting at them – literally shouting: 'YURI!! IT'S TOM. GET A PEN AND PAPER. I'VE GOT INFORMATION THAT COULD MAKE YOU A MILLION. YURI! I'M NOT MESSING ABOUT. GET A PEN AND PAPER FOR CHRIST'S SAKE!'

What makes Tom's accounts of these conversations so disconcerting is that he's not playing by the normal social rules of our species. Ordinarily if someone talks to you at length about your passions and pursuits, you'll assume that they have a genuine interest in them. Ordinarily, but not always. We're monkeys who have evolved complex social structures and whose brains are shaped to deal with that complexity. So things aren't always simple. Perhaps a certain sort of conversation indicates a kind of flirtation. Or an attempt to create an alliance. Or it's leading up to a request for help. We navigate situations of this kind all day, every day, without thinking anything of it.

What's not quite so usual in regular social intercourse is the sheer brazen nakedness of Tom's deception. He cared nothing about that old lady. He hadn't heard of Schubert before typing the name into Wikipedia. If Yuri had liked whispering not shouting, then Tom would have been the breathiest whisperer in the land. The outrageously goal-oriented nature of Tom's sales tactics takes the ordinary rules of human interaction and trashes them. In the evolutionary environment of the African savannah, when humans hung out in groups that were maybe 150 strong, people like Tom couldn't have thrived. The nakedness of his deceptions would be exposed so soon, would leave him so friendless, that he'd have had to conform, at least to an extent, with the prevailing rules.

Indeed, much of the literature of salesmanship is purposely designed to help ordinary human beings over their savannah-designed mental circuitry. Those who teach salesmanship talk about overcoming 'sales call reluctance'. That's sales-speak for the ordinary human shyness when it comes to promoting oneself, one's company, or one's product. In savannah-world, where everything that goes around comes around, where reputations are quick to form and hard to shake, we're right to have that shyness. It's not that we're not taking care of our own interests all the time. Quite likely we are. But if your tribe is just 150 strong, taking care of your own interests also means building a reputation for being a trustworthy person; it means making friends and working for others. A shyness over self-promotion is part of the complex set of mental tools and dispositions that guided our ancestors through that maze.

That was then, however. In today's world, where Tom has a few million potential punters to part from their cash, the ancestral safety-check has pretty much stopped working. If a saleswoman allows her 'sales call reluctance' to get the better of her, then she'll either move to a more congenial job – or be fired – or buy some books which will teach her, step-by-step, how to overcome her instinctive mental-emotional circuitry.

Nor is it just her emotions that she'll be learning to deal with. She'll be learning to manipulate ours as well. For example, you know those little consumer competitions where you have to write in 'just 15 words or less why you love' a particular product? They feel like a throwback to some older, gentler world of consumer marketing, an anachronism. Yet research shows that if you can get someone to write about their love for (let's say) a breakfast cereal, then their resulting purchase behaviour will reflect that 'love', no matter whether or not they believed what they wrote when they wrote it. The act of writing itself cements a relationship that might not even have existed beforehand. That's why those contests endure.

Or why is it that a competent car salesman will seek to *avoid* discussion of all those optional extras that come when you're buying a car (paint finishes, alloys, extended warranties, and the like)? Surely, he should want us to expand our shopping lists. Again, however, consumer research indicates that if you introduce these extras too early, they become confusing – and the sale is less likely to happen. Once the sale is agreed, however, all those options come straight back onto the table. They're no longer confusing. They're complementary to the decision that's just been made; they confirm and complete it.

The list of such sales tricks is ever-growing and many of them are now widely known. We know what a supermarket is doing when it pumps fresh bread smells out around the bakery, or positions the premium variants of a particular product at eye-level, or packages its value brands in a way deliberately designed to look cheap and unappealing. On the other hand, though we know these things, we are still influenced by them. Our savannah-designed brain circuity doesn't rewire itself simply because we're aware of some of its fallibilities.

If modern consumer marketing can sometimes come to seem like scientifically developed mind (and wallet) manipulation, it's also too simple merely to blame the seller. As I read

Tom's memoir of his time at the rough edge of sales, it became clear that at its most elemental, sales is a game played out between buyer and seller, a kind of seduction. It's not that the buyer has no interest at all. If they didn't, they'd simply hang up. There wouldn't be a sales tactic that could influence them to buy. But each buyer also has an obstacle, a resistance to that sale. The salesman's task is to find that resistance and overcome it. Yuri liked to be shouted at, so Tom shouted. The elderly woman wanted a friend, so Tom became her friend. The bargain hunter wanted a bargain, so Tom transformed his sales patter into a dumb story about a once in a lifetime bargain. And so on. Each form of resistance met with Tom's inimitable response.

I don't even think that those lured into buying necessarily *believed* Tom. Did that old lady believe Tom was nattering away to her about fox-hunting because he really cared about her and her interests? Almost certainly not. From the way Tom reports the conversation, she was elderly and lonely but of perfectly sound mind. In effect, she was allowing Tom to talk her into making an investment (the thing that mattered most to him), because he was giving her the thing that mattered most to her. It was a tit-for-tat bargain, where the rules were understood by both sides.

Viewed like this, the artificiality of Tom's sales techniques didn't much signify. For sure, that elderly lady would have preferred a genuine friend to a phoney one, but a phoney one was better than no friend at all. Yuri would probably have liked being shouted at in any context, but if all that was on offer was being shouted at in a way likely to cost him several thousand euros, well, heck, he'd take whatever was going.

Just to be clear, I'm not suggesting that this collusion between buyer and seller made Tom's activities ethical. They were nothing of the sort. Coke-dealing also works off collusion between buyer and seller. So does prostitution, illegal gambling, backstreet abortions, and plenty else. From a business perspective, though, the real problem is the essentially ephemeral nature of any scam. The businesses that Tom worked for and created so outraged the responsible authorities that they were certain to act and act aggressively. No successful business can operate unless it's animated by a strong sales impulse, but if that sales impulse is permitted to run riot, it'll end up throttling the business.

The way that successful entrepreneurs resolve this paradox is with integrity. Nearly all the businesspeople I spoke to talked unprompted of the importance of straight-dealing, of decency, of doing things right. For a fair while, I simply didn't understand why this theme should recur. I hadn't been accusing my interviewees of anything. Why were they so keen to defend themselves? When I met Tom and read his account of his life on the dark side, I understood. *All* business people are caught in a tug of war. On one side lies the lure of the easy sale, the slick deception, the deliberate manipulation of the buyer. Quick sales and fast profits are the potential reward. On the other side lies integrity: the desire to build a business that buyers will respect and return to; a business whose sales tactics are professional and goal-directed, but not abusive; a business that largely respects the unwritten rules of our savannah-society. More than the rest of us, entrepreneurs are subject to temptation and, more than the rest of us, entrepreneurs need to guard against that temptation by disciplining themselves to think, be, and act in an upright way. That's not to say that all businesspeople always get it right. They clearly don't. But few businesses of any size or duration have got where they've got without at least some attempt to do things right.

Risk-taking, drive, and the ability to persuade: these three traits lie at the heart of the entrepreneurial instinct, a kind of holy trinity of business. But the trinity would be radically incomplete without the joker, the maverick, the upsetter of norms – the entrepreneur's appetite for invention. It's to that restless and renewing talent we turn next.

FOUR

Invention

> Hell, there are no rules here – we're trying to accomplish something.
>
> – THOMAS EDISON

Entrepreneurs are, by and large, straightforward people. Whereas with the large companies I have spoken to there has been a certain amount of bureaucracy involved in securing an interview, entrepreneurs did not mess about, even if it was to say no.

In thinking about my chapter on invention, however, I found myself stumped. It wasn't that people were refusing to talk to me; it was more that I was uncertain who to ask. I wanted to find inventor-entrepreneurs; people who could spout patents and new technologies and visions of the future and have utterly novel ways of attacking old problems, not simply tweaking existing designs to make them work better. Furthermore, I wanted companies that were still in start-up mode. Although there are dozens of big, inventive technology companies who'd have been happy to show me around, they have existing technologies to trade off, existing brands and dominant market positions. I wanted to talk to the people who had started out with an idea and nothing else. No money, no market position, no brand, no sales force. But how was I to find such people?

Then I realized I was being a twit. I live close to Oxford, home to one of the world's great universities and the hub for scores of high-tech businesses. Almost certainly the people I wanted to meet were living right on my doorstep and before long I found exactly what I was looking for. An Oxfordshire-based company, Reaction Engines Ltd is a young start-up that boasts a small but select group of engineers and technologists. Their website baldly summarizes the corporate mission: 'to design and develop advanced space transport and propulsion systems'.

Now, I feel my duty to my readers very keenly. Rocket scientists aren't exactly two a penny, even in Oxfordshire, but at the same time I wasn't going to be happy with a common or garden rocket scientist, the sort that makes nose cones for NASA or the type that spends zillions of pounds tweaking the guidance systems for nuclear missiles. No. As I saw it, my readers deserved a *proper* rocket scientist, the sort who wants to take tourists into space, revolutionize rocket design, mess around with ridiculously dangerous fuels and plant colonies on Mars.

Reaction Engines ticks those boxes, and then some. To get cheap access to space, you need single-stage, reusable rockets. As it stands today, in the absence of such a technology, the cheapest available commercial launch costs around $100 million. A single launch of the NASA space shuttle costs about $700 million. Because booking cargo space on board a rocket is so expensive, a satellite becomes incredibly expensive too, because a vast amount of quality assurance has to be done to make sure that the satellite will function precisely as intended for a very long time. If the cost of access to space were to fall, then the amount of over-engineering and quality assurance involved in making satellites would also fall. The cost of communications would come down. Atmospheric monitoring would become cheaper and simpler. And so on. In a small but real way, the world would become a better place.

The trouble is that there's simply no way to load enough fuel on a rocket to carry it into space and bring it back again. The fuel load becomes so heavy that you have to add more fuel to lift the extra fuel and before you know it the maths has spiralled off into infinity and the job just can't be done.

The fuels involved, however, aren't hydrocarbons – even jet fuel doesn't pack enough of an energy punch. Rockets burn a mixture of hydrogen and oxygen. Since there's already a whole lot of oxygen in the atmosphere, if you can find a way to capture some of it on the way up, then you need to carry a whole lot less to start with, and all of a sudden the maths becomes doable again. What you need, in fact, is a hybrid, an engine that's half 'air-breather' and half rocket,* able to switch from one mode to the other as soon as the outer atmosphere is reached. Reaction Engines reckons it has just such a hybrid and it's busy with the detailed work of going from concept through to manufacture-ready design. The engine is called the SABRE and would power a launch vehicle to be known as SKYLON.

While I was beginning to think that the company's technologies might just about be strong enough for me to present to my reader, I still had doubts. Cheap satellites and colonies on Mars are all well and good, but was this company ever going to produce a genuinely iconic, era-defining product? Did its stuff *look* cool, as well as *sound* cool? Did it have other interesting projects or was this just a one-idea outfit?

Well, there too and no matter how high I was determined to set the bar, the company made the grade. Its air-breathing rocket is, in principle, capable of travelling through the atmosphere at hypersonic speeds – that is, at speeds of around Mach 5.5, so fast that Concorde would seem like very third rate transport. A hypersonic aircraft capable of carrying 300 passengers

---

* Reaction Engines' literature refers to existing technologies as 'conventional rockets'. Pah! Conventional rockets are *so* yesterday.

should be able to fly from London to Sydney in around two and a half hours, except that, as the company literature glumly admits, it might be better to set aside four hours to allow for air traffic control delays. If such an aircraft were chased by an F-22 fighter plane with afterburners on full (an impossibility, in fact, since an F-22 doesn't have the range), you'd have time to pass through customs, ride a cab to your hotel, take a shower, order dinner, dispose of your soup, and be halfway through your kangaroo *à l'australienne* before the fighter plane was even radioing ahead for a landing slot.

As for looks – well, Reaction Engines' rockets look like an 8-year-old boy's idea of the coolest thing in the entire world. Imagine a very elongated cigar shape, pointed at both ends and with just enough wing to nudge you into noticing that there are hardly any wings there at all, and you have the design exactly. If the jumbo jet was the transport icon of the twentieth century, then Reaction Engines might just be developing the transport icon for this one.

As for the fertility of its ideas, it was hard to fault the company there either. Not being an engineer myself, I don't understand half the things the company does, but I do know that when the 'Current Projects' tab on a company's website lists eight major projects, the last but one of which is entitled simply 'Orbital Base Station', then I know I've found a winner. I made some phone calls, and before too long I was on my way to see the company's managing director and chief technologist.

His name was Bond, Alan Bond.

If I was expecting something out of an old Sean Connery movie, then the business park where the company had its headquarters was hardly disappointing. Showing my identity documents at the gate, I drove slowly through a campus where the signs all said things like 'FCS Forensics', 'ABSL Space Products', or 'Culham Electromagnetics and Lightning'. One large and windowless building was adorned with a sign that simply read

'NUCLEAR FUSION'. All that was needed to complete a Connery-era stage set was a mag-lev monorail, some tanks full of bubbling liquid and lots of bad guys in easily identifiable bad-guy suits.

Alas – or fortunately, depending on taste – these thoughts were quickly dispelled. Alan Bond came bounding to meet me at the door to his offices. 'What's the time? Eleven. Ha! You're just in time for cake.' In a scene that was more *Wallace and Gromit* than *Doctor No*, the company's finest bundled into a conference room to raid the tea trolley and carry away piles of stodgy baked goods. Over tea and (in Bond's case) a squidgy appley-creamy thing, he started to tell me about his career and his company.

His interest in space began at the age of about 4, when he first encountered the 'Twinkle, Twinkle, Little Star' nursery rhyme. He asked his father – a fitter – what stars were and his father took him outside to introduce him to the concept of outer space. The boy was entranced. At age 8, he came across the exploits of Dan Dare, 'Pilot of the Future'. A lifetime's obsession was born.

He studied maths, joined the aerospace company Rolls Royce and began to learn what real engineering was all about. Still in love with the idea of space, he managed to get himself assigned to the most interesting projects going. He worked on the RZ2 rocket engine that powered Blue Streak nuclear missiles and (later) satellite launchers. He became section leader of the cryogenic performance office, which meant messing around with the complex thermodynamics of burning liquid hydrogen with liquid oxygen.

He was good enough at what he did that for four years he found himself working for a British weapons programme, which he can't say much about even now and couldn't talk about at all at the time. He also worked with the British Interplanetary Society to design a plausible unmanned starship.

Since the design involved helium-based nuclear fusion, and since a shortage of helium on earth was to be overcome by sending robot factories to Jupiter to extract the stuff from the Jovian atmosphere, and since those factories were to operate for twenty years while suspended from hot air balloons, then it's probably not unfair to suggest that the notion of 'plausible' in interstellar transport design is still somewhat elastic.

To his relief, his stint at the weapons programme ended. Bond messed around in the world of nuclear fusion for a while, then became closely involved with a British Aerospace/Rolls Royce programme to design an air-breathing, single-stage, reusable satellite launch vehicle, named HOTOL. It was the project which Bond had been dreaming about. In the inevitable way of such things, the engineers worked hard, drew up designs, came across problems ... and the government and the project's two commercial backers got cold feet and withdrew. It was Bond's moment of truth, the equivalent for him of those lumps of glittering stone brought to Knox D'Arcy by a trio of wild-eyed miners.

He had two choices. He could do what he'd spent his life doing up to this point, working with some of the world's most technologically advanced companies and agencies, doing the things that they wanted him to do. Or he could do what he had wanted to do ever since he'd first encountered Dan Dare: he could strike out on his own to design and build a spaceship. Reason and good sense pointed in one direction. Passion and conviction pointed in the other. There was no contest. Bond had money in the bank from having sold a crucial patent to Rolls Royce. Using that cash, and in the company of two rocket-scientist colleagues, Bond set up Reaction Engines.

For a while the company lived hand to mouth, selling bits of consultancy, living off capital, but at the same time managing to revise the old HOTOL design in a number of crucial respects. The difficult thing about building an air-breathing engine is that air heats up as it's compressed. At Mach 5.5, the heat generated is sufficient to melt any normal engine. Bond's design gets around this problem by using liquid hydrogen to cool the air. In a cunning move, the heat stolen from the air is then used to power other bits of the engine. The result is stunningly efficient. Provisional calculations suggest that the thrust to weight ratio is about fourteen times, or about three times better than regular jet engines and about seven times better than scramjets (another innovative propulsion technology currently in development elsewhere). Private investors began to get interested and funded further work. The European Space Agency has donated money too. By 2012, the company hopes to be well beyond the proof-of-concept stage for every element of their design. From that point on, they'll be busy with the slow and expensive business of turning engineering drawings into cost-effective, space-going reality.

I don't know if that rocket will ever fly. I hope it does, but slipping the surly bonds of earth isn't easy, cheap, or riskless, to put it mildly. I do know, however, that Alan Bond is an extraordinary individual, one of the few authentic geniuses I've ever met, perhaps the only one. If SKYLON flies, Bond (who is no spring chicken and may not live to see it happen) will become one of the most famous inventors in world history. If it doesn't – well, he'll still be a genius and rocket scientists of the world will always know it.

But his company is not a company. He is not an entrepreneur. He does not, if truth be told, belong in the pages of this book.

To be sure, Reaction Engines is, legally speaking, a limited liability company registered at Companies House. It has a board and sets of accounts and everything that the law requires. But companies are there to make money. Reaction Engines is there to build something amazing. In due course, if it gets it right, it'll create a huge amount of value. Some people will get rich off the back of it. But none of those involved with it today care about the money. Bond himself doesn't give a damn. Even the private investors who have part-funded the project are doing so because they want to do something extraordinary, not in the expectation of any near-term return. Investors whose motivations are coldly commercial have stayed away from the project and will continue to stay away until the technology is a lot closer to being proven. A former colleague of Bond's told him sadly that SKYLON would 'fly higher and faster' than anything Rolls Royce could plausibly invest in. That phrase could be used to summarize the position of industry generally towards any genuinely cutting edge research. High and fast is not where money is reliably made.

From high and fast to noisy and slow.

Not long after seeing Bond, I met up with a man called Paul Luen, the CEO and founder of a small, innovative marine safety company, Martek Marine. Like Bond, Paul Luen came from a fairly humble background. Like Bond, he got an excellent degree in a tough discipline (chemistry, in Luen's case). Like Bond, he ended up knocking around in the kind of companies that could make use of intelligence and drive. Unlike Bond, however, Luen had an interest in making money. He worked in sales, not product development. When the opportunity arose to invest money in the company he was working for, he borrowed £10,000 and made the investment. He worked hard selling gas-detection equipment to industrial users. The company had a handful of customers in the shipping business, but not many; its focus lay elsewhere.

Then Paul noticed that the shipping industry was gradually tightening up its somewhat antiquated safety rules. The new rules would impose higher standards on, among other things, gas detection procedures. Paul believed that the company could develop equipment designed specifically for the marine market, and that it could make a lot of money in the process. His boss didn't see things the same way and before too long Paul and two of his colleagues had quit to set up in business on their own. They invested £6,000, which was pretty much all the spare cash that they had. They worked for six months on no pay. The company started out with no products, no sales agents, no brand, no finance, and no reputation. It did, however, have plenty of competition. The area that Paul was keen to enter was one dominated by large, established companies, well known to shipping firms around the world.

The tiny start-up had to design and manufacture a range of entirely new products, for a market that had never previously existed, and beat a host of well-resourced competitors as it did so. A ridiculous challenge, of course, and yet one that Paul's team met with style.

Their first major product was something called Bulksafe, a system designed (literally) to ring alarm bells if water started entering the ship's hold. Detecting water is not, in itself, a particularly tricky business but, like any vaguely technical product, this one had to meet a whole slew of further parameters. The system needed to be maintenance free. It had to be corrosion proof. It should be able to operate in dusty conditions (because the ship's hold might, for example, be full of coal). It needed to be proof against chemical contamination. It should be able to withstand tough handling. It had to be something that you could install quickly, cheaply, and without starting to mess around with the ship's hull. It had to be something that would meet all the new safety regulations and carry a lifetime warranty. When the new regulations were finally published, at the end of a long consultation process, Paul's team was ready. Ages before its competitors were in position, Martek Marine launched Bulksafe. No other product could do what it did. Orders started to flood in.

The same thing happened with a gadget called MariNOx, a system designed to monitor emissions from marine engines.

Within just three weeks of the relevant regulations being published, Martek had MariNOx on the market and, again, its competitors were nowhere. People came to Martek because they had the first available product. They stayed because it also had the best one.

By now, the company has won fistfuls of awards for its innovations and export prowess. Perhaps more to the point, the company has grown fast and profitably, without taking on a single penny of debt along the way. By 2012, the company is aiming to have sales of £20 million and an operating profit of £4 million, the largest single slice of which will be Paul's. I spoke to the company when panic about the recession was at its highest, but Paul told me that both sales and profits were growing; the only downside was that some of its new product launches would need to be put back by a matter of months.

If Reaction Engines was the perfect example of a highly inventive company, then Martek Marine is a textbook example of a highly innovative one. Its products have all been developed from scratch. It's always been first to market. It's always taken and held a position of market-leadership. Yet the most striking thing for me in talking to Paul was simply this: product development was the easy bit. The international bodies responsible for regulating safety at sea had issued consultation papers indicating the likely drift of regulation. Paul and his team looked at options for meeting those requirements. They created a concept and spent time talking to a dozen or more consulting engineers about implementation. They outsourced much of the prototype work and any machining tasks that they couldn't sensibly take on themselves. And they developed a product.

In one sense that product was entirely innovative because it solved a hitherto unsolved problem. In another sense, they simply took existing concepts and bits of expertise, and assembled them intelligently into one simple-to-use package. The way Paul spoke about it all, invention of this sort is a business process like any other; one that needs thoughtful and attentive management, but no more or less than anything else. Martek Marine doesn't have a single engineer with Alan Bond's genius. It never will because it doesn't need to. What the company needs to succeed is a tenacious grip on what its customers want today or may need tomorrow. The rest of it is simply a matter of management. Indeed, if the company had wanted to outsource its product development – that is, outsource all the genuinely creative work involved in designing a new product – it could easily have done so. Consultancies exist which offer exactly that service. You can find websites where different bidders compete to solve a given product development challenge. Even innovation can be specified, outsourced and put out to tender. Just put 'product development solutions' into Google, if you don't believe me.

If that seems to take all the fun, all the sexiness out of entrepreneurial innovation – well, it shouldn't. It doesn't really matter whether an entrepreneur is engaged in a technically led business or not. *All* entrepreneurship is innovative *always*. It cannot not be. When Paul and his colleagues started Martek, they started with nothing: three blokes and an idea, sitting in a pub. They didn't know how to start a company, plan a product, get it certificated, organize manufacturing, retain sales agents, arrange logistics, rent premises, budget cash flows, compile tax returns, or anything else. In the first months and years of a start-up's life, no problem has ever been solved before. If something needs to be done, then someone has to figure out how to do it. Sometimes that's a phone call to a known expert. Sometimes it's something that can be worked around. Other times it's something to do yourself. Whatever the solution, there is never an established precedent, no one whose job it is to take care of the issue except you.

Indeed, speaking to Paul, I realized that for him creating a product had been straightforward; creating the company had been the challenge. Take, for example, the matter of marketing. Shipping is a global industry and Britain no longer has a significant merchant navy. If Martek wanted to sell its kit, it needed distributors in Singapore, Taipei, Oslo, Rotterdam, Mumbai, Hong Kong, Cape Town, Rio de Janeiro and a whole host of other places besides. That meant somebody – often Paul – climbing onto a plane and looking for local agents. How do you find the right kind of sales agent in Taipei? How do you know you can trust him? What kind of contract should you sign? What kind of income split makes sense? What kind of literature do you need to supply with the product? If you're part of an established company, then all these questions have answers. There are existing agents, existing contracts, and a body of experience. When change happens, it tends to be incremental, building patiently on the lessons of the past.

An entrepreneur has no such comfort – and no such shackle. Martek's success demonstrates that more often than not it got the answers right. But not always. No sooner had it launched its products, than rival producers in India simply copied them. The products were securely protected by patent, but all a patent really means is that you have a right to sue. Indian courts can easily take ten years to come to a verdict and the ultimate recovery of funds is highly improbable. Paul didn't know all that to begin with and spent a few thousand pounds finding out. A more established company would have known that; it would have had a procedure in place telling it what to do.

I left my conversations with Alan and Paul reminded of a basic truth. Entrepreneurs are only rarely and accidentally inventors. Ford did not invent the car. Hoover did not invent the hoover. Rockefeller did not invent any oilfield or oil transport technology. Carnegie was no technologist, nor is Lakshmi Mittal, his modern-day counterpart. Paul Getty, it's true, did invent the John Paul Getty Special, but that hardly qualifies him for induction into the inventors' Hall of Fame. Knox D'Arcy,

Gerry Lambert, Richard Branson, and Warren Buffett invented nothing. Mr IKEA, Ingvar Kamprad, invented nothing. Michael Dell and Michael Bloomberg invented nothing. Retail billionaires Walton, Sainsbury, and Albrecht (in the United States, the UK, and Germany respectively) invented nothing. They're not unusual. Most entrepreneurs never do.

Indeed, if we tend to think of invention and entrepreneurship as running hand in hand, that's partly because there have been one or two major historical exceptions to the rule (notably Edison) and because the modern software industry has made a number of inventive types very rich indeed. If you put the software industry aside for a moment, then not one of the richest people in the world made their money primarily or even largely from invention. Even in software, few people would suggest that Bill Gates or Larry Ellison or Paul Allen have been the most *inventive* people around. Their skills have been in turning their perfectly acceptable, but not highly innovative, products into the dominant brands of their respective markets. In fact, if you comb the lists of the world's richest people for genuine inventors, then the only two names that truly qualify are Sergey Brin and Larry Page, the Google twosome – and it's not a coincidence that the software industry is one where the gap between initial idea and market-ready product is an exceptionally narrow one.

Yet to focus on a lack of invention is to miss the point. For one thing, innovation doesn't have to be about invention, in the Patent Office sense of invention. Richard Branson of Virgin reinvented long haul air travel, without needing to build a different sort of plane. He simply understood that business travellers were human too, that humans can get bored but like pampering, and he arranged his airline around those insights. Two American entrepreneurs, Herb Kelleher and Rollin King, reinvented short haul air travel via almost exactly the reverse insight: that radically simplifying air travel could hugely lower costs and thereby attract customers. Two sharply different business models. Two hugely successful challenges to the incumbents. Innovation without invention.

It's this sense in which entrepreneurs most typically innovate. It's what they do. There is no pre-existing structure so they *cannot* not innovate. Yet many of the entrepreneurs I met (Paul Luen included) are compulsive innovators in another respect as well. They innovate because existing structures bore them. The joy of creating something entirely new is far deeper than the pleasure of running something already established. It's an attitude which in many cases will cause them to leave successful businesses before they should, nudge them into over-investing in risky projects. It's the attitude which makes them what they are. It's also the attitude which has turned the crazy inventions of others into products that work and sell and fill our homes. It may one day be the attitude that takes Alan Bond's genius and makes it fly.

FIVE

Bastards

> For wheresoever the carcass is, there will the eagles be gathered together.
>
> – MATTHEW 24:28,
> King James Bible

The entrepreneur of these opening chapters seems to be quite some person. He or she needs to be restless and risk-taking, driven and organized, a persuader and innovator and doer all rolled into one remarkable person. You'd think such people would be rare indeed, but you don't have to be a Carnegie or Edison to make the grade.

Take, for example, one Michael Mastromarino, formerly the CEO of Biomedical Tissue Services of Fort Lee, New Jersey. Mastromarino's business involved the sale of human tissue – not exactly the kind of business to satisfy a childhood dream, but a perfectly legal one under US law. Sales of skin, bones, ligaments, arterial valves, and other bits and pieces are needed for a whole variety of surgical procedures. Although it may sound a bit creepy to have a free market operating in such things, there are some perfectly sound arguments in favour of the idea and Mastromarino did well at the business. His firm notched up millions of dollars' worth of revenue and he himself made over $4 million. A textbook example of a free market solving an issue of scarcity, bringing vital products to those in need of them, at a reasonable cost, and driven by no more than a profit-maximizing firm's desire to make a buck.

Alas, the textbook in question would need to be one in psychopathology. Mastromarino had started out as a talented and capable maxillofacial surgeon, whose main claim to fame was a chapter on bone-grafting in the promisingly titled *Smile: How Dental Implants Can Transform Your Life.* After suffering a painful fall, he started to dose himself with Demerol, an opioid-type painkiller. He got addicted, his professionalism suffered, and he ended up losing his licence and his livelihood. Fortunately, Mastromarino was restless and a risk-taker. As a surgeon, he'd interacted with tissue banks as a buyer – so why not as a supplier? He had the contacts, the surgical expertise, and that entrepreneurial vim and vigour so essential to the enterprise.

So he set up shop. He found undertakers willing to alert him when they had corpses available. He used his excellent surgical technique to extract good quality tissue, rapidly and without damage. He sold his material to a thoroughly reputable outfit, Regeneration Technologies, Inc. He was in business again. Nothing stood in the way of his success but the lack of raw material.

Driven and well organized, Mastromarino soon found a way round that particular problem too. He started to offer undertakers cash for every corpse they brought in. In poorer parts of the tristate area – the Bronx, Harlem, and Newark primarily – undertakers found the money too good to resist. Of course, there were problems. Tissue needs to be harvested very fresh, and from corpses that weren't compromised by infectious disease, cancer, or the like. But that's where the invention and risk-taking came in. Mastromarino learned simply to forge consent forms, to ignore warning signs of disease and cancer, to operate in rooms that were non-sterile on corpses that weren't refrigerated.

As soon as he or one of his operatives got a call from an undertaker, they were there, scalpels flashing, ready to slice and dice. When leg bones were extracted, they were replaced with PVC tubing and the slits stitched up so the corpse would look OK in an open casket. The undertakers made about $1,000 per corpse, the mortuary nurse about $300 plus salary, Mastromarino somewhere between $7,000 and $15,000. Police later stated that some of the procedures had been carried out so sloppily that surgical gloves were found sewn into the cadavers.

It's not a story that gets nicer with closer acquaintance, so I won't go on, suffice to say that Mastromarino ticked every single box on the checklist for entrepreneurs that began this chapter. Risk-taking is only a breath away from dangerous speculation or law-breaking. The drive to build and organize is only a whisker away from a drive to dominate and control. Persuasiveness can also be about lying, creativity about coming up with new and nasty ways to make money or pervert the law. Those entrepreneurial virtues of the first four chapters aren't actually virtues at all. They're talents or dispositions which can be put to good use or bad; which can be perfectly judged or wildly excessive. Arguably, the risk-taking aspect of an entrepreneur's make-up is one which, if unguarded by law and meaningful enforcement measures, will always tend towards the reckless.

Anecdotal evidence for the All Businesspeople Are Bastards theory isn't hard to find. D'Arcy was reckless, Carnegie a liar, Rockefeller (once) a perjurer, Vanderbilt a bully, Ford an anti-Semite – the list could be extended almost indefinitely. Even today, when ethical standards in business are far higher than they ever used to be, we look at modern day giants – Bill Gates, Steve Jobs, and their ilk – with a weird mixture of admiration and loathing. We admire what they've achieved yet can't help giving credence to the whispers which tell us that Gates is aggressive, Jobs an egomaniac. We tend to believe those whispers regardless of the evidence, because we find it all but impossible to believe that entrepreneurs can be both successful and nice. The strange result is that while the extraordinary improvement in living standards of the last 250 years has come about very largely because of entrepreneurs and business types, nobody seems to love them for it.

Some of our ambivalence comes from reasons that have a lot more to do with us than with any sensible estimation of Messrs Gates, Jobs et al. For starters Bill Gates is obviously a very rich man. Humans are perfectly well used to the fact that we're not all equally well endowed, but the scale of inequalities in wealth runs far beyond ordinary biological diversity. Take speed, for example. I'm 43. I go jogging occasionally, but I'm far from obsessive. Even as a youngster, I was never a particularly fast runner. Usain Bolt, on the other hand, is a sprinter so prodigiously gifted that he can simultaneously win an Olympic gold, break a world record, and fool around ten metres before the finishing line. Yet, viewed in terms of cold mathematics, Usain Bolt isn't all that much faster than I am. He can run the hundred metres in about ten seconds. I could comfortably run it in twenty. On that simple measure, Bolt is twice as good as I am.

Or take looks. Jude Law and Brad Pitt and a young Paul Newman are all, I'm happy to admit, better looking than I am. But how much better looking? We've all got the same numbers of eyes, noses, mouths, and ears. None of us are deformed or have a skin condition or any startlingly displeasing physical feature. The differences in our physiognomies come down to tiny differences in the exact weight and balance of our features – a matter of millimetres here, a shade of colouring there.

When it comes to money, these happy resemblances are entirely absent. A careful cross-country study of household wealth conducted in 2000 put the median household wealth in the United States at about $39,000. (Median is the 'man in the middle' way of looking at averages, so that exactly 50 per cent of households has total wealth above the median level, and exactly 50 per cent has total wealth below that level. The British median household wealth, by the way, was a few thousand dollars *higher* than in the United States. America is richer in aggregate, but wealth in Britain is more evenly spread.) Now, $39,000 is a perfectly nice amount of assets. You yourself may be poorer or richer than that, but, almost by definition, the chances are that you know somebody whose household is not so far off that level of aggregate wealth. Unless you are a hermit, or hang out exclusively with the very rich or the very poor, then you can't help bumping into somebody who's on or around that median level.

To Bill Gates, however, that $39,000 is an entirely trivial sum. He's worth around $60 billion. That's almost two million times better off than the 'man in the middle' median. If Usain Bolt was that much faster than me, he'd be running the hundred metres in one one-hundredth of a millisecond. If Jude Law was that much better looking than me – well, he just couldn't be. Most ordinary human attributes just aren't scalable in that way. Because financial wealth is conjured from far beyond the reach of biology, aggregating profits over the entire globe and then capitalizing them to reflect a value of all future profits too, it produces outcomes that nothing in nature has ever accustomed us to. Evolution simply hasn't given us a template for dealing with a message which, crudely interpreted, reads 'you are two million times worse than that geeky bloke with the unfortunate glasses'. And, naturally enough, humans being human, we tend to react to the unfamiliarity of that message in the simplest possible way: by disliking the unfortunate person who delivers it.

There are other reasons why business types are generally unloved. The good that entrepreneurs do goes largely unnoticed – even by themselves. When I spoke to entrepreneurs and asked them about their own contribution to the wider public good, they all, every one, began by talking about their charitable and philanthropic work. Money donated, time given, organizations put to work. And they all missed the point. Missed it by a mile and two hundred and thirty-something years, because back in 1776 Adam Smith wrote:

> It is not from the benevolence of the butcher, the brewer, or the baker, that we expect our dinner, but from their regard to their own interest. We address ourselves, not to their humanity but to their self-love, and never talk to them of our necessities but of their advantages.

These lines can't be too often repeated. Entrepreneurs don't have to be nice guys to do good. They do good by being entrepreneurs.

An example: one of those I interviewed was a serial entrepreneur called Martyn Rose, a vigorous fifty-something who's donated a large amount of time and cash to a number of charities. Back in the 1970s, Martyn made his first investment in a company that made waterproofing chemicals. He invested during a recession – invested everything he had and borrowed heavily on top – and discovered that waterproofing chemicals sold well in times of hardship. Instead of chucking stuff out when it started to leak, consumers bought something to patch it up and keep it going. The investment did well. He reinvested his profits. He improved his products. He made some efficiency savings. The company grew and went on to make his fortune. (His first fortune, that is; he made a few more after that.)

In speaking about, and disparaging his achievement, Martyn said that if he hadn't done what he'd done, then someone else would have done it and that, in any case, it was only waterproofing materials, for crying out loud. It wasn't a cure for cancer. It wasn't cheap energy. It didn't put food in the mouths of the starving.

That's all true, but Adam Smith teaches us to think differently. When Adam Smith wrote, the world around him was desperately poor. Poor in all kinds of things including, as it happens, cheap and effective waterproofing materials. The lack of those materials wasn't a particularly significant part of the problem. You could have made a list of the hundred things that the world back then most needed and waterproofing materials would not have been on the list.

Yet, even if things only matter a bit, they still matter. We value those things enough to want to buy them, even though we have only a limited budget and plenty of other things we could spend our money on. Add up all a company's sales, knock off the cost of its inputs (raw materials and the like), and you have a fair measure of how much value – as measured by us, the buyers – that company has brought into the world. And the magic of capitalism is its win-win nature. It's not just consumers that are made happy by all their tins of waterproofing kit. It's the people who make them, who are given a decent wage in exchange for their labour, who are able to raise their families without want or worry. And, magic upon magic, the whole merry-go-round whirls round happily enough that the government can take its share of everything in tax, so that schools can be run and roads built and soldiers paid and the sick cared for.

That's a pretty mighty amount of good, yet it's a contribution that doesn't fit our model of what do-gooding should look like. Martyn didn't personally nurse the sick or bring soup to the homeless. And his motivations were never selfless, based not on 'our necessities' but on his 'advantages', advantages which ended up making him a wealthy man. Because his contribution didn't fit our, essentially pre-capitalist, model of what these things should look like, we tend simply to ignore it.

But if the good that entrepreneurs do seems invisible, the harm that they do is very much in evidence. Sometimes workers have to be fired or factories moved. Sometimes competitors are put out of business or raided and broken up. If the benefits of capitalism are so diffuse they become almost invisible, the costs are often painfully obvious and personal. That's not a good recipe for universal love.

It gets worse. Senior management types are renowned for a kind of cheese-paring pettiness, always inclined to quarrel over pennies where any decent person would just show a little human generosity. Examples are legion. Call a phone company – a company whose business is based, you'd have thought, on permitting two humans to communicate by phone – and yet you have to plough your way through a million menus to get through to an actual human and by the time you do, you've got so lost that you've been pressing buttons at random and end up being put through to the Major Emergency Response Team when all you ever wanted was to change your calling plan. Or you can maintain a positive balance with your bank 364 days a year, then you go into overdraft for just one day by just one measly pound and you'll all of a sudden see a whole spatter of charges arise that you probably gave your theoretical consent to somewhere sometime, but whose sheer gall still takes your breath away.

These things are outrageous, at least in the sense that I personally get regularly outraged by them. Yet, in my rational moments, I know why these things happen. Where consumers are happy to measure things in pounds, business types are forced to measure them in pence. A typical phone company might make a net profit of only 7p in the pound, a supermarket more like 4p, a bookstore maybe 2p. An airline is lucky to make anything at all. A bank has a return on assets of around one-third of a penny in the pound. If companies like these start being generous about trifles – a fifth of a penny here, a quarter of a penny there – they'll destroy their profitability at a stroke.

The British cycling team knows a thing or two about winning. British cyclists destroyed their competition at the 2008 Olympic Games and they're expected to do the same again in London in 2012. Their performance director, David Brailsford, summarizes his philosophy of success very simply as the 'aggregation of marginal gains' – tiny little advantages that cumulate into one insuperable one. The doctrine precisely summarizes the route to nearly all business success. When John D. Rockefeller built Standard Oil, his contemporaries were most often struck by the Napoleonic speed, scale, and completeness of his victories. Yet, as in war, Rockefeller's strategic successes were built on the finest attention to detail: railroad tariffs, still design, mechanical sludge removal, barrel manufacture, tank storage farms, tank car loading systems, piping costs, shipping operations, international distribution – there was nothing too trivial to deserve his relentlessly efficient attention. Where he led, almost every competent business since has followed.* Hence the cheese-paring and the ungenerous obsession with trifles.

This chapter has spent most of its time explaining why businesspeople may be admired but are seldom liked. It's been an extended apology for the entrepreneur weeping tears of rejection into her Château Lafite Rothschild, for the unloved industrialist forced to comfort his grieving soul with another Rolls Royce and an extensively customized private jet. So it's perhaps time to admit one further truth: that one reason why successful businesspeople are often not liked is that they are often not at all likeable.

I haven't read many 'How To'-type books in my life for the simple reason that I don't believe most such books have anything useful to impart. But one book I did read and learn from is titled simply *How to Get Rich*. Its author, a magazine

* The prominence of technology-based successes in recent years has slightly drawn attention from this basic truth, because Microsoft and Google and eBay and their peers have triumphed for largely non-Rockefellerian reasons. But they're not typical. If you're about to invest your all in a business start-up, model yourself on Rockefeller not Gates.

publisher named Felix Dennis, has absolutely no professional or academic qualifications to justify his lecturing me – *me*, a highly rated investment banker and Oxford-educated economist – on the topic, but since he does sit atop an entirely self-made fortune of around £750 million, I'm prepared to extend him the benefit of the doubt.

And Dennis is blunt about what it takes to succeed. Among his words of wisdom:

> - If you care about what the neighbours think, you will never get rich.
> - If you cannot bear the thought of causing worry to your family, spouse or lover while you plough a lonely, dangerous road ... you will never get rich ...
> - If you are not prepared to work longer hours than almost anyone else you know ... you are unlikely ever to get rich.
>
> The truth is that getting rich means sacrifice. And the worst of it is, it isn't always *you* that's doing the sacrificing. You must get used to that, or give up the quest.

In another chapter, Dennis is talking about ownership and tells us:

> You must strive with every fibre of your being, while recognising the idiocy of your behaviour, to own and retain control of as near to 100 per cent of any company as you can. If that is not possible, in a public company for example, then you must be prepared to make yourself hated by those around you ... That is the dirty, rotten secret of it all, my friend.

His book is, in fact, 'an *anti*-self-improvement book' – because it admits openly that the chances of anyone reading it and then becoming rich are minuscule. 'The vast majority of you are far too nice.' If it's any consolation, however, Dennis doesn't regard you as rich until you're worth £40 million or so, or a whole lot more than that if you're American. So you can be nice and still worth £39 million or, let us say, a round $100 million, which is the kind of compromise I could probably bear to live with.

The lack of niceness you need to succeed doesn't need to be very profound – and certainly there are plenty of entrepreneurs who rediscover their inner niceness once they've made their pile. But it's a rare entrepreneur who isn't somewhat obsessive; who doesn't downgrade their personal relationships while hot in pursuit of the almighty dollar; who doesn't put aside a concept of 'fairness' while at the negotiating table; who isn't perfectly ready to fire people, close factories, hand out rollickings, or make other tough decisions. Most of the entrepreneurs I spoke to told me that, at the time when their careers were first taking off, they were either single, or had relationships that failed, or had a partner of extraordinary forbearance. Marriages are best formed after the entrepreneurial furnaces have burned back a little.

An obsessive temperament is at work here, of course, but so is a kind of motivational minimalism. The emotional and ethical thickets that the rest of the world blunders around in don't confuse the entrepreneur. If a particular action is good for the business, then it's an action that needs to be taken. It ought to be taken with due regard for others – there are good ways to fire people and bad ways; nice ways to negotiate and terrible ones – but the need for the action is never in doubt. That's why you'll find that businesspeople tend towards a radical simplicity in the way they talk, negotiate, and operate. That simplicity isn't the product of either idiocy or genius. It's simply the result of having only one goal that truly matters.

The same thing lies at the root of another disconcerting characteristic of most successful entrepreneurs: their truthtelling. Most of us like to tell the truth, of course, but we're caught up in a web of human complexity at the same time. We might know that, let's say, a particular product line is underperforming, but we also know that Jenny has tried her hardest on the marketing side and the real problem person, Jake, feels a lot of guilt at his failures, and we prefer him by a long way to that creepy person from production who's just waiting to stick his nose in. On top of which we have convinced ourselves that this year, surely, the market is finally going to improve. At a meeting where these things are being discussed, it's not that we'll hold back from the truth, but our expression of it will be compromised by all those other things that compete for our attention. It's not that entrepreneurs aren't aware of all those facts about Jenny, Jake and the creepy guy from production; it's just that those facts, to them, are background. If a product isn't selling, then it isn't selling. If the line needs to be axed, it needs to be axed. What is to be done about Jake, Jenny, and the others becomes a secondary problem to be sorted out once the primary decision is taken.

The breathtaking simplicity of this approach is something most of us find uncomfortable, because it relegates to the sidelines all our human emotionality and complexity. That conflict, between business goals and human complexities, lies at the heart of almost every drama about tough businesspeople, from Dickens's *Hard Times* to contemporary TV drama like *Mad Men*. It's also why businessmen have a reputation for crassness, and an addiction to numbers and facts. The addiction to numbers is certainly there, but that's only because numbers don't lie about profits and profits are all that ultimately matter. It's not crassness that's to blame, but a frightening simplicity of goals.

Yet for all the discomfort that we may feel around formidably successful businesspeople, there is almost always a respect that goes with it. Martyn Rose's factories made all those tins of waterproofing gunk. Rockefeller's refineries turned crude oil into usable fuel. Felix Dennis churns out his magazines. Michael Mastromarino – well, it's hard to like the fellow and I'm not even going to try, but even he found ligaments for those in want of ligaments, skin for those in want of skin. However complicated our reactions to entrepreneurial success, we can at least see the stuff that's produced as a result of their endeavours, or the difference made by the services that they've provided. Our respect may be grudging, but it's usually there, however buried.

No such sympathy, however, shelters bankers and investors, traders and hedge fund managers, the dark magicians of all things financial. They're doubly or trebly cursed: Cursed once for being richer than we are. Cursed twice for their inhuman intensity of focus. Cursed three times for practising an art apparently both magical and pointless. King Edward I of England expelled the Jews because he owed them money and because there is no good PR to be enjoyed by a usurer. Philip IV of France disbanded the Knights Templar and tortured many of their members for the same two reasons. The modern hedge fund manager is unlikely to be expelled or tortured, but governments still tremble at their power. It's to that power, and to the people who exercise it, that we turn next.

PART TWO

The Money Men

SIX

Bankers

> Why did I rob banks? Because I enjoyed it. I loved it. I was more alive when I was inside a bank, robbing it, than at any other time in my life. I enjoyed everything about it so much that one or two weeks later I'd be out looking for the next job. But to me the money was the chips, that's all.
>
> – WILLIE SUTTON, *Where the Money Was: Memoirs of a Bank Robber*

When I was a baby investment banker, my employer, J.P. Morgan,* was a baby of sorts as well. Although the company had a huge balance sheet, a mighty reputation, and offices all over the world, it was a business in transition. It had made its name as one of the world's biggest and best commercial banks – that is to say, a bank which takes deposits and makes loans but doesn't do all the crazy, sexy things that Wall Street investment banks get to do – but its core business was rapidly changing.

Big firms, the sort of firms who had long made up J.P. Morgan's global client base, were increasingly borrowing direct from investors, by issuing bonds and other types of security, thereby cutting J.P. Morgan out completely. The bank had two options. It could keep hold of its existing clients and try to sell a whole new range of products to them. Or it could do less and

* Now J.P. Morgan Chase, but I'll refer to it by its shorter, older moniker.

less business with its old clients and move down the food chain to smaller corporations which were (and are) more reliant on bank borrowing.

Needless to say, 'moving down the food chain' is not an appealing prospect to any self-respecting Wall Street ego, and since J.P. Morgan was a firm whose power had once made governments tremble and stock markets blanch, that option was never likely to appeal. So it went for option one. The firm wasn't about to give up its existing profitable business, but it wanted to supplement it with a full range of investment banking services as well. Because the regulatory hurdles were higher in America than they were in Europe, it was Europe which acted as laboratory for the New Way.

But what exactly was the New Way? No one quite knew. There wasn't so much a master plan as a determination to grope profitably towards a new business portfolio. Experiment was in the air and that meant a willingness to take risk, which is where this particular story begins. This was the time of 'Barbarians at the Gate' – the era-defining deal which saw a private equity firm, KKR, acquire an American conglomerate, RJR Nabisco, for an eye-popping $25 billion.* It was a deal that had Wall Street's finest crawling all over it and was therefore presumably the sort of deal that the new look J.P. Morgan should be getting involved with. So J.P. Morgan duly decided that it should do Leveraged Buyouts (LBOs) too.

People were hired, budgets agreed, targets set. Before too long, a deal presented itself, and it was a strange beast. A Swedish company, Stora, had a consumer products division which boasted two main arms. One arm made matches, such as you might use for lighting cigarettes or bonfires. The other arm

* Eye-popping for then, I mean. In recent years, that kind of money wouldn't have done much more than cause an eyebrow to be raised – and then only in a languid, 'is that all you've got' sort of way.

comprised the Wilkinson Sword shaving products company. Stora itself, however, was a paper company, turning Swedish trees into reams of photocopy paper.

The whole set-up was a mess. The match business had nothing to do with making paper. Making paper had nothing at all to do with making razor blades, and razor blades and matchsticks only go well together in the hands of teenage hoodlums and arsonists. The commercial logic for separating all those disparate businesses was compelling.

The strange bit, however, was that Stora's consumer products division was to be bought by a consortium led by none other than Gillette, Wilkinson Sword's major competitor. Because Gillette was already a dominant force in world shaving, the competition authorities in Europe were never going to allow it simply to snap up one of its main rivals, so Gillette said that it would minimize its involvement. Roughly speaking, it promised to put up a big chunk of the money and then stand well back. The whole deal was to be very heavily reliant on bank borrowing.

The question that was put to the buyout team at J.P. Morgan was simply this: did the firm want to help? The total transaction amount was to be a shade over $600 million, of which about $400 million was to be made up of senior debt. That phrase, 'senior debt', has a nice reassuring ring to it, somehow suggesting the responsible, grown-up sort of debt that wears leather patches on its sleeves, smells of pipe-tobacco, and has a perfectly manicured lawn. Alas, all it actually means is that, in the event of bankruptcy, the senior lenders get paid out before the junior sort. And there was going to be plenty of junior debt as well: approximately $138 million of it. Alert mathematicians may already have noticed that $138 million of junior debt added to $400 million of senior debt amounts to – a lot of debt, especially when the total transaction size is just $600 million or so. You might think that a venture financed by piles of borrowing tottering on top of a teeny sliver of good old-fashioned cash was asking for trouble.

Maybe so. That's certainly what the competition authorities believed, because they took a highly sceptical view of Gillette's motives in backing the transaction. After all, if Wilkinson Sword was struggling underneath a mountain of debt, it would hardly be the feistiest possible competitor to Gillette.

That, however, was not the question which faced J.P. Morgan. The question which faced us was: would we lend the money? On the one hand, it wasn't the kind of deal that the bank had financed often in the past. On the other hand, this was surely a lovely stepping stone towards the New Way. It was a deal that still involved lending money – the bank's old business – but in a high risk, high fee, very Wall Streety sort of way.

As the baby banker involved in the deal, I was assigned the task of building the spreadsheets. I did my job and the spreadsheets grew. I developed the kind of ratios that bankers liked to look at: interest coverage, gearing, debt to equity, cash flow coverage. All good solid concepts, most of which would have made sense to a medieval Italian banker.

My spreadsheets, inevitably, announced all the right things. Interest would be covered and gearing would come down. All would be for the best in the best of all financial worlds.

At the same time, everyone involved in the deal knew that spreadsheets are simply the world's most complicated way for converting Garbage In to Garbage Out. They're a way, if you like, not so much of predicting the future as specifying exactly what would happen if various different futures unfolded. And nobody knew what the future held.

The J.P. Morgan team divided two ways. On the one hand, there was the group of people putting the deal together, the Structured Finance team, who were representatives of the New Way. They were young, smart, driven, and they wanted to make money. The fees that banks can earn on transactions of this sort are huge, and although I forget what the precise percentages concerned were in this instance, quite likely there was an entire percentage point available to play with, probably even more in the case of the junior debt. The interest rate on the debt would also generate large annual margins for the bank. If all went well, there would be big bonuses for the bankers who had put the package together.

On the other side of the divide stood just one person: the Chief Credit Officer, Europe. He didn't look anything like an investment banker. He wasn't young and wasn't hungry. He looked, indeed, exactly like what he was: a middle-aged British banker, complete with dark suit, receding hairline, big old-fashioned glasses.

When my spreadsheets were completed, and the Structured Finance team was ready, a meeting was set up at which credit approval would be formally requested. The Chief Credit Officer, I assumed, would be a kind of spreadsheet dynamo, ripping into suspect figures, attacking inappropriate ratio calculations, challenging my working capital assumptions. I couldn't have been more wrong. I imagine he knew how to turn his computer on in the morning, but I wouldn't be totally surprised if his secretary had performed that chore for him. Certainly he'd never created a complex financial spreadsheet in his life. His career had begun long before such things came along. Nor was he chock full of the kind of faux-expertise that investment bankers rapidly acquire about any new industry. The Chief Credit Officer didn't have a headful of difficult facts about the shaving industry: frightening new data about the popularity of beards in Germany or the rise of disposable razors in Scandinavian bathrooms.

On the contrary, his technique was simpler and more dazzling. He listened to the rest of us make our case, armed only with common sense and a kind of relentless scepticism. Any team working hard on a major project goes through waves of communal emotion before settling on a consensus position. In the case of this project, the Structured Finance team had come to be Believers and individual doubts faded away in the presence of so much confidence. The Chief Credit Officer, however, hadn't been a part of the project team and even if he had been he was genetically inoculated against flightiness. He just sat and listened and disbelieved. In his presence all the stuff which had looked so good in a spreadsheet or loan prospectus simply sounded contrived and implausible.

That's not quite the end of the tale, however. Although I don't believe that the Chief Credit Officer ever liked that deal, and although his word was almost always law, credit approval was given nevertheless. I don't know why. The bank had a close relationship with Gillette which it was reluctant to put at risk, but perhaps the bank sensed that it needed to take bigger risks in search of the New Way. In any case, the deal was done. J.P. Morgan was the chief lender of the senior debt. It also participated in the junior debt and bought a chunk of equity. These were big bets – and they went wrong.

The equity investors were wiped out completely. The providers of junior debt lost very heavily. The senior lenders, I believe, ended up recovering their money, but only after years of effort and fraught negotiation. This wasn't by any means the worst moment in J.P. Morgan's lending history, but the transaction was still a very costly, very regrettable error. It came about because the boosterism of a bunch of smart investment bankers overcame a traditional banker's relentless scepticism.

This story encapsulates almost everything that matters about the banking disasters of 2007 and 2008. They were disasters that came about because the boosters got the upper hand over the sceptics. Paul Moore, once the head of Group Regulatory Risk at HBOS, a large and aggressively run British bank, was a sceptic. He warned loudly and clearly about the bank's sales-driven culture and its indisposition to challenge; he issued his warning through the normal channels for such things, he did so long before the crisis struck, and he was fired for his pains.

HBOS, at the time, was an institution where selling mattered more than anything else. Bank clerks who sold heavily would be rewarded with cash prizes. Those who failed to meet their targets would be given a cabbage, by way of public rebuke. When Moore conducted focus groups with bank staff at different branches he was told, 'We'll never hit our sales targets if we sell ethically.' When he had a disagreement with a senior saleswoman in the bank, she leaned over a table, saying, 'I'm warning you, don't you make a fucking enemy out of me.'* Admittedly, those who make their living from selling products never quite see eye to eye with those whose job it is to apply the brakes but, when I met him, Moore didn't strike me as anti-business, just anti-bad business. In a better run bank, he'd have fitted in just fine.

The people at HBOS and RBS and Northern Rock and AIG and Lehman and Bear Stearns and Fannie Mae and Freddie Mac and Washington Mutual and all the other financial supertankers that steamed at full speed onto the rocks made the same basic error. They began to *believe*, and they lost their inner sceptic. The problems of Western banking – and not just of Anglo-American banking – have been so profound that it has been easy to believe that everyone went wrong, that an entire industry wandered off to perdition.

But that's not true. In search of a bank that had never forgotten the essence of banking, I knocked on the doors of Nationwide, a British building society. This is a company, please note,

---

* I only have Paul Moore's side of the story here. I asked HBOS for an interview so they could offer me their version of events, but I never got an answer to my requests. Funny that. And, by the way, contrary to myth, top businesspeople do not tend to swear much. In my ten years of investment banking, I seldom came across genuinely bad language. I suspect that there's a correlation between management teams that swear a lot and stock prices that are about to fall off a cliff.

whose core businesses are in residential lending and property loans, the businesses at the heart of the hurricane, the worst possible place to be when the storm clouds burst. What's more, Nationwide is hardly a newfangled sort of place. It is a mutual society, owned by its customers, a nineteenth-century institution still afloat on the British high street.

Yet when a twenty-first-century disaster tore into Nationwide's Victorian rigging its balance sheet was solid. The firm made a profit. It increased its market share, but not impetuously. Since its mortgage arrears weren't alarming and its funding base was excellent its loan book was fine. You could read its financial statements for the period spanning the worst financial crisis for eighty years and arguably the worst crisis in history – a crisis whose violent epicentre lay right on top of the Nationwide's core business – and you'd hardly get a sense that anything was awry. In fact, the worse everyone else did, the easier it was going to be to take advantage of other opportunities as they became available.

I spoke to a man named Jeremy Wood, one of Nationwide's longer-serving directors, about how it had managed. After all, banking is a tough sector, in the sense that the more crazily your competitors behave, the harder it is for you to do your job sensibly. When the bank around the corner has slashed its lending rate, how do you persuade anyone to borrow more expensively from you? When the bank around the corner is willing to lend money to anyone able to stand upright, then how do you manage to insist on decent lending standards yourself?

The answer, as with most things in business, was beautifully simple. Nationwide just did what it had always done, and tried to do it as well as it possibly could. If it wouldn't compete insanely on price and didn't feel like compromising its lending standards, then it had to have outstanding customer service. It knew that if it served a customer well with, let's say, a mortgage product, then that customer might come back for some house insurance or a savings plan or something else.

The strange paradox at the heart of banking is this. Until just recently, bankers were thought of as boring, conservative, risk-averse, and square. They were the sort of people who'd carry a brolly to work on a sunshiny morning because it just might rain in the afternoon. These stereotypes are – or were – basically accurate. Yet they came to develop their habits of risk-aversion because they live, move in a world of towering risk.

Think about it. With most businesses, if you make a sale, you make a sale. Your product leaves the warehouse, cash comes into the business, thank you very much, job done. Sometimes, occasionally, you may send out a defective product and need to make a refund, or there may be other glitches that cause the orginal transaction to be reversed, but these are rare events, and in any case, your loss is limited to the cost of the item in question. If you earn a revenue of $10, then your loss is limited to that $10. If no one has asked you for a refund within a few weeks or months of making the sale, then the chances are they never will.

None of this is true in banking. Let's suppose a bank extends a loan facility to one of its customers. The bank will get an arrangement fee – let's say, half a per cent. It'll also earn a little margin between the interests that the customer pays the bank and the interest that the bank has to pay to get its own financing. Let's suppose that in a given year, the bank makes a total of 1 per cent on that loan. That would be decent business, as it happens. A return on assets of much less than 1 per cent is perfectly common.

Now consider what happens if that loan goes bad. You've made a loan of a million dollars and your revenue is 1 per cent of that, so $10,000. The company you lend to goes horribly wrong – perhaps its accounts are fraudulent, or competition blasts it from the market, or exchange rates move against it, or it suffers a surge in its input costs – and even in compiling a list you suddenly start noticing how multifarious are the ways in which disaster can strike. You can 'call in your loan', but you only ever get the chance to call in your loan at a point when it is unlikely to respond to your whistle. It's also true that once a company is in default, then bankers get a large amount of say when it comes to determining strategy, but again, this privilege doesn't help you very much. You understand your industry, banking, but you don't particularly understand the ins and outs of the industry which is slowly killing your borrower. If your borrower's management can't sort the mess out, then it's most unlikely that you can.

If the worst comes to the worst, then your borrower will go bankrupt and you may be able to retrieve as little as 10 or 20 cents in the dollar. That means that on a transaction where you earned just $10,000 in revenues – before your admin costs, before you've paid for branch staff and paper clips and fancy stationery – you stand to make a loss of $800,000 or $900,000. That's an eye-wateringly painful outcome. To earn that money back again, you have to conduct a huge amount of further business and pray that none of it comes back to bite you. To earn revenues of $800,000, you have to earn that $10,000 eighty times over – but, in fact, it's profits that matter here, not revenues, so you'll have to earn that $10,000 maybe 200 times over (all the time praying that no further disasters strike) before you've even made it back to square one. That's why most bankers are conservative and clasp their brollies tighter as the sun beats down. They're like that because they go to work in a gunpowder factory where only the safety-conscious survive.

The most mystifying – and disturbing – aspect of the period leading up to the credit crunch is what happened to all that bankerly caution. My brother-in-law is a long-haul pilot for British Airways. Every few months he has to sit in a simulator and work his way through a flight in which everything that can go wrong, does go wrong: air traffic problems, instrument failures, storms, engine cut-outs, bird strikes, you name it. He emerges from these sessions soaked in sweat and physically exhausted because they're designed to push him to the limit and they work. When pilots sound calm in the face of minor events during a routine flight, nothing likely to happen on board a real-life aeroplane compares with the disasters that strike the average simulator flight.

Banks all run their own version of these simulator sessions. They take their balance sheets and put them through simulator sessions ('stress tests') in which everything hits at the same time: recessions, property meltdowns, market collapses, and the rest. Goldman Sachs, known for the excellence of its risk management systems, used to run a WOW simulation, a Worst Of the Worst. The bank took the worst events that had taken place in the last ten years in each of the markets in which it was active. It then assumed that each event was 30 per cent worse than it had been in the past. Then it assumed that all those events struck at the exact same time and sought to ensure that its balance sheet would survive these shocks unharmed. In actual fact, when crisis struck in 2008, the effect was worse, much worse, than the WOW simulation had ever predicted. Goldman Sachs came through the crisis badly scarred, but just about OK. Far too many of its lesser brethren failed altogether.

There are some technical reasons behind those failures.* but it's not the technicalities which matter most. What really

---

* One of the key problems, for example, was that much of the 'toxic debt' was made up of mortgage loans that had been bundled up, repackaged, and then sold as securities on the bond markets. Because such securities could, in principle, be sold in a matter of seconds, it didn't quite seem sensible to carry out the old-fashioned credit analysis beloved of traditional bankers. Instead, banks looked at how much they might lose because of adverse changes in the market for such securities. They did their calculations and adjusted their balance sheets accordingly. The trouble is that when disaster struck, the markets for those securities simply froze – and by that point it was far too late for credit analysis.

matters is that *bankers forgot they were bankers* and they forgot that they went to work in a gunpowder factory. They did this because they started to behave too much like top executives in other businesses – concerned about market share, and earnings growth, and foreign expansion, and punching aggressively into new markets. That's all well and good and no successful bank should be heedless of such things. But if you work with gunpowder, safety is the first consideration, everything else comes second. As governments get on with the monster task of rejigging the way banks are regulated, there'll be a million tiny and important questions of detail to deal with and get right – and yet not one of those questions will matter as much as ensuring that banks rediscover the *spirit* of what it means to be a banker: the relentless scepticism of a capable Chief Credit Officer, the immunity to hype, the search for the lone cloud on every sun-filled horizon. Above all, it means pessimism. It means remembering that human beings screw up, that ventures fail, that spreadsheets lie, and that all foolproof systems are just waiting for the right fool.

I speak from experience.

The $600 million buyout of Swedish Match should never have taken place and I helped to make it happen. Boring bankers are good bankers. Exciting ones aren't bankers at all.

SEVEN

Investors

> I never attempt to make money on the stock market. I buy on the assumption that they could close the market the next day and not reopen it for five years.
>
> – WARREN BUFFETT

If Hollywood were to make a movie about Bill Browder, the one person they would not think to play him would be Bill Browder himself. He's in his mid-forties and looks kind of ordinary. He's not overweight, but he's not some kind of gym rat either. He's lost a little hair on top. If you met him and he told you he worked as a reasonably successful executive in the sort of Chicago-based multinational that makes its money from selling tinned meat or industrial fasteners, you'd have no reason to disbelieve him. There's no hint of a Charlton Heston in his demeanour, no Sean Connery, no Harrison Ford. But that only goes to show that Hollywood casts for box office appeal, not truth to life, because Bill Browder once wrestled the devil and almost – briefly – came out on top.

His story is a strange one and it starts with his grandfather, Earl Browder, an American and a communist. Earl Browder wasn't just a red, he was a red who rose to become head of the US Communist Party and who stood twice for President of the United States. (He lost on both occasions, in case you were wondering, to Franklin D. Roosevelt in 1936 and 1940. He was the first presidential candidate in history to have a black running mate.)

Browder senior had three sons, one of whom, Felix, was a brilliant mathematician who was perhaps the most promising talent of his generation at Princeton. When, after Princeton, he sought an academic post to further his career in the 1950s, just as McCarthyism was getting going, he found that the political affiliations of his father ran against him. His applications for work were all turned down.

There was a military draft at the time and, not having an exempt occupation, Felix was called up. Seeing that their new recruit was unusually intelligent, the army had the bright idea of placing him in Military Intelligence. Then, noticing belatedly that their unusually intelligent new recruit had a father who was the head of the US Communist Party, the army thought again and set Browder to work pumping gas on an army base in Fort Bragg. Browder might have spent his entire career pumping gas, consoled only by a succession of victories in the World's Most Intelligent Gas Station Attendant Awards, had it not been for Eleanor Roosevelt and his own persistence.

His persistence drove him to keep sending out job applications, one of which ended up being reviewed by a senior committee at Brandeis University. Almost unanimously, that committee wanted to reject Browder's application on the grounds of his father's affiliations. The only hold-out was Eleanor Roosevelt, who sat on the university's management board. She pointed out the obvious, namely that Browder was, by far, the most qualified applicant they had for the job. She also suggested that the national security superstructure of the United States was unlikely to collapse if he was given it. Since she and her husband had won the Second World War, her credentials were difficult to argue with. The committee gave way and Felix Browder got the job.

Felix's son, Bill, had a less challenging start to his professional career, and boasted some fairly regulation views about capitalism. He studied economics at the University of Chicago, which as well as being possibly the best economics school in the world is also, emphatically, the leading cheerleader for free market capitalism. Like so many of his peers, Browder got a job with Bain, a major management consultancy, and after a couple of years working all the hours of the clock, Browder did just what the rest of his peer group did and applied to business school. He got in, and started working all the hours of the clock there too. The school he chose was Stanford, not just a terrific place of learning, but also an institution which worked hard to instill a sense of specialness in its students.

A sense of specialness which Browder already had. But the key moment in his career, from which everything else kicked off, had been back in that first stint at Bain. Here's what Browder told me about that moment:

> There is this moment at Bain [we're all having lunch ...] and this woman comes in all bubbling with excitement at this big advance they've made on one of their projects. I say, what's so great? What happened? She says, well, we added so much value to our client. It was a yellow-pages publisher, and she was so excited like she had just changed the world. And I thought to myself, by adding value to one yellow-pages publisher she had just subtracted value from another. So that doesn't make the world a better place and she personally hadn't gotten any richer and she hasn't done any good for anybody else, so I thought what's so great about that? I thought that's just the dumbest business in the world. I thought either one has to do something really good for the world or one has to do something where there's a direct monetary reward for the good work you do. On the back of that, I thought when I go to business school, that's going to be the prism through which I look at things ... You

shouldn't just settle into something, you should do something that you want to do.

Notice here the element common to every genuine entrepreneur, the moment of Me-ness, the inner refusal of the role of employee.

On leaving business school, Browder needed to ask himself what his goals were. What really mattered to him? What was his life going to be about? The simple fact is that Browder didn't leave business school with some inner voice guiding his destiny; he chose to go ahead and create it. Among the crowd of smart, educated, motivated, career-minded young men and women around him, there wasn't all that much to distinguish him as someone special – except one thing: his family past.

It was the end of the 1980s. The Berlin Wall was crashing down, and with it the whole brutal edifice of Soviet communism. Browder didn't speak Russian or any other Eastern Bloc language. His grandfather was not able to give him a little black book containing the home phone numbers of the new power brokers. Nevertheless, Browder wanted to pursue a path that was *his* path, and he decided that its first windings should unfold in Eastern Europe.

He worked first as a management consultant, based for months on end in a remote part of Poland, trying to salvage a fast-decaying bus manufacturer. While he was there, the first round of voucher privatizations took place. Newspaper ads allowed ordinary punters to buy shares in a slew of formerly state-owned companies, and it was just a question of filling out a form and sending off some cash. Browder had a total of about $4,000 to his name. He was aware that, away in Warsaw, British consultants were advising the government on its privatization programme. He also knew that their strong advice to the new Polish government would be to ensure that the privatizations would deliver value to ordinary investors in Rzeszów and Szczebrzeszyn and other places more unpronounceable yet. In short, the government was being told to sell its assets off on the cheap.

The government took that advice with an astonishing degree of literalness. It sold off its holdings at a price equal to half a year's profits. In Browder's words, 'now I wasn't an investment expert ... but I figured that all these companies needed to do was stay in business for more than half a year and I'd make a profit'. So he decided to invest his money, all of it, in Polish shares. The shares were duly launched on the stock market. They rose in value, not 10 per cent, or 50 per cent, but more like 1,000 per cent. His $4,000 became $40,000. All of a sudden, Browder's search for a life plan took on a new clarity. He'd invest in the privatizing industries of the ex-Soviet Bloc countries. He'd make a fortune.

He returned to London. Almost no one was investing in Eastern Europe in those early days, except the newspaper magnate Robert Maxwell, so Browder worked for a while with the Maxwells investing in the East. When that came to an end,* he took a job with Salomon Brothers and agitated successfully to be allowed to invest in Russia. At first he was seen as a bit of a nut. The communist system had collapsed because its economy didn't work, right? Why invest in something that didn't work? But persistence paid off. Browder was given $25 million to play with – chicken feed, really, in the context of a major investment bank. Browder turned that $25 million into $125 million in the space of little more than a year. He was given a bonus of $500,000.

Now you don't have to be all that good at arithmetic to notice that half a million dollars, nice as it is, does not constitute a very

* Drowned, bloated, and enmeshed in scandal, in case you'd forgotten. A quick internet search will remind you of the rest.

large chunk of that $100 million profit. Worse still, Salomon Brothers didn't seem ready to offer Browder the degree of independence that he craved.

So, his entrepreneurial mindset again in evidence, Browder chose to set up in business on his own. He jumped on some planes, talked to some investors, found a well-connected businessman to partner with and he was off. The Hermitage Fund was born.

In its early years, the fund did well, largely because the privatizations which took place were priced extremely cheaply. All you had to do was fill your pockets with any half-decent looking buy and let time and markets do the rest. At this stage in its life, the Hermitage Fund was a very prosperous outfit, blessed with excellent timing and some well above-market returns, but it was not yet extraordinary.

Then came the emerging market turbulence of 1997/8. The smaller Asian countries were the first to suffer, while giant Russia with its massive oil and gas reserves was seen as largely immune. Alas, Russia had made the mistake of funding its external debt largely with short-term bonds. When financial turbulence struck, the country found itself excluded from the debt markets and a short-term liquidity glitch spiralled quickly into crisis. The Russian stock market collapsed, and with it the value of Hermitage's holdings. For the first time in his life, Browder had failed and failed big. It was a moment which also demonstrated how much his previous run of success had depended on being in the right place at the right time. When he was in the wrong place at the wrong time, he suffered. Most of the western investors who were with Browder in Moscow simply packed their bags and took themselves off home.

So what next? Clearly, Russia was still an important stock market and could only become more important with time. There was nothing to stop Browder going on doing what he'd been doing. He was already well off. He could go on having a safe, lucrative, self-directed life. Or he could get mean. The great Russian privatizations of the Yeltsin era were marked by gross conflicts of interest, by theft, by blatant greed and outrageous breaches of company law. In short, a handful of super-wealthy managers and investors were systematically fleecing companies in which Hermitage was invested. Since Browder himself owned a reasonable slice of Hermitage, these so-called oligarchs weren't just stealing in the abstract, they were stealing *from him*.

No one likes to be stolen from. It's not simply a question of the money, it's a question of good faith and decent human behaviour. There's a moral indignation at work, as well as simple self-interest. On the other hand, when those stealing your money are Russian tycoons, stealing in their own country, almost certainly with the connivance of the authorities, and almost certainly backed by the fearsomely dangerous Russian mafia, it's not everybody who seeks to kick up a fuss. In a country that lacks any real rule of law, where judges take political instructions, and where politicians and oligarchs dance some shadowy but intimate *pas-de-deux*, people who make a fuss are liable to meet with nasty ends. People like Mikhail Khodorkovsky, the multibillionaire who's now in jail for 'tax evasion' (read: annoying the Kremlin). Or like Anna Politkovskaya, the crusading investigative journalist shot dead by unknown assassins. Or like Alexander Litvinenko, the Russian spy-turned-whistleblower who was killed in London, James Bond style, by a splash of polonium-210 in his tea. Russia was and is the sort of country where sane men and women generally tiptoe quietly away from confrontation.

Bill Browder is not sane, but then no true entrepreneur is. He couldn't get over the fact that 'these bastards were stealing from *me*'. (Browder, like most entrepreneurs, doesn't really do circumlocution. It's one of the nice things about talking to them.*) Financial theory is full of ratios and accounting concepts. Price to earnings, profits before interest, and tax – that kind of thing. Browder and his colleagues evolved a new pair of concepts: 'profit before stealing' and 'profit after stealing'. If you could buy shares in a company with modest 'after stealing' profits but excellent 'before stealing' profits, and if you could find a way to reduce the level of theft in that company, then profits should go up and so should the price of its shares. In fact, the price of its shares should go up by *more* than the rise in its profits, because Western investors will pay more per unit of profit for a well-governed company than a badly governed one.

Nice idea. The next step was to put it into practice. The first thing on Browder's side was that Russia was an ex-police state with most of the old repressive and intrusive apparatus still functioning in one form or another. That meant that when transactions took place, they weren't done orally and in secret. There were documents made, records lodged, forms filled out, and it was generally possible to track those documents down and bring them to light. Browder did his detective work and sought to piece together exactly *how* these bastards were stealing from him: the management companies that siphoned off profits, the share issues that massively diluted existing shareholders, the asset sales transacted at prices that were beyond the absurd.

There wasn't much point in releasing this information to Russian journalists, as it would never have been made public, so Browder learned to trickle his information out to the Western press – the *Financial Times*, the *Wall Street Journal*, and a

* Hermitage's newsletters make good reading for the same reason. One of their classic quotes runs as follows: 'Investors are valuing this company [gas giant, Gazprom] as if 99 percent of its assets have been stolen. The real figure is around 10 percent so that's good news.'

handful of other similarly influential papers. There was no point giving too much information out all at once, as Western journalists had little interest in fact-checking an overcomplex story. Equally, there was no point in giving a spicy bit of information to just one newspaper and hoping that it would print it. The trick, it seemed, was to leak a bit of information to one paper and threaten to give that same titbit to a competitor, if the information wasn't acted on in a timely way. Even a free press has its limitations.

The strategy worked magnificently. Villainous Russian corporations were all of a sudden exposed to a wholly new kind of assault: truth. The truth wasn't physically injurious. While it might add somewhat to the cost of bribery, it was nothing that couldn't be handled. It wasn't likely to result in a string of convictions – indeed, Browder himself once noted that of thirty-two court cases he'd been involved with, he'd been the loser thirty-one times over.

All the same, truth mattered. It mattered because it made Western investors wary. While those Russian oligarchs didn't care about the delicate feelings of Western investors, they certainly cared plenty about the share price of their companies. Browder's agitation embarrassed Russian politicians by making them look impotent; it threatened to enrage the general population, shocked by the scale of the corruption. In addition, the Russian super-wealthy had goals other than money. They wanted to hang out with the Western super-rich at Davos. They wanted to be able to buy Western assets without questions being asked about their reputations. Browder's activism made them look bad. To be precise, Browder's activism exposed them for the bandits that they were.

So they changed their behaviour. Not all the way, but they toned down their thieving and share prices reacted accordingly. Browder's stake in Gazprom climbed from its initial $150 million to become worth $1,500 million. Some of his other investments also became dramatically profitable. By the end of 2001, Hermitage was by far the most successful hedge fund operating in emerging markets.

If the story ended there, it would have a wonderfully happy ending. Alas, it didn't. Russia is still Russia. At the turn of the millennium, Putin's Kremlin wanted to rein in the freewheeling oligarchs so that power could once again be concentrated at the very centre. Browder's activism supported that broader political goal, so he was permitted to remain active. When the Kremlin's mood changed, Browder was out favour. In November 2005, Browder was abruptly denied entry to Russia under a regulation probiting foreigners who pose a threat to national security, public order, or public health. His offices were raided. Ludicrous tax charges were brought and one of Browder's lawyers was badly beaten by police*. In that sweetly persuasive Russian way, the raids were telling Browder that he was no longer welcome in Moscow and he took the hint. He's still active in the emerging markets, still ready to raise a rumpus, but his targets now lie in countries less extreme, less violent, less unpredictable than Russia.

This tale is a wonderfully rich one for countless reasons. There's a beautiful, almost novelistic symmetry in the family's story. Browder's grandfather was sent away from Soviet Moscow in order to run as communist candidate for President of the United States. Seventy years later, Browder would be expelled for bringing too much capitalism to a theoretically capitalist Russia.

There's a lovely parallel too in what it tells us of the rule of law. Browder, though he talks like an American and holds char-

---

* Since writing this section, the story has grown worse. Following an attack on one of Browder's investment vehicles *by the police*, a lawyer named Sergei Magnitsky had the courage to testify against them. The same officers against whom he lodged his complaint then arrested him, and pressured him to withdraw his testimony. He refused. After 11 months in pre-trial detention, he died. He had been tortured to death.

acteristically American views about many things, now holds a British passport. That could just be a matter of convenience for someone forced to endure the queues at Heathrow once too often, but it's more than that. Russia lacks any rule of law, and is a dangerous place to live and do business for that reason. When commodity prices flag, the appalling weaknesses of its economy are likely to be vastly more visible than they have been in the years of plenty and those weaknesses are attributable more to the country's lawlessness than to anything else.

But the United States also failed Browder's family. His father was a mathematician, whose own father happened to be a communist. The mathematician should have been able to pursue his career to the maximum extent of his abilities, unhindered by his father's political affiliations. He should not have to have been given a security clearance for anything. He should not have been allowed to fool around with nuclear technology or arms deals or missile firing codes, but higher mathematics involves none of those things. The best universities in the world should have been looking to hire the best talent in the world. It took Eleanor Roosevelt, a woman large enough of vision to see beyond the fear of a controversial hiring, to point out the obvious and restore sanity.

The episode reminds us that the rule of law isn't just a matter of rules and regulations, it's a question of mindset and culture too. Those things need to be nurtured and guarded and they can't just be left to lawyers and courts. Browder holds a British passport because, for all its deficiencies in other areas, the country boasts the strongest, longest, and deepest rule of law tradition anywhere in the world. As it happens, no rich economy can manage without a serious commitment to the rule of law, but it's important for more reasons than that. Freedom depends on it.

Browder's story also repeats and emphasizes some of the points already made about entrepreneurship. Robert Knox D'Arcy, the speculator and oilman of our opening chapter, took financial risks on a prodigious scale. Browder is a more sober investor on every financial count, but his risk-taking involved playing hardball with the Russian mafia, the Kremlin, and the oligarchs. If it's risk you're after, then no one mentioned in this book can beat Browder for sheer ballsy audacity. There's also that quality of Me-ness. That sense of wanting a life shaped by one's own desires and motivations, that sense of personal affront when losing money.

Yet for our purposes here what really matters is something else: the nature of investment in a modern stock market economy. Formidably successful as Browder has been, he's not typical. In fact, he's about the least typical investor I could think to find. Browder made his money by fighting wrongdoing. That wrongdoing was financial and economic in origin, but it had far broader ramifications. In a lawless economy, where corporations can do what they like so long as they've paid off the right people in government and the criminal underworld, then any kind of behaviour is OK. It's very hard to assess how serious the problem is because you need a certain level of law-abidingness in a nation even to collect accurate data. Nevertheless sober estimates suggest that a million tons of oil is spilled from Russian pipelines each month. That's twenty-five Exxon Valdez spills a month, more or less one a day, often straight into aquifers and water supplies. At the nuclear waste complex in Chelyabinsk, management of radioactive material is so bad that a nearby lake ranks as the worst polluted spot on earth, containing seven times the amount of strontium-90 and cesium-137 that was released at Chernobyl, an accident that released as much radiation as the atomic bombs dropped on Hiroshima and Nagasaki combined. By 2020 or 2030, half the children in the area are expected to be born with serious genetic deficiencies. The point here is that though dilutive share issues or dodgy asset sales sound like the sort of thing that only a professional investor could care about, those things are part of a corporate and political philosophy which says it's all right to poison the water supply or cripple babies. Responsible corporate governance wouldn't solve all those problems on its own, but it would be a very good start.

Instead of walking away from the challenge, Browder took a stand. He fought the devil and won his first few bouts. He made money for himself along the way, but he also had a palpable effect on the level of wrongdoing in an economy that seethed with it. He made money *because* he had that effect. The money-making and the crusading-for-justice were two aspects of the same thing. If the political winds had stayed more favourable, Browder and his allies could have been one of the most important forces driving Russia towards a law-bound, freedom-loving society.

And who were his allies? When Browder agitated for change in Russian companies, he naturally wanted to build coalitions of like-minded shareholders to support him. In his early days Browder figured that any Western shareholder would support him. Why not? Browder would do the work, all the others had to do was sign their names to petitions, vote their shares in particular ways, and pick up the profits. To his surprise and dismay, however, Browder discovered that the average passive investor had no stomach for the fight. Fights meant hassle. They meant legal conflict. They meant exposure. Most Western investors took Browder's calls, exchanged politenesses, and did nothing.

The exception was wealthy individuals who cared about their money with the same hot passion as Browder cared about his. Also there were hedge funds, whose activist principals likewise saw their funds' cash as a proxy for their own. These people acted like their own money was at stake, because big chunks of it *were* at stake. They signed Browder's letters. They agitated for change. They voted in the way most likely to procure it.

It would be easy to tut-tut at the apathy of most investors, without dwelling on the matter – but the issue is worth thinking about for just a moment. If you had invested any money in a mutual fund towards the end of the 1990s or the start of the Noughties, and if that fund had international exposure or an emerging markets focus, then quite likely you had some money sitting alongside Bill Browder's Hermitage Fund money. If you had any significant pension fund assets in the period, then some of those assets might well have been sitting in Russia, even if you never knew about it.

That's the sober way to put the issue, but not the clearest. To put the matter in Browder's own language, those bastards weren't just stealing from him, they were quite likely stealing from you. They were stealing *your* money. It wasn't a one-off thing. They stole and stole and stole and stole and stole.

That's bad enough, but here's something that should annoy you even more. *You* paid *your* fund managers to look after *your* money. That's their job. You can't legitimately expect them to do all the hard work that Bill Browder put in, since Hermitage, like any hedge fund, charges a pretty fancy price for its services – but still, they didn't have to do that work. They had to sign letters and vote shares. That was all.

And they didn't do it. They did nothing. They didn't refrain from action because they thought Bill Browder was wrong, since everyone knew he was right. Your fund managers just thought it was OK to take your money and then let a bunch of Russian gangsters steal it, because anything else was too much hassle. No financial regulator has ever challenged such behaviour and no one has ever been fired for it. No one has ever lost a bonus, missed a promotion, or even endured the most tepid of wrist-slaps and no one ever will. It's how the industry works.

All this should anger you. Although those 1 per cent fund management fees are largely hidden from our eyes, because they're skimmed from our assets rather than presented by way of an annual invoice, they amount to a lot of money. If you have any significant funds under management, then those fees probably constitute one of your larger annual expenditures. You quite likely think that if you were as indolent in your own job, you'd have lost it some time ago.

The investors I met while writing this book were all successful in their fields. Many of them were very rich to boot. But whereas the entrepreneurs I met were recognizably similar in temperament – on the whole being restless, risk-seeking, needing to take control, obsessive, and direct – the investors were more diverse.* I met buccaneers and I met bean-counters. I met people with a swaggering sense of self-worth and people who'd have faded into anonymity in a room full of actuaries.

Needless to say, Bill Browder is every inch the entrepreneur. It so happened his entrepreneurship took a financial form, but if his stint at that Polish bus factory had thrown up interesting opportunities in bus-manufacture, or structural steelwork, or something completely else, then I've no doubt he'd have been more or less equally happy to leap on those instead. And his success as an investor is due almost entirely to those entrepreneurial genes. His investment strategy was driven by a philosophy, *his* philosophy. He was never going to end up following the herd, because every important decision in his career was centred on a sense of Me-ness. Not selfishness, you understand, but a sense of being his own boss, determining his own destiny, making his own decisions. When the investment herd stampeded out of Russia in its hour of crisis, Browder wasn't even listening to the hoofbeats. They didn't register. Why would they? They never had done before.

* There's not a perfect distinction between the two breeds, by any means. Any halfway successful entrepreneur will have become an active investor of their own money. Most able investors will have set up their own investment companies, thereby becoming entrepreneurs. But still, a fuzzy dividing line is still a dividing line.

Plainly enough, that aloofness from the herd hardly guarantees you success. Browder could easily have failed, and the common view is often the right view. But you can't be a successful investor unless you dare to be different, and if being different involves you in a storm of emotional complexity – a desire to prove yourself; a terror of failing; an anxiety about the respect of your fellows – then you're entering the field of combat with the battle already half-lost. The best investors are entrepreneurs too.

Alongside that rare ability to be different lies the possession of a philosophy, an outlook, an investment *raison d'être*. Those books with titles like *How to Turn Yourself into Warren Buffett Only Richer and with Better Hair* misunderstand this. They mistake philosophy for strategy, as though it's something you can select from a menu, like choosing between sole meunière and steak au poivre. And that's wrong. Bill Browder's investment strategy reflects Bill Browder himself. Other investors are different. Warren Buffett's most successful ever investments include the acquisition of stakes in Coca-Cola and Gillette, two of the most stunningly visible companies in the corporate world. If Browder's investment philosophy has to do with slaying dragons, Buffett's can perhaps best be summarized as seeing the obvious: finding strong and enduring businesses, buying in at sensible prices, preferring humble managers and sober business plans. If Browder tried to be Buffett, he'd almost certainly fail (as well as getting bored so quickly that he'd hardly give himself a chance). If Buffett tried to be Browder – well, it's inconceivable. It's about as unlikely as Barack Obama trying to remake himself as P. Diddy.

These things run so deep that they go deeper than money alone. I realized this in conversation with Michael Jackson – not the late King of Pop, but a technology investor with the unusual distinction of having been chairman of not one but two new entrants to the FTSE-100. Jackson talked about his time as chairman of one of those two, a software and services company called Sage. As stock prices in the technology sector surged prior to the new millennium, Jackson's investor-brain knew that prices were becoming inflated. As an investor, he knew he should sell down all or part of his long-standing (and very successful) holding in Sage. If he'd been flicking through the pages of *How to Turn Yourself into Warren Buffett Only Richer and with Better Hair*, he'd almost certainly have done just that.

But Sage meant far more to Jackson than merely a financial play. He had been with the company from its youth. He had been a small but important part of its success and he had worked with management to shape strategy, to influence decisions, to create a culture. Jackson held on to the bulk of his holding out of a sense of something like loyalty. When I quizzed him about that decision – and I pressed him fairly hard – he was clearly torn. He said several times that he should perhaps have sold earlier and more heavily than he did – but each time he said it, he looked uncomfortable. He didn't *look* like a man who'd have been happy to sell, and I suspect that if he'd been investing his money alone (as opposed to having to consider the interests of the other investors in his fund) then he'd have taken the hit with a wince but without real regret. In short, Jackson's philosophy impelled him to hold stock when reason told him to sell. Philosophy trumped money.

Jackson, Buffett, and Browder are all hugely successful investors, who'd have made huge profits for you if you'd been lucky enough to invest with them at the right time – not *despite* the occasional clash of philosophy and cold financial logic, but *because* they are driven by something beyond mere money. Mostly that philosophy will deliver financial gold. Occasionally it will not. The great investors don't care, or don't care deeply, because for them the whole game is about more than just cash. That's why they end up winning.

The huge majority of investors are not like this. One of the strangest interviews I conducted was with a senior fund manager at a well-known fund management firm. I can't give either the individual's name or that of the firm he worked for, because in order to get the interview in the first place I was obliged to engage with a long email correspondence in which I foolishly undertook not to print anything without getting the thumbs up from him first. When finally I met him, he seemed bored and arrogant and vaguely angry. The boredom seemed to say, 'I don't particularly want to be here talking to you.' The arrogance seemed to say, 'I'm more important than you are, and I'm not remotely interested in your project.' But I was mystified by the anger. Why be angry? What was there to be angry about? Here was a guy responsible for funds worth well in excess of £1 billion. He had loads of responsibility, an excellent pay packet, an opportunity to show off a little. Why be angry?

As I left the building, relieved to be away from it, I helped myself to some corporate brochures on the way out. I noticed that the average performance of the company's funds fell below that of the broader market. The Great Man who had just granted me an audience had actually destroyed value for his investors, who'd have done better (on average) if they'd used a team of monkeys to pick stocks for them. That's not unusual. Because professional investment managers are responsible for almost all stock market activity, they can't as a group achieve more than an average performance *before* management charges are taken into account. Since they all charge management fees, then the 'average' fund manager will paradoxically always perform worse than the underlying market.*

---

* I don't want to get all mathematical on you, but those management charges destroy far more value than you might imagine. A management fee of 1 per cent a year sounds like it's going to eat up just 1 per cent of your portfolio. Not so. You pay that fee each and every year, so it's nibbling at your portfolio each and every year. The net present value of those fees can easily amount to 25–30 per cent of your portfolio's overall worth. Not something they tell you when you hand your money over.

I can't prove it, of course, but I suspect that the Great Man's anger was born of an inner insecurity. His arrogant tone – the charts that he flipped at me – the drawling way he spoke of company managements the way that other people might talk about their cleaners – all sought to imply that here was a Master of the Universe going about his godlike business. At the same time, however, he knew that equipping the doorman downstairs with a blindfold, a dartboard and a list of stock prices would generally achieve a performance that was no worse than his own – indeed, rather better, if the doorman was prepared to forgo a fee.

Underperforming the market is something that can and will befall any capable investor. Browder has had horrible times in the markets as well as good ones. When I met him, stock markets in Russia and the other emerging markets had plunged catastrophically, ripping a huge hole in Browder's personal net worth. Buffett's tastes are less exotic, so his bad times have been less bad, but he too has known what it's like to lose. So has Jackson. So has every other investor of any experience.

Yet those guys invest with a passion, as an expression of themselves. Losing money, for them, isn't as bad as losing a sense of who they are. The Great Man never started out with any such sense. He talked to me about selecting investment strategy as though it were like picking out a pair of socks. The Great Man, in fact, was paid bundles of money to perform worse than his doorman and without the consoling knowledge that what he did was charged with any important inner meaning. There are worse fates in life than that, but I still wouldn't like to be inside the Great Man's head, not for all his turbocharged salary.

EIGHT

Masters of the Universe

> At other places management says, 'Well, gee, fellas, do we really want to bet the ranch on this deal?' Lewie was not only willing to bet the ranch. He was willing to hire people and let them bet the ranch, too. His attitude was: 'Sure, what the fuck, it's only a ranch.'
>
> – Senior trader at Salomon Brothers talking about Lew Ranieri, creator of mortgage-backed securities. Quoted in Michael Lewis, *Liar's Poker*

In 1991, I was on the point of quitting the development bank where I'd been working for the last couple of years and was interviewing for jobs back in investment banking. These days, investment bankers are somewhere down with child-molesters, tobacco-marketers, and human-traffickers in popularity. Back then, no one really loved a banker, but at least you could walk down a street without having to wipe spit off your face. I interviewed with a number of firms, including at Goldman Sachs, the Holy of Holies, the most highly regarded investment bank in the world.

It was a strange experience. To say that Goldman took its interviewing seriously would be a pallid understatement. I had a total of fifteen interviews, most of them an hour long, and nearly all with front line bankers, some of them very senior. The interviews passed in a kind of blur. Imagine, if you will, a succession of good-looking, very international, very intelligent, very dedicated young people doing their very best to instill in you a sense of deep inadequacy.

'*Hola*! My name is Vicente Juan Jesus Maria del Prado Dos Cerveza y Paella. I speak twelve European languages to fluency, so please. Tell me. How many European languages do you speak?'

'Morning. Johann von Clausewitz-Fürstenberg. I graduated first in my year from the University of Heidelberg and have a PhD in Quantum Physics from MIT. So, *bitte*. Enumerate your principal qualifications in the field of higher mathematics.'

'Harry! Hi! Jane Kravitz. Good to meet you. I dropped out of Harvard to build up a financial services boutique. Did very well. Goldman bought me out last year. Now, Harry, why don't you share with me your experience of creating multimillion dollar businesses from scratch?'

After two days of this, I felt like a tent peg being slowly hammered into compacted clay. That wasn't the end of it, though. A week or two later I got a call. Goldman were obviously on the lookout for a monolingual Brit of no particular mathematical gifts who had managed to stumble through life without creating a single noteworthy enterprise, because I was told that they were interested in taking me on. Specifically, I was told that they thought I had the aptitude for the job, but that they weren't too sure that I was a 'Goldman man' and would I mind very much coming back in for another two days of interviews? Now, if it had just been a question of acting the tent peg for another couple of days, I could probably have managed it, but that phrase 'Goldman man' gave me the shivers. The way I understood it was that a Goldman man needed to place work over friends, work over family, work over life. It wasn't me. I told Goldman that I wasn't for them and ended up going to back to work for J.P. Morgan, a decision I never regretted.

These days, it's become a media truism that investment bankers have been greedy and stupid. Let me tell you right away that that's wrong. Investment bankers are many things, but not stupid. If there were a kind of business Olympics, then Goldman would be a perennial gold medallist, its major competitors coming only a whisker behind. And greedy isn't quite right either. Investment banks are profit-maximizing businesses, but then what business isn't? Bankers like money, but then again, most of us do. For what it's worth, I've never encountered a business with a more unified, more focused corporate culture than Goldman Sachs. Everything, but everything, was a team effort. Every decision of significance sped round the firm by voicemail and email, being shaped and refined until a genuinely joint decision was made. I knew one Goldman banker who returned from holiday yachting around the Greek islands to be formally rebuked, because he hadn't taken enough care to ensure that his mobile phone had had adequate reception while on board. Holidays, for Goldman people, are just a sunnier kind of office.*

Perhaps it's best to start with some explanations. At the heart of investment banking lie three basic activities. The first is helping companies raise money on the stock markets, by underwriting and selling equities. The second is helping companies borrow money from the bond markets, by underwriting and selling bonds, a kind of corporate IOU. The third is advising companies on buying and selling other companies. That's the heart of it. That's what investment bankers do.

Needless to say, though, it's more complex than that and those core activities are surrounded by a whole host of others. For example, you're not going to be in a position to underwrite

---

* At least they have holidays. I once interviewed a banker who was leaving Wasserstein Perella, a Wall Street boutique. He had been there two years and had spent fifty-one of his first fifty-two weekends at the office, including one of his two Christmases. It had taken him that long to realize that he wasn't a Wasserstein Perella man.

equities or bonds, unless you're active in the market for equities and bonds. That means you need a trading floor filled with folk who buy and sell these things, plus plenty of sales folk looking for people to buy and sell them to. You don't need to be an investment bank to run a trading floor, but investment banks tend to be in the thick of the action all the same.

If you think that issuing and trading bonds and shares sounds like a lucrative business but not a complex one, then you're right. It also won't entirely have escaped your notice that in recent times bankers haven't exactly confined themselves to the simpler, older ways of making money. Things started to get complicated in the 1980s, a time of expanding international trade and investment, and a time when capital controls still impeded the easy flow of money. It sounds strange to say it now, but back then the world needed investment bankers.

Let's say, for example, that you were a large German company looking to expand in the United States. You could have borrowed in Deutschmarks from investors in your home market, but that would have left you with a pile of Deutschmarks that wouldn't have done you a whole lot of good in Albuquerque or Little Rock. You could, of course, have used your Deutschmarks to buy dollars in order to fund your investment in those fine places – but that would have left you with a dangerous mismatch between your assets (in dollars) and your liabilities (in Deutschmarks). If currencies moved the wrong way, a normally cautious borrower could suddenly find themself in a potentially perilous situation. That was option one.

An alternative strategy would have been to borrow in US dollars. That would have been fine, except that American investors are most familiar with American companies and would demand an extra risk premium for lending money to a relatively unknown (to them) German company. That premium meant higher interest rates for foreign borrowers, driving costs up and investment down. That was option two.

Neither option was attractive but that was just the way it was and there was nothing that could be done about it.

Then, in the 1980s, a solution emerged, simultaneously ingenious and delightfully simple. Suppose that your German company, Deutsches Ungeheuer GmbH, wants to borrow $100 million to invest in the United States. At the same time, perhaps there's an American company, American Muscle Inc., which wants to invest the equivalent sum in Germany. Bankers realized that American Muscle could simply borrow in dollars from the investors that knew it best; Deutsches Ungeheuer could borrow in Deutschmarks from the investors that knew *it* best; and the two companies could simply swap their obligations. It was one of those little capitalist miracles. Investors would be investing with the companies they felt were safest and borrowers would get the currencies they wanted. By reducing the costs of finance, investment was encouraged, thereby helping ordinary folk in both economies. And needless to say, the bankers who made the whole thing happen ended up getting a lot, lot richer.

This new financing option was such a sweetly simple solution to a perennial problem, that it became explosively successful. Quite soon, it wasn't necessary for Deutsches Ungeheuer to wait around until it found a partner to dance with, because banks themselves began to take to the floor, using their own balance sheets to tango with all and sundry. As the market grew, it became boring, but in a good way. Competition increased. Profits fell. Contracts became standardized and banks learned how to manage the risks. Currency swaps became a standard financial tool. It was a clever, valuable, helpful innovation.

The same basic insight – the notion that financial instruments could be sliced up into bits and repackaged in a way that was of benefit to everyone – led to countless further innovations. If you happen to have a fixed rate mortgage, then you are taking advantage of those innovations. If you have money invested in the stock market in one of those funds that guarantees to return 100 per cent of your capital, no matter what the future holds, then you are taking advantage of those innovations. If your gas supplier offers you a deal where you can put a ceiling on your fuel bills, no matter what, then you are taking advantage of those innovations. Needless to say, the potential benefits to companies, with their much more complicated sets of exposures, were very much greater still.

From our post-credit-crunch standpoint, it's clear that, for all the cleverness of those innovations and for all the real benefits they brought, they were also creating a powder keg, buried right at the heart of Wall Street, which, when detonated, would threaten to blow the whole of Western capitalism to shreds. We've picked at some of those issues already, and will get to still others in later chapters. For now, however, our focus is on mindsets, on what makes those investment bankers tick. They're clearly smart. They work phenomenally hard. And, as the currency swap episode indicates, the best banks possess a kind of relentlessly innovative culture.

These observations, however, don't quite get to the heart of the matter. There are lots of people who are clever, innovative, and work hard, yet what is so distinctive about investment banking culture that it has spawned an entire literature of its own? (The title of this chapter, for example, comes from Tom Wolfe's *Bonfire of the Vanities*. Wolfe couldn't have known that the real bonfire wouldn't take light until 2008, though.)

A good way of getting to the heart of that culture is to simplify the question. In Elizabeth Gilbert's phenomenally successful *Eat, Pray, Love*, she suggests that all major cities possess a code of values which can be boiled down to a single word. Thus Rome is SEX, the Vatican is POWER, New York is ACHIEVE, Los Angeles is SUCCESS, Stockholm is CONFORM. (The examples aren't mine, they're Elizabeth Gilbert's. She doesn't discuss London, but when I discussed London with my wife, she came up with SELF-EXPRESSION, while I reckoned a cabbie's uninterested shrug just about conveyed it all. The nearest city to me is Oxford, whose word is obviously THOUGHT.)

To adopt the same approach then, if investment banking were boiled down to a single word, what word would it be? The most obvious word is MONEY. Bankers are obsessed with it. Most employees in most companies will face some sort of regular appraisal from their employer. In investment banks, though, those appraisals couldn't have a stronger grip on consciousness if they were iron bands around the skull. When I was at J.P. Morgan, every banker was obliged to submit a written review on at least fifteen of their teammates, and obliged to solicit a whole bunch of reviews on their own work. Anyone could review anyone. If you were a fifty-something managing director with oceans of experience and I was a junior analyst whom you had offended, then I could write a review on you that stated just exactly what I thought of you. The vast majority of these reviews were secret, but every boss had to collate and summarize them for each of his or her subordinates. Committees were in place to ensure that the bosses applied broadly similar appraisal standards. At J.P. Morgan the process kicked off in autumn and didn't really end until Christmas, but it loomed throughout the year in much the same way as the Day of Judgement must have loomed for medieval Christians.

Like the Day of Judgement, the outcome of your personal appraisal process opened the doors either to heaven or to hell. As a rough guide, in top level investment banking jobs, about 10 per cent of the bankers can expect to be fired each and every year. They aren't being fired because they're drunk on the job, or botched an assignment, or nicked too much stationery, or groped the wrong person at the Christmas party. They're being fired because they're intelligent, hard-working and competitive people who have been deemed slightly less intelligent, hard-working and competitive than their friends and colleagues. That's enough for them to be kicked out, or at least to be given a very strong indication that now would be a good time to start talking to friendly head-hunters. A further 10 per cent will be given a strong message to do better next year or else.

At the top end, on the other hand, rewards are huge. Bankers receive large salaries but bonuses for the most successful performers are multiples of those salaries, sometimes large multiples. The top 10 per cent will do phenomenally well. The next 10 per cent will do very well. The next 10 per cent down will be given plenty of encouragement and (by ordinary mortal standards) plenty of money but nothing approaching the vast rewards of the very top tier. In 2007, Goldman Sachs shared a bonus pool of $18 billion among its 30,000 or so employees, a sum equal to more than $600,000 per head. Most of those employees, however, were support staff (who are well paid, but not crazily well paid), junior analysts (ditto), or bankers being nudged out onto the street. At Goldman Sachs and at rival banks, it's the top performers who scoop the pool.

The reward structure is hopelessly unbalanced because its entire purpose is to foster a culture in which excellence is rewarded and an ordinary, capable and committed performance is left feeling inadequate.

Hence the obsession with money. If bankers don't start out obsessed by their end-of-year bonus cheque, then the system is carefully designed to make them that way. I'm not a materialist sort myself. If I have books, a log fire, and enough to eat and drink, then I've got most of what I need to be happy. But when I was at J.P. Morgan then I too, if not exactly obsessed, came to care very much about that end-of-year cheque. I didn't care about it because I was desperate to get myself kitted out with the Armani, the Rolex, the Porsche and all the rest of it.* I cared because the cheque was an accurate assessment of my performance, and represented a tangible measure of my value to the firm. Throw the same petrol on flames that are slightly readier to leap, and it's hardly surprising that plenty of bankers develop their money obsession to ugly heights. Perhaps the word that best summarizes the industry isn't MONEY but GREED.

Perhaps – but I don't think so. For one thing, it's not just the bonus culture which causes bankers to obsess so much about money. It's an obvious point, but an important one, that bankers deal with money all the time. Journalists will obsess over stories. Ad men will obsess over brands, architects over buildings, doctors over treatments, and so on. Anyone lucky enough to be engaged and challenged by their occupation will often come across as unreasonably interested in the stuff of their professional life. In the case of bankers, that comes over as a tendency to view the world through financial spectacles, which is hardly edifying, but isn't any weirder than, say, a journalist's tendency to view the world as a succession of stories, angles, and issues.

For what it's worth, I'd also say that bankers are generally sane enough to know that they're the lucky denizens of an ecosystem that's awash with money. I was in my twenties when I first 'earned' a six figure sum. I didn't think that I had some moral claim on that money. Nor did I think it was a measure of my contribution to society. I definitely didn't think that the world needed more people like me and fewer of those ill-paid types like nurses, care workers, midwives, and the rest. On the contrary, I knew I was hideously overpaid and I felt extraordinarily lucky to

* My suits came from Marks & Spencer. My car was a second-hand VW. My watch cost me $10 from a roadside stall in New York's Chinatown and looked nice until all the fake gold rubbed off, at which point it just looked odd. It went on working for ages, though. A good $10 worth, if you ask me.

have a job that I enjoyed and that paid me so well. I can honestly say that the vast majority of my former colleagues would have said something similar. (In their more reflective moments, anyway. Grumbling about bonuses was pretty much mandatory, but only when the yardstick of comparison was internal to the banking industry. As soon as outside comparisons were invoked, then no one that I worked with was dumb enough to complain.) Needless to say, bankers that I knew weren't so overwhelmed with gratitude that they felt obliged to hand their bonuses over to charity, but then nor do premier league footballers, or manufactured pop stars, or underperforming chief executives or any of the other folk whose incomes vastly exceed their contributions.

For this reason I think that the word which best encapsulates the industry is simply COMPETITION. The money obsession arises simply because money is what bankers are competing for. If the best bankers were rewarded with chocolate bars, or scented bath foam, or 6-week-old puppies, then they'd start to care mightily about chocolate, puppies, and bath foam. In Bret Easton Ellis's *American Psycho*, the repellent protagonist, Bateman, and his equally repellent friends start to become competitive around their business cards. In the book version of the scene, Bateman introduces his business card to his peers in a fever of anxiety about their response:

> 'New card.' I try to act casual about it but I'm smiling proudly. 'What do you think?'
>
> 'Whoa,' McDermott says, lifting it up, fingering the card, genuinely impressed. 'Very nice. Take a look.' He hands it to Van Patten …
>
> 'Cool coloring,' Van Patten says, studying the card closely.
>
> 'That's bone,' I point out. 'And the lettering is something called Silian Rail.'
>
> 'Silian Rail?' McDermott asks.

'Yeah. Not bad, huh?'

'It *is* very cool, Bateman,' Van Patten says guardedly, the jealous bastard, 'but that's nothing …' He pulls out his wallet and slaps a card next to an ashtray. 'Look at this.'

We all lean over and inspect David's card and Price quietly says, 'That's *really* nice.' A brief spasm of jealousy courses through me when I notice the elegance of the color and the classy type. I clench my fist as Van Patten says, smugly, 'Eggshell with Romalian type …' He turns to me. 'What do you think?'

'Nice,' I croak, but manage to nod, as the busboy brings four fresh Bellinis.

'Jesus,' Price says, holding the card up to the light, ignoring the new drinks. 'This is really super. How'd a nitwit like you get so tasteful?'

I'm looking at Van Patten's card and then at mine and cannot believe that Price actually likes Van Patten's better. Dizzy, I sip my drink then take a deep breath.

'But wait,' Price says. 'You ain't seen nothin' yet …' He pulls his out of an inside pocket and slowly, dramatically turns it over for our inspection and says, '*Mine.*'

Even I have to admit it's magnificent.

Suddenly the restaurant seems far away, hushed, the noise distant, a meaningless hum, compared to this card, and we all hear Price's words: 'Raised lettering, pale nimbus white …'

'Holy shit,' Van Patten exclaims …

I am unexpectedly depressed that I started this.

Ellis has this about right. Bankers really are this competitive, albeit oftentimes less psychopathic than Bateman. I worked with one good soul who had turned up for his first day at university with bright red hair, a denim jacket, and a motorbike. By the time he'd been in investment banking for a year or two, he was addicted to expensive men's tailoring and had advanced views on the right cut for a shirt collar and whether it was correct to have your handkerchief match your tie. I bet that his deepest soul still thrums to the sound of a 500cc engine and smells of denim, hair dye, and bike oil. But bankers can't easily compete on these fronts, so he turned his attention to shirt collars and handkerchiefs instead. Business cards were standardized at J.P. Morgan (and everywhere else that I know of), but if they hadn't been, then beyond doubt bankers would have been competing furiously to have the most expensive, most tasteful, most wonderful business cards ever.

The culture owes nothing to chance. When bankers are recruited, the recruiters are in large part looking for a track record that indicates an unhealthy obsession with competition – in sport, in exams, in business, in almost anything. Once you assemble a bunch of highly competitive people in one place, each of whom has excelled in their life so far, then a competitive culture will spring up almost automatically. When that culture is fed and watered by a crazily lopsided reward system, then strange blooms and extreme growths are the inevitable result.

We're accustomed to thinking that competition is a good thing, and, indeed, it mostly is. The restlessness and innovation that characterizes investment banking has also characterized every ground-breaking entrepreneurial innovation ever. That doesn't, however, imply that competition must always and everywhere be helpful.

The quote from Michael Lewis's *Liar's Poker* at the start of this chapter is a good example of the less-than-helpful aspect to it. Following the financial crisis, there has been a good deal of talk in politics and the media about the importance of ensuring that bankers' bonuses are properly long term, and linked to personal performance and that of the firm. That all sounds great in theory, but is largely nonsense in practice. Long before the financial crisis, most senior bankers would have been paid a large chunk of their bonuses in the form of shares and those bonuses wouldn't fully vest (that is, be available to the individual) until three years or so after the bonus date. There may be some sensible ways to tweak the mechanics of all this, but the mechanics are hardly the main issue.

The point is that you can tweak bonuses all you like, but as soon as you let the unholy god of competition free to rampage through a herd of some of the world's most competitive people, then don't be surprised at behaviour that would shock and appall the rest of humanity. Lew Ranieri – the guy who thought, 'what the fuck, it's only a ranch' – was simply doing what he'd been hired, trained, and incentivized to do. To be the World's Best Trader, a person would need to be shrewd, would need to understand markets, would need to work tremendously hard, and so on and so forth. But Ranieri knew that there are plenty of people on Wall Street and in the City of London and elsewhere in the world who have those qualities to a high degree. He also knew that traders can be differentiated according to their willingness to take risks on a massive scale and (you'd hope) being lucky when the roulette wheel stops. Ranieri and his colleagues weren't there to be second best, and so they went for it. If by chance they were to bankrupt themselves, the firm, and its investors – well, at least they went for it.

What's more disturbing is the effect that excessive competitive zeal can have on the world beyond Wall Street. In *Traders, Guns and Money*, the derivatives guru Satyajit Das describes a world where competition has gone seriously awry. The book opens talking about a lawsuit brought by a bank against an Indonesian company which made noodles. OCM, the company in question,* wasn't in rosy good health and its noodle-making profits had largely dried up. The company had been looking around for ways to save money and its finance types noticed that the 12 per cent cost of borrowing in Indonesian rupiahs

* OCM is not the company's real name. Das gave it a pseudonym to protect its identity, and I've followed suit.

was about twice what it would cost them to borrow in dollars. So they went to Highly Innovative Bank who arranged a currency swap for them. OCM was now able to meet its funding needs by borrowing dollars at around 6 per cent, a huge saving. No doubt their finance director felt very pleased with himself. All this took place in 1995 and the rupiah was 'fixed' against the dollar.

Please note the inverted commas around the word 'fixed'. Mostly we call something fixed if it's not movable. The word suggests something screwed, bolted, nailed, glued, cemented, soldered, welded, riveted, or otherwise bonded in a once-and-for-all kind of way. Currencies aren't like that. Central banks will do what they can to keep a currency anchored to a certain benchmark, but if the seas rise and the winds blow, then that anchor can rip away. When John Major and Norman Lamont tried to keep the British pound 'fixed' against a basket of European currencies, the seas rose and the anchor failed. Britain is a big country, with a well-run central bank, mighty reserves, and loads of financial sophistication. Indonesia, in 1995, was none of those things. The rupiah, in fact, was not fixed at all.

Back to OCM. So pleased was it with its first transaction, that it went back for more. It entered into a more complicated derivatives transaction with the same a Innovative Bank. It so happened that the way financial markets moved in the wake of that second transaction allowed the noodle maker to sell out at a profit. Two deals, two very satisfactory outcomes. The Indonesians must have been delighted.

Highly Innovative Bank was pleased as well. They'd made nice fat fees twice over and now had a client who believed in every product they presented. So they came up with a whole new deal. The structure of that deal is too complex to describe here, but the critical part of it is easily related. The noodle maker had originally borrowed $300 million. In this new deal, they rearranged the financing to lower the interest rate, but with the proviso that *if dollar interest rates fell, then the noodle maker's borrowing would double to $600 million.* There were specific wrinkles in the deal that made it even worse than that. In Das's emphatic but unexaggerated words, if things went wrong 'OCM would not only be dead, it would be hung, drawn and quartered'. Roughly speaking, OCM had entered into a contract which pushed its borrowing costs down in the short term by taking a gargantuan amount of risk. From here on, everything lay in the lap of the gods.

The gods were not kind. This was the late 1990s, and a succession of Asian economies started to suffer exchange rate crises. The first Asian country to run into trouble was Thailand. The Thai baht, like so many Asian currencies, was 'fixed' and the Thai Central Bank was so committed to keeping the baht fixed that it spent the country's entire stock of foreign currency reserves trying to keep it that way.* The money was wasted. The anchor ripped out. The Thai baht was now floating.

Where Thailand led, others followed. The Korean won was abruptly devalued. So were the Malaysian ringgit and the Philippine peso. The Indonesian rupiah – the currency that was 'fixed'against the dollar – fell so far that, at its worst, it went from 2,000 rupiah to the dollar to around 12,000. OCM's decision to borrow in dollars not rupiah had just *sextupled* the effective size of its debt.

Or had it? Wise heads in the United States were watching chaos unfold across the Pacific, and they did what they could to help. Tossing a lifeline to a region in turmoil, the Federal Reserve cut interest rates. It was a nice gesture, appropriate and helpful. Good old Fed. Unfortunately, the consequent drop in dollar interest rates caused that vicious little clause in OCM's last deal to kick in and OCM's debts now doubled, from $300 to

* If that sentence hasn't made your jaw drop, then reread it.

$600 million. Measuring from peak to trough, OCM had just increased its debt burden by a factor of twelve.

The exact calculations are a little academic. OCM was finished. On the face of it, it had been blown so far out of the water, they might still be picking bits out of the stars. In its small and noodly way, OCM's fate prefigured the destruction wreaked on the financial system in 2008 and 2009.

Once again clever, hard-working, and innovative bankers had wrought their havoc. More specifically, three toxic ingredients came together in the same place. The first was an imbecile client. OCM didn't understand what it was getting into and it should never have signed a contract that it didn't understand and there's simply no excuse for such idiocy. Whatever your feelings may be concerning the bankers in this sad little story, you should keep your sympathy for OCM in severely short supply.

The second ingredient was possibility. If it hadn't been for the uprush of innovation from the 1980s, Highly Innovative Bank simply couldn't have engineered the transaction that it delivered. In the decade or so since Highly Innovative Bank sold its financial weapon of mass destruction to OCM, the envelope of possibility has moved much, much further out.

The third ingredient was the culture prevalent in Highly Innovative Bank. The bankers were *bankers*. Spurred on by their ethos of relentless competition and given huge profit targets by their annual review process. Pushed by a distorted – a *consciously* distorted – appraisal system into believing that being averagely good was not enough. In this strange world, ethics are hard to sustain.*

---

* Hard, mind you, not impossible. The very best investment banks have always had a genuine corporate commitment to ethical behaviour. I don't want to suggest that those banks never put a foot wrong, but at least their corporate cultures try hard to accommodate values other than just next quarter's profit number. That's why their quarterly profit numbers tend to be so good.

It's easy to see this matter in purely corporate terms – bad bank, foolish noodle maker, big mess – but we need to delve into the underlying psychology. Let's say you're that Highly Innovative Banker returning from Jakarta. You're flying long-haul business class, and you tried to get that upgrade to first class (as you always do), but didn't get it. You had to run for the airport after your meeting and this is the first moment since signing the deal with OCM that you've really had a chance to relax and contemplate. You're offered champagne and you take it. You've kicked your hand-made shoes off and have pulled a lambswool sweater on over your shirt for comfort on the flight. The champagne bubbles start to relax you. You review the day.

They signed the deal! You had thought they would but you're never certain until you've actually secured that signature. The contract did not contain a line for fees. That is, the contract never stated, 'We, OCM, pay you, Highly Innovative Bank, the sum of $x million for selling us a product which may well blow our company sky high', so OCM never knew how much you were earning on this deal. But you, of course, know perfectly well and it's an enormous amount. The deal isn't just a ludicrously complex and inappropriate one, it's also been priced outrageously. Quite likely, this is the most profitable deal of your year so far, perhaps of your career. It goes a huge way towards satisfying your annual profit target, and your bonus this year is going to be a monster one. You like the prospect of the money but, much more than that, you love the sense that you are excelling in a world of the excellent. You feel rewarded. You feel valued. It would be easy to mistake that feeling for a sense of being loved.

Somewhere, however, another line of thought is nibbling away. You have just mugged these people. You've sold them a potentially lethal product at a shamelessly exploitative price. You have, naturally, set up certain defences to this line of thought, defences which are necessary for legal reasons, but which are psychologically valuable too. Those defences come down, in effect, to the old saw, *caveat emptor*, buyer beware. OCM signed a piece of paper which said they understood what they were buying, that they didn't rely on Highly Innovative Bank for advice, and which provided enough other legal jargon to protect your butt. However, it can't quite bury the truth. *Caveat emptor* also applies when double-glazing salesmen give the hard-sell to old grannies, when car dealers sell vehicles that they know to be at death's door; it applies, in theory, to every awful product sold by every awful sleazeball to anyone naive enough to be taken in. That doesn't make it right and you know it.

When these two grindstones are active at the same time – the lure of reward and the warnings of conscience – something has to give. Sometimes, people do the right thing, and for all I know, there were a stream of people leaving Highly Innovative Bank because they wanted to do something more productive with their talents. Other times, conscience just gives way. A kind of self-chosen moral coarsening goes on. That's why any tale about banking excess almost invariably involves an excess of drink, drugs, spending, sex, and gambling too. Those other excesses are a way of drowning out the guilt. If you had, indeed, been the banker leaving Jakarta that night, then you were going home rich, you were going home drunk, but you weren't going home happy. On the inside, you were screaming.

The story of the Unwise Noodle Maker is a useful way of illustrating what happens when excellence overreaches itself but, like all good stories, it has a twist in the tail.

No noodle maker, no matter how unwise, ill-led, or mediocre, likes being swatted from existence. If OCM had chosen to honour its contract it would have gone bankrupt, so (to simplify a more complex story) it chose not to. Highly Innovative Bank sued. On the face of it, the bank had an overwhelmingly powerful claim. The contracts were unambiguous, the paper trail relentless in its logic. OCM owed the bank money.

But Highly Innovative Bank was regulated by the British Financial Services Authority, which required that licensed banks and other financial entities operated according to a defined set of standards, one of which was 'suitability' – that is, the principle that banks should not sell unsuitable products to their clients. The noodle maker's legal team argued that the suitability test had been so grossly breached that the derivatives contract was null and void.

The case went to court. Lawyers argued and expert witnesses disagreed. Legal fees rose and rose. And then – a miracle. Highly Innovative Bank had appointed a new chief executive who wanted to sweep away all the clutter that remained from the old order; he wanted the bank to refocus on its clients and did not want toxic arguments from the old days to poison the new era. Consequently, the bank came to OCM with an offer to settle. A deal was struck, that left neither party particularly happy, but allowed OCM to get on with life once again. It took a loss in its financial accounts, and returned to its core business with a new keenness. The noodle maker was back a-noodling.

This was a grotesque case, as bad as they come. But let's be crystal clear about something: in a competitive world, ethics do not always win; or rather, they never win absolutely. Ethics come with a price tag and the price is not always affordable.

Let's take a trivial example to start with. When investment banks compete for bond issues, one of their key selling tools is league table positions. Every bank likes to show itself in one of the top three positions. The argument, roughly, is 'everyone else obviously trusts us, so you should do'. As far as it goes, the argument is a perfectly strong and appropriate one. But how do you measure league position? It's not like football, where there is one and only one official league table each season. There are a variety of different tables that can be compiled, and your presentation will always pick the one that shows you to best advantage. Equally, if your bank happens to come out well on the rolling three month statistics, but badly on the twelve month ones, then you can bet that your presentation will show only the figures that are most flattering to you. This much is just ordinary competitive argy-bargy.

But take things a little further. An issuing bank is there to sell bonds to third parties. That's its job. At the same time, if a bank handles a bond issue, there'll be times when it doesn't sell the full issue. Not immediately; perhaps not for some time. And that doesn't have to be a crisis. Big banks have big balance sheets. They can hold bonds by way of stock and sell them over time as the market permits. Again, nothing wrong so far. It's just business.

But when it comes to compiling league tables, what matters is the number of bonds sold promptly *to third parties*. The bonds marooned on a bank's balance sheet shouldn't figure. But how does anyone know? The folk who compile the league tables know that Bank ABC has been awarded the right to issue $500 million worth of bonds on behalf of XYZ Corp. That's all. The only way that the league table people can know that Bank ABC failed to sell $200 million worth of the bonds is if Bank ABC tells them. And I have it on good authority that all banks routinely portray their sales figures more positively than is in fact the case. To put the same thing more bluntly: they lie.

Arguably, no one is harmed. Arguably, league table positions wouldn't even be much different in a world where everyone lied and a world where nobody did. You could well say that it's naughty, but just one of those things. The sort of thing that will give a bank's ethics committee a headache for a few weeks then be forgotten about.

But let's crank it up another notch. There have been markets in the past (notably mortgages) and there will be markets again in the future, where the game being played is 'Find the Dummy'. So to take a typical example, a bond whose value is $100 and whose value everyone knows to be $100 is put through the investment banking mill. It's bundled together with other bonds. Special purpose vehicles are created and contracts are written. What come out are five new bonds, whereby each bond is worth $20, but they look very different to the original plain vanilla variety. This type of financial engineering isn't bad in itself. It may even create a limited amount of value for reasons too technical and too boring to get into here. But the new bonds are much harder to value than the original one. Four out of five buyers will be perfectly clued up. They'll value a $20 bond at $20, and a sale is made that's fine and fair for both parties. But then there's the dummy. That dummy might be a dozy state-owned bank in China. It might be a European retail buyer. It might be the sovereign wealth fund of a poorly managed oil producing country. It might be anyone. But whoever it is, that last bond is sold not at $20 but at $25. Entire chunks of the mortgage market operated like this and could only do so because there were enough dummies to fuel it.

Once again, I am not asking you to feel sorry for the dummies. If they didn't understand a financial product, then they shouldn't have bought it. No excuses. But the bankers here have now gone a step further than just fiddling their league table positions. They're actively engaged in selling a product to people at a price they know to be unfair, and they've selected the buyers they have precisely for their ignorance, doziness, and stupidity. Like any con-artist, they'll be gifted in their patter. The dummies will be complimented on their financial astuteness. They'll be wined and dined and they'll be filled with stories of success and spectacular profits. The con will be deliberate, ongoing, and meticulous. (Which provides you, incidentally, with two sure fire ways of working out whether you're the dummy. If you're receiving compliments during a fancy meal that you're not paying for, then that's strike one. If you think you know who the dummy is, but you're not completely sure, then buy a mirror. You're looking at him now.)

One senior banker who was involved in the mortgage market – and this was years before the crash – told me that he wrote a paper for top management explaining that the bank's participation in the mortgage market could only be maintained by finding and exploiting the dummies. The banker who wrote the paper was of the view that such participation was unethical, and it should be terminated forthwith. This was a bank that took ethics with very great seriousness. Its senior management reviewed the paper and they agreed with the basic assertion that the entire mortgage market was a 'Find the Dummy' game. But they also recognized that if you wanted to be a major player in the Wall Street bond markets, then you needed a mortgage desk. If that meant flogging rubbish to dummies – well, *caveat emptor*. It's fair to say that every major investment bank in the world took this view. Competition precluded taking any other.

As for all those people who once interviewed me for Goldman Sachs – the Cerveza y Paellas, the Clausewitz-Fürstenbergs, the Jane Kravitzes, and the rest – they were good people doing a tough job within a corporate culture that fosters both excellence *and* ethics. Yet competition will always push those ethics as far as they can go, and sometimes a little further than they should. As far as I know, all leading banks fiddle their league table positions. As far as I know, all banks play 'Find the Dummy'. That game will end up with losses for the fall guys, but those losses will typically affect institutions with very large portfolios, which won't be structurally impaired by the loss.

The noodle story is a little different, because this was a deal where the buyer was being sold a weapon of mass destruction, with its timer already ticking. The buyer's corporate viability was at stake. Ordinary people with ordinary jobs were facing catastrophe – and that in a society very much less wealthy than our own.

I am convinced that the best banks on Wall Street would never have done that deal. And if perhaps they did in the go-go days of 2007, then I trust that they'd never do it again today. But the worst banks have to compete too. They don't have the brains, the networks, the track records, or the sheer excellence of their most able rivals. But one competitive avenue open to them is the ethical one. If ethics cost money, then ditch the ethics. Find the dummy. Do the most outrageous deal you can. Then get out. One day the waste will hit the air-conditioning, but you'll be long gone by then with your bonus cashed and your yacht remodelled. The bad old days of 2007 may seem a long way away from us now, but they're coming back because competition will see that they do.

Two last thoughts to finish with.

Number one, the financial industry is an extreme example of competition because of its wealth, its prominence, its bonus systems, the consequences of financial disaster, and for other reasons besides. But it is not alone. In the early 1990s, I was working in mergers and acquisitions, with an especial focus on the airline industry. In the course of that work, I got to know a number of airlines remarkably well. And they fiddled things too. I knew airlines that did third party maintenance work on aircraft and found ways to diddle their clients. (Not, let me add, ways that remotely compromised safety. They would never do that.) I knew airlines that found ways to steal confidential data. I knew airlines that contrived dodgy deals that got them round awkward international rules on ownership. These were often first class airlines with impeccably respected management teams. Insiders in every industry under the sun could mention similar sins, because that sinning comes with the territory. It's like it or lump it and as a society we have, probably rightly, chosen to lump it.

And a second closing thought. Or rather, hope.

When currency swaps took off in the 1980s, a profit boom was quickly followed by the commoditization of the industry. Currency derivatives went from being something complicated and hard, to complicated and easy. Those early, giant profits were soon eroded by competition. The hopelessly lopsided, competition-encouraging bonus structures of investment banking were well adapted to a world where giant profits were available to the most ambitious, capable, and aggressive banks. They are poorly adapted to a world of financial commoditization. If the dummies wise up and stop paying over the odds for financial products, if issuing companies get tougher about the amounts they'll pay for a service, if the financial markets generally start to look a little more like the market for beans or toasters or daffodils, then banks will change too. And they'll change not because some bureaucrat in London or Washington has decided to take charge of such things, but because banks themselves will figure out that they don't make sense any more. If that happens, then the world will be a less colourful place; it'll be a world where books like *Liar's Poker* and *Bonfire of the Vanities* and *American Psycho* can no longer be written. It'll also be a safer world, a world worth working for. And if every new era needs a slogan to define it, then may I humbly offer my own suggestion: 'Save the noodle maker, save the world.' I don't think that'll happen, but I'd like it if it did.

NINE

Bean-Counters

> Vocational Guidance Counsellor: 'Yes Mr Anchovy, but you see your report here says that you are an extremely dull person … Our experts describe you as an appallingly dull fellow, unimaginative, timid, lacking in initiative, spineless, easily dominated, no sense of humour, tedious company and irrepressibly drab and awful. And whereas in most professions these would be considerable drawbacks, in chartered accountancy they are a positive boon.'
>
> – From the Lion-Tamer Sketch, *Monty Python's Flying Circus*

One of the least probable facts in all of history is this: that double-entry bookkeeping was invented by the Italians.

Don't be deceived by that term 'double-entry' which calls to mind terms like 'double-cross' and 'double-agent', and suggests that those cunning medieval Italians had already figured out how to cook the books more cleverly than their dull northern neighbours. On the contrary, 'double-entry' simply refers to the yin and yang of accounting. When we're thinking about balance sheets (that is, what a company owns and owes at any particular moment in time), the yin and yang are called assets and liabilities. When we're thinking about income statements (that is, about revenues and costs), then the yin and yang are called credits and debits.

In this Zen world, there is no good and bad, only the simple click of figures as they snap into place. So, for example, you might think that owning an asset is a purely good thing. To an accountant, however, an asset can be defined as an unexpired cost, which not only sounds like a bad thing, but a bad thing that hangs over you and gives you nightmares. Equally, you'd think that debits would have to be a bad thing and credits would have to be a good thing, only you have to debit cash to increase it and crediting your bank debt pushes it up not down.

Fortunately, this is not a textbook on accountancy and all that matters for present purposes is that double-entry bookkeeping is a way of ordering the financial mathematics in such a way that it always works. Specifically, if you do your accounts right, then two Great Truths will always hold. The first Great Truth is that your balance sheet will balance. That means that your stock of assets will always be equal to your stock of liabilities plus your company's equity. The second Great Truth is that at the end of any given time period, the company's equity will have increased by an amount equal to the profit earned and retained in that period (capital-raising and other complicating factors aside).

When these two Great Truths are taken together, it means that every single transaction a company makes is taken into account when calculating its final profit numbers. That is, when you start to contemplate it, a remarkable fact. Measuring profit is a little bit like calculating sea levels. It sounds like an easy enough thing to do until you get down to the level of practicalities. If you want to measure the sea level, it's not enough to go down to the seashore with a measuring rod, you have to think about tides and seasons. You have to think about whether the land in this part of the world is being lifted or depressed by geological forces that have nothing to do with the sea level. What looks like a simple business of just sticking your rod into the water and taking a reading has become nightmarishly complicated.

It's the same with profit. How do you know if a business is making a profit? The simplest version of the answer is to look at the company's bank balance and see if it's going up or down.

But cash is hardly the only valuable asset that a company possesses. It might choose to hold other financial assets or pay down some debts or buy some new equipment. Indeed, a fast growing company may very well be permanently short of cash, because it's investing more rapidly than it's earning back in profit. When the investments come good, then profits may be much higher than they are now, but in the meantime a profitable, fast-growing company will be 'burning' cash, not accumulating it.

The same is true the other way round as well. If a company is only weakly profitable, or, indeed, downright loss-making, it may nevertheless contrive to generate cash by simply avoiding capital expenditures. This isn't a theoretical example, it's a very real one. The US airline industry has long been troubled by appalling profitability and a succession of high profile bankruptcies (or Chapter 11 reorganizations if you want to be technical about it). Since buying aeroplanes chews up a lot of cash, American airline companies have tended to defer aircraft purchases as late as they possibly can. In the early 1990s, the period when I was most in touch with these things, a well-managed European airline might have an average aircraft age of just five or six years. In the United States, that average was closer to twelve. Aircraft are still perfectly good to fly at that age, of course, but an *average* age of twelve years means that a typical fleet contained some brand new aircraft and some aircraft with well over twenty years of flying in their rivets and wing joints. That's what happens when lousy profits and the need to generate cash come together in the same industry ... and is a thought to keep firmly out of mind as you step on board a domestic flight in the United States.

Because cash is so unreliable as an indicator of profits, the Zen masters of accountancy prefer to overleap it altogether.*

* An exaggeration. Actually, tidy souls that they are, they like to produce a cash-flow statement.

Using concepts of capitalization and amortization, accountants divide expenses into those that relate to the present time period, and those relating to the future or past. Accountancy, in fact, is the art of allocating transactions through time, thereby wiping out the distortions of a bank balance that bounces around like sea levels, in order to arrive at the unembellished fact.

This level-headedness is accountancy's great achievement. Let's say that the company chief executive decides to buy a Picasso for his office wall, because he thinks it'll impress clients and cause them to buy more widgets from the firm. Is he right or is he wrong? Just how many extra widgets are bought as a result of that particular piece of corporate braggadocio? The answer is that, in one sense at least, no one knows and it doesn't matter. It doesn't matter because that particular transaction is recorded the way every other one is and the final profits number is what it is. Accounting, when done properly, isn't about persuasion or oratory or argument or reasoning or causality or strategy. It's about a set of rules and the unerring implication of those rules. Accountancy will never be able to tell you whether the Picasso was a good buy or an atrocious one, but it will deliver its coldly steady verdict on the company's performance as a whole. Accountants are unloved in part because they are truth-tellers. The numbers never lie.

That's one version anyway. It's the version which is right, very much more often than not. Ninety-nine point something per cent of what accountants do is to apply largely non-controversial rules in a disciplined way to achieve a truthful result. There's always scope for different judgements, but usually not much.

Needless to say, though, there's another version of the story, a darker and more controversial version altogether. Take, for example, an issue which came to the fore during the credit crunch. Let's say Boring Bank makes a loan of $100 million to a corporate borrower. The borrower gets into trouble and won't be able to repay the loan. Wise heads inside Boring Bank reckon, on the basis of financial analysis and past experience, that the borrower should neverthless be able to repay about $80 million if given time to do so. Boring Bank's accountants will probably want to check that that $20 million loss seems about right, but they're accountants not bankers. In the absence of any powerful argument to the contrary, they're likely to agree with the estimates made by Boring Bank. If they do, they'll recognize a loss of $20 million in the year when the borrower ran into trouble.

It *sounds* sensible. But it's not the only way to look at things. At the same time as all this was going on, Zippy Bank bought up $100 million worth of bonds issued by the self-same corporate borrower. When the borrower got into trouble, panic set in. Everyone, but everyone, was trying to unload their bonds. As a result of massive selling and the absence of any buyers, those bonds dropped in value to just fifty cents on the dollar. It might well be the case that those bonds would, in fact, return eighty cents on the dollar if you held them to maturity but financial markets, you may have noticed, aren't about the long term. They're about what people are prepared to pay right now.

Consequently, when Zippy Bank sits down with its accountants, it'll find that they want to use the prevailing market price as a way to measure its losses. This is called mark-to-market accounting and implies a loss of $50 million. It's no use Zippy Bank talking about the long term and the economic value that could be realized by holding their assets to maturity. That's not something Zippy Bank has ever spoken about before and their accountants aren't going to be swayed now.

The loan made by Boring Bank might be, in economic terms, almost identical to the bonds acquired by Zippy Bank, but the way those transactions are accounted for leads to enormous differences in reported profitability. And reported profits *matter*. In the context of the credit crunch, it potentially spelled the difference between life and death. The $20 million loss reported by Boring Bank led to an ugly profits number but, assuming that Boring Bank had been a good and prudent bank, wouldn't lead straight to insolvency. Given a few more quarters of steady income, Boring Bank stood every chance of earning its way out of trouble.

Not so Zippy Bank. That $50 million loss, when combined with all the other losses it was making at the same time and for the same reason, threatened to blow a hole right through the ship's hull. That's why Lehman died. That's why Bear Stearns had to sell itself for a song. That's why Merrill Lynch flung itself into the arms of Bank of America. That's why even Morgan Stanley and Goldman Sachs, the very zippiest of zippy banks, ended up having to seek new capital on humiliating terms. These things happened because their accountants wanted to do things the zippy way not the boring way. Other things mattered too (notably the reluctance of anyone to lend money to those zippy banks once these problems began to get out of hand), but the use of mark-to-market accounting was unquestionably a critical factor in the whole debacle.

It would be easy, however, to draw the wrong conclusion from all this. The wrong conclusion runs, 'There you go! There are no certainties in this world, only matters of judgement. That's why you get disasters like Enron, where accountants were too lenient, and disasters like the credit crunch, where accountants were too harsh. The accountants just cook the books anyway. They're told what numbers to produce and they'll crank them out.'

There are particles of truth here and one overwhelming falsehood. The truth is that accountancy is, has been, and always will be dependent on the prudent judgements of fair-minded people. It's also true that accountants are always running to catch up. As corporations deploy new strategies, and as the world changes, accountants need to change their methodologies too. That much is true. The false bit is everything else. Corporate accounts are masterpieces of concise and accurate reporting.* Refinements over the last twenty or thirty years have made them much better still, especially in previously dodgy jurisdictions like Italy or Belgium, whose accounts used to be so weirdly opaque that you wondered why anyone bothered.

That's not to say that accounts offer a complete or uncontestable picture of anything, but in this world of tears they're as close as we're likely to get. Even where accounting rules embody value judgements or seemingly irrational differences of approach, the judgements tend to be sane and the differences justified. For what it's worth, there were excellent reasons why the accountancy rules pertaining to zippy banks and boring banks were different. If zippy banks went bankrupt as a result – well, that was their fault for being so damn zippy. The accountants were just doing their job.

If all this seems too tidy to you, then you're probably right. Accountants, you may have noticed, are figures of fun. They are famous for being dull, timid, trivial, rule-following, number-obsessed, creativity-suppressing bean-counters. When the Monty Python crew wanted to do a sketch in which someone inappropriate seeks a job as a lion-tamer, they had that person be an accountant. The term 'bean-counter' itself is doubly derogatory, because who would want to spend all day counting?

The ferocity of these stereotypes suggests that something's going on, that the world has somehow not understood or not

---

* They are, for example, vastly more accurate than government accounts which simply ignore many liabilities accrued in the course of a year. In the United States, the national debt equates to about $80,000 per family. But that's just the bit the government is prepared to admit to. If you add in the unfunded liabilities of pensions and health care, the total is more like $500,000 per family. Other governments are just as bad – while any business larger than a cornershop is legally prohibited from such distorted accounting. Governments should do better.

warmed to the heroically truth-telling Zen masters of accountancy. All true – and the clues that unlock the riddle can be found among the criminal masterminds of Enron and in the honest, hard-working, and productive travails of a man called Paul.

Enron first. Once upon a time, when Ronald Reagan snoozed in the Oval Office and *Dallas* was the world's favourite soap-opera, Enron (then known as plain old InterNorth) was a good, boring, safe company. It ran power stations and transported natural gas through its network of pipelines. Because such activities tend to create large local monopolies, they are highly regulated ones, not just in the United States, but all over. A well-managed Enron would make a little more money than a badly-managed one, but not a huge amount. Enron was run perfectly well. Its shareholders hardly made out like bandits, but they did fine. Its customers were well and diligently served. Reagan went on snoozing. Bobby Ewing died and was resurrected. All was well with the world.

Then, in 1985, a new chief executive was appointed called Kenneth Lay. Lay didn't like sensible and he didn't like boring. He should have been a parachute jumper or a snowboard star or an investment banker. Instead he found himself at the helm of a sensible, boring, modestly diligent company that pumped gas and burned oil. What to do?

Lay's answer was to transform his company. His Enron wasn't going to be boring; it was going to be sexy. 'Sexy' is an odd word to apply to companies and yet it would be hard to relate Enron's history – or, indeed, corporate history generally – without making full use of it. The new Enron wanted a racy price/earnings multiple on the stock market. It wanted to be involved in high-growth businesses. It wanted to avoid intrusive government regulation. It wanted to use brains, financial leverage, and risk-taking to create profit.

All well and good in theory, but when a boring company in a boring industry decides it wants its share of the designer frocks and red carpet glamour, then trouble is almost bound to come a-knocking. Lay decided to turn Enron from a pumper of gas (dull!) into a trader of energy (sexy!). It would buy and sell energy futures, the way that hedge funds buy and sell currencies. That felt good to Kenneth Lay and his friends, so why (they figured) stop there? Why not buy and sell steel? And petrochemicals? And pulp? And coal? And – they were having fun now – why not wheat and coffee and sugar and pork bellies? And why the heck not buy and sell the weather as well? (Weather-based derivatives if you want to be pedantic about it.) Things were rocking now, but they'd rock a whole lot more if the company took on a bundle of debt. So it took on a bundle of debt.

Enron Towers was now a happening kind of place. Year after year, Enron was named America's most innovative company. This, in a way, was perfectly true, given that even the company's accounts were becoming progressively more imaginative. Some of the accounting techniques used were technically allowable. Others defied all sanity and logic. Losses were buried in Enron group companies which were kept 'off-balance sheet' – that is to say, hidden away from the shareholders who actually owned the whole merry-go-round.

Risk turned to foolishness; foolishness turned to criminality. The whole enterprise spiralled out of control and ended up destroying the company. At its peak, Enron had 22,000 employees and a stock price of over $90. Now Enron's employees can comfortably fit into a single room and and it has no stock price at all. The firm's many creditors have so far received payments equalling about thirty-six cents on the dollar.

Personally, I don't get over-exercised by any of this. There are some clever, foolish, unethical people in the world and every now and then they're going to do some clever, foolish, and unethical things. When such things happen, it's important that lessons are learned, that stable doors are duly bolted, and that the malefactors are properly punished. In Enron's case, all that duly took place. Kenneth Lay was found guilty on ten different counts of conspiracy, fraud, and false statements. His chief financial officer, Jeffrey Skilling, was found guilty of nineteen such charges, was fined $45 million and is currently serving a twenty-four year prison sentence. In a final tragic act of this drama, Lay himself neatly side-stepped the rules one last time by dying of a heart-attack before he could be sentenced. Because he hadn't yet exhausted the legal appeals process, the court was obliged to erase his conviction and no fine could be imposed.

Of more interest to me, and of greater relevance to this chapter, is the role of Arthur Andersen, an accountancy firm, in all this. Each time a company releases its annual accounts, there is a one page facsimile of a letter signed by its accounting firm, to the effect that the accounts are a true and fair representation of the company's finances. That letter is sacred. It's the single most important page in any set of annual accounts, because if it isn't there, then everything else could simply be moonshine and hogwash. Sure enough, each and every time Enron released its accounts, it boasted a letter from Arthur Andersen (motto: 'Think straight, talk straight') duly confirming that its accounts were true and fair representations of reality.

Now, to be absolutely fair, Arthur Andersen could only work within the standards set by the accounting trade and those standards, at the time, weren't as tight as they are now. Furthermore, although the company was convicted of obstructing justice by shredding piles of Enron-related documents, the conviction was subsequently overturned because of shortcomings in the instructions given to the jury. But the bigger issue is this. Enron's accounts were ludicrous misrepresentations of the underlying state of the company and Arthur Andersen's 'true and fair' statements allowed those misrepresentations to grow like Topsy. Arthur Andersen knew that and let it happen. They wanted to be sexy too.

So much for Enron. The second tale concerns Paul Luen, the driving force behind Martek Marine, the company we encountered in the chapter on invention. When Paul was setting up his company, he had to think about his products, about his marketing, about his suppliers, about his competitors, about his workforce, about his premises, about his distributors, and much, much else. He also had to think about bookkeeping and accounts. Now Paul is an entrepreneur, a risk-taker. If you remember, he hurled his limited cash at a brand-new enterprise and worked for six months without salary. Now just take a wild guess whether Paul was more concerned with his products/marketing/suppliers and so on, or with his bookkeeping. Do you think Paul emerged from his intensive period of early start-up with a gleamingly efficient accounting system and rubbish products, or with a collection of industry-leading products and accounts that did not please the good men and women of Her Majesty's Revenue & Customs?

Of course Paul's accounts left much to be desired. Not because he was remotely Enronian but because, number one, he had other more important things to think about and, number two, he's an entrepreneur. To be a good entrepreneur, you need to be a risk-taking, restless, creative, imaginative rule-breaker. To be a good accountant, you need to be a risk-averse, disciplined, tidy-minded, factual rule-follower. The two mindsets are just about as far apart as they can be, while still sharing recognizably human DNA.

What happened next in Paul's case is what happens next in the evolution of every capable entrepreneur. The tax inspectors were both patient and insistent. They were patient, in that they had the wit to recognize that substandard accounting processes are part and parcel of business start-ups. They were nevertheless, and rightly, insistent that Paul shaped up. So he did. The whole accounting issue morphed from the least interesting and least pressing item on the 'to do' list into a business challenge needing prompt and capable management. Given that prompt and capable management is what Paul does, he hired the right kind of expertise, invested money in the right kind of systems, and let capable bookkeepers do the rest.

These two stories together tell you everything you need to know about our ambivalent feelings towards accountants. They're seen as the antithesis of the questing, risk-taking, free-wheeling spirit in us, because they are.

Yet when accountants, like Enron's Arthur Andersen, decide that, to hell with it, they're going to be entrepreneurial too then disaster looms for one and all. That's not to say that an entrepreneur faces only two choices, between Enron's crookery on the one hand and Paul's managerial good sense on the other. A middle way does, indeed, exist: it's known as 'being Italian'. A friend of mine once worked at the investment bank Morgan Stanley. For one long year, she worked on a project involving one of the great Italian industrial clans – let's call it the Tagliatelli clan. She worked as an analyst; that is, the junior level number cruncher whose job was to provide the financial modelling on which everything else in the project would depend. She entered a world she had never encountered before. It was a world of dozens of companies, cascades of ownership, peculiar voting structures, incomprehensible management contracts, weird jurisdictions, bizarre accounting policies, and byzantine tax arrangements. For about six months, she wondered at each new marvel, convinced that behind this spider's web of intrigue lay a spidery mastermind, a genius of finance.

Finally, after six months, she figured out that she was wrong. Not only was there no presiding genius, there was no one in the entire group structure who understood the system. None of the family. None of the chief executives. None of the finance officers. If the web had a spidery mastermind at all, then it was her. She herself had become the shadow she'd been so long pursuing.

That moment of revelation cast the entire corporate structure in a new light. She now saw it for what it was: a corporate plumbing system where every new leak had been met with a temporary patch which, being badly designed and inappropriate, would sooner or later lead to more leaks and more patches. The real wonder wasn't the genius of its structure, but the fact that anything worked at all. Indeed, the whole reason why the group had called Morgan Stanley in was precisely because the good ship Tagliatelli had become so barnacle-encrusted and encumbered that she was becoming impossible to steer. Given that success in business generally requires a kind of Napoleonic speed and decisiveness, the middle way – the Italian way – is generally a path to short-term convenience and long-term ruin. Italy's twenty-first-century business leaders would do well to go back to the disciplines that served them so well in the Renaissance.

That, in the end, is why bean-counters matter. Entrepreneurs are more brilliant, no question. Brilliant in the sense of attracting and emitting light. Brilliant in the sense of moving fast and flashily, producing dazzling outcomes. The entrepreneurial mindset may be the very opposite of the bean-counting one, but both halves need each other the way flowers need bees. Entrepreneurs, businesses, and entire economies fail without bean-counters. Sexy is good; boring is essential.

PART THREE

Firms and Markets

TEN

Markets

> Trying to stop a market is like trying to stop a river.
>
> – Vietnamese proverb

In thirteenth-century England, markets mattered.

For one thing, they were physical locations: market squares or broader than normal streets where goods were traded. Back then, agriculture was the only significant industry around, so the goods in question were agricultural ones: bushels of wheat and rye, pecks of oats, quarters of peas, live chickens, and so on. These things mattered, because those buying them needed them to live; those selling them obtained their livings that way. The market itself was seen to matter so much that settlements weren't permitted to create one unless they could show that they were a minimum travelling distance away from the nearest alternative. Indeed, the majority of early markets were set up by royal charter, so that the king himself needed to approve their existence.

Numerous place names in the UK still honour that medieval past. Market Harborough was so pleased to get its charter in 1204 that the town's name was changed so that it could boast about it. The nearest town to me in Oxfordshire is Chipping Norton – 'Norton' meaning simply North Town, while 'Chipping' is derived from the old Anglo-Saxon verb meaning 'to buy'. The architecture of many of these old British market towns also pays homage to their medieval pasts: grand inns, grain stores, and corn exchanges. In those days, as I say, markets mattered.

These days, the word 'market' has almost completely lost its original sense of a physical location for trading goods. We're happy to talk about the 'labour market' although there are no slave markets any more and no 1930s-style mobs crowding the factory gate to offer labour. Indeed, the 'markets' which so dominated headlines in 2008–9 have dematerialized completely, involving neither physical locations (because they take place over the phone or in cyberspace), nor physical goods (because they involve financial derivatives), nor physical buyers and sellers (because the trading is conducted between corporate entities), nor even physical money (because it's all done electronically). Markets have gone from being places that smelled of turnips and chicken shit to places that aren't places selling goods that aren't goods.

Nevertheless, those early chicken-scented markets tell us a great deal about the way we think about markets today. Even then, the power of free trade was frightening, something to be constrained. Though national laws set the framework, local regulations tightened the rules almost to beyond breathing point. In one Wiltshire market, for example, grain sellers had to agree their selling price with magistrates beforehand. No transactions could take place before nine in the morning, at which point a bell would be tolled twenty times to indicate the start of trading. For the first two hours, the largest transaction permitted was two bushels and then only if the grain was for the customer's own use.* After eleven in the morning, the trading

---

* If you're in danger of muddling up your bushels and pecks, then a British bushel is equal to approximately 2,219 cubic inches, while the lesser American bushel clocks in at a mere 2,150 cubic inches. A bushel is worth exactly four pecks, while the word itself comes from the old French *boisse*, meaning one sixth of a bushel or one and a half pecks. Got that?

bell would be tolled another twenty times at which point other buyers (such as bakers and brewers, for example) were allowed to enter the market, but only if they met a whole slew of further conditions (they had to be licensed by a magistrate, could only buy on the day of the market, and so on).

In theory, it was legal to buy grain for resale – those who made their living this way were known, entertainingly, as badgers – but the laws around badgering were so tight that it suggested the occupation lay somewhere close to prostitution in the public esteem. In 1563, for example, an Act of Parliament required badgers to be licensed by no fewer than three Justices of the Peace, to be married householders, to be at least 30 years old, and to be resident in the local county for at least three years. Local regulations might be more burdensome still.

Badgering might have been frowned upon, but at least it was just about legal. Middlemen who 'forestalled' goods – that is, who bought them en route to market and not at the market itself – were lower than low. An edict of 1275 thundered:

> It is especially commanded, on behalf of the lord king, that no forestaller should be allowed to stay in any town, who is manifestly an oppressor of the poor and a public enemy of the whole commonalty and country. Thirsting for evil profit he hurries out before other men, sometimes by land and sometimes by water, to meet grain, fish, herring or other kinds of goods coming for sale by land or water (oppressing poorer people and deceiving those better off) and he contrives to carry off these goods unjustly and to sell them much more dearly.

Poor old Stephen Speare of Exeter was condemned to the pillory in 1266 because he 'took wheat on the River Exe' – before, that is, it had arrived at the designated market.

The medieval theory behind all this legislative activity was, on the face of it, a good one. If poor people were deprived of food, they would starve. Therefore, food should be made available first and foremost to those in need of it. The regulation of badgering, forestalling, regrating (don't ask), and engrossing (ditto) was aimed at preventing bad people from making speculative profits at the expense of the poor and needy. It's astonishing and rather impressive how much energy the emerging state put into guarding its weakest citizens. It's hard not to sympathize.

Yet it's a good rule in history and a good rule in economics and a *very* good rule in economic history, to ignore the regulations and look at the outcomes. Historians have examined the pattern of grain prices across England in an attempt to determine whether there was a genuine national market in food, or whether there was just a patchwork of local markets that operated largely independently from each other. Amazingly, it seems that England's market in food was almost completely national as far back as you can look. (The data goes back to about 1200.)

That's an astonishing fact. It means that, in broad terms, grain prices in London and Oxford and York and Durham and Bristol and everywhere else all rose and fell together. The pattern of agricultural production itself could never have produced such an outcome. A bad storm in York might be depressing harvests (and boosting prices) in the self-same year that Gloucestershire farmers were seeing bumper crops (and slumping prices). If grain markets had been left to the weather gods, there'd have been huge variability in production, huge variability in prices. That's not what happened. And the only way that prices could have been smoothed out as much as they were was through people buying grain in one market and selling it on in another – by badgering, in fact. Indeed, those medieval grain markets worked even better than that, because there wasn't even much seasonal variation in grain prices, implying that engrossers were hard at work buying grain at harvest time and reselling it nine or ten months later when stocks were low.

So busy were these agents of the free market that one historian has gone so far as to say, 'as early as 1208 the English grain market was both *extensive* and *efficient* ... There is, indeed, little evidence of any institutional evolution in the grain market between 1208 and the Industrial Revolution.' Indeed, you could go even further and argue that the market in food was freer in AD 1200 than it is today: back then there were no production subsidies, no tariff barriers, and no farm inspectors. For all the effort put into medieval regulation, the evidence suggests that its effect was roughly nil.

All this is disconcerting. The motivations of those medieval regulators were so transparently good – they were trying to stop poor people dying, after all – that it's tempting to assume that the failure of regulation must have had calamitous consequences for the worst off. But it didn't. It was the best thing that could possibly have happened. The precocious development of the English food market wasn't just some empty victory for early Thatcherites; it meant that the English were much less likely to starve. As late as the eighteenth century, continental Europeans continued to suffer from occasional famines brought about by the failure of the local harvest, while such famines hadn't been known in England for centuries. In England, whenever a local harvest was bad, grain poured in from elsewhere to make up. When food stocks began to run low in late spring, there were merchants ready to sell the grain which they'd been storing over the winter.

Widows and orphans didn't survive despite the failure of price regulation. They managed to feed themselves because of it. If you want an illustration of the good that free markets do, you can't do much better than those medieval grain markets. Because food merchants did what they did, despite a deeply hostile climate of opinion, prices were kept low and kept steady. People still died of starvation from time to time – these were the Middle Ages after all – but you'd still prefer to have been a peasant in England than in most other parts of Europe.

You might well think that the food market operates differently today, but you'd be wrong. The essentials are identical. You may never have heard of a company called Cargill, Inc., but it's the largest private firm in the United States and one of the largest private firms anywhere. It has revenues of $116.6 billion, profits of $3.3 billion, a workforce that's 159,000 strong spread over sixty-eight countries worldwide – and it's a badger. It makes its money by trading in food: by badgering, engrossing, forestalling and regrating, not to mention all the ancillary activities to be expected of a modern agricultural behemoth. And at the heart of all that activity is the same thing that took Stephen Speare to the pillory – in the words of Cargill's CEO, Greg Page, helping 'food commodities to move from places of surplus to places of need'.

All this matters, because it demonstrates some fundamental truths in the most graphic possible way. Markets aren't good because they satisfy some weird Anglo-Saxon antipathy to government meddling. They're good because they stop people dying. Traders don't need to be driven by some higher purpose in order to achieve good ends. They do good by buying low, selling high, and pocketing the difference. The more traders are allowed to get on and trade, the more those differences will be competed away. The most that regulation is likely to achieve is to make it harder – and therefore more profitable – to be a badger.

Trading is such an ordinary part of capitalism that we often no longer see it for what it is. Take publishing, for example. Publishers don't write books. They don't print books. They don't retail books. Those functions are all conducted by others. Things like cover design and PR work are usually conducted in-house, but not always. There are specialist agencies aplenty who can handle those functions effectively themselves. So what – and I'm not the first author to pose this question – what does a publisher actually *do*? If all their chores can perfectly well be handled by others and in many cases already are, then why don't publishers just tiptoe silently from their offices, leaving a list of useful phone numbers taped to the front door?

The answer, of course, is that publishers are traders. They buy intellectual property from artisans and sell it in bulk to retailers. Along the way, they 'add value' to the package, just as those medieval grain merchants added value by looking after storage and transport. But those other bits and pieces are sideshows that can be parcelled out to others if it makes sense to do so. The core of what any publisher does and has always done, the bit that can't be outsourced, the bit that makes a publisher a publisher, is the wholesaling aspect, the trading part, the part that has to do with helping stories 'to move from places of surplus to places of need'.

There are plenty of other businesses in a similar position. Mobile phone resellers buy large blocks of airtime from the networks (from 'proper' mobile phone companies, that is) and sell it on to business or retail users. Some fund management companies do much the same thing: they take money from retail investors but hand over the actual management of those funds to another firm. Any advertising company will offer a 'media buying' service, which is essentially the resale of other people's advertising space. And so ad (almost) infinitum: logistics companies which own no trucks, travel agents that have no planes, holiday companies without hotels.

Despite our post-medieval sophistication in all things capitalist, it's hard to resist a sigh of understanding when faced with facts like these. We want to exclaim, 'Ah! So they don't actually *do* anything.' That's what the magistrates thought when they sent Stephen Speare to the pillory. It's what we think now, when we discover that a well-known brand is merely on-selling a service which it does not itself provide.

We're wrong. A senior executive from a major American mobile phone company told me that, in the early years of mobile telephony, his firm had resisted the lure of 'resellers' for a long time. Then a company with deep roots in the African-American community came with a proposal, the first part of which was a demolition job of that phone company's approach to black Americans. How the tariff packages were wrongly pitched. How the advertising was inappropriate. How obvious marketing opportunities were being missed. The executive told me that he'd made up his mind to say yes to the proposal before they'd even started to talk terms. The Big Phone Company was never going to be able to reach all the various micro-communities that made up its territory with a single universal message. So it invited in the resellers and its share of the relevant sub-markets started to grow and phone users enjoyed a service that was tailored to them. The Big Phone Company got to sell airtime that would otherwise have gone unused. The reseller made money. Everybody involved did better.

So markets matter. Traders matter. The trading function is an indispensable, if only semi-visible, part of almost every modern industry.

These thoughts are worth emphasizing because they're about to be tested almost to destruction, as we come to consider the whole business of trading on financial markets. Take, for example, the foreign exchange market. Clearly, Chinese buyers of fancy German machine tools need to find some euros with which to pay for them. A bank seems like a good place to find such things. And a bank, therefore, needs to be able to buy and sell foreign currencies in order to meet its customers' needs. So far, so ordinary. No need for the pillory just yet.

But the foreign exchange market is strangely large. The *daily* turnover of foreign currencies is approximately $4 trillion.* The daily movement of goods is approximately 1 per cent of that volume, at just under $40 billion. If you take account of services too, then you get to slightly more than 1 per cent – but that still leaves ninety-eight point something per cent unaccounted for, and when you're talking about $4 trillion every day, then failing to account for ninety-eight point something per cent of it is liable to make most people feel a little queasy. Other 'legitimate' reasons for foreign exchange buying – such as cross-border investments and acquisitions – will shave a few further billions off the unaccounted for total, but not many.

In the end, that money moves around because traders and investors and banks and hedge funds are seeking to make a buck. Some of them will be gambling outright that the dollar will rise against sterling, or fall against the euro, or whatever. Others will have their eyes focused on other cross-border bets, but need to ensure that they have the right currency at hand to make them, or perhaps want to protect themselves against currency risk when they do. All these things require dabbling in the markets and account for the vast bulk of those daily $4 trillion.

The conventional attitude to trading on this scale is one of puritanical disapproval – our instinctive, medieval-style aversion to trading in evidence once again. It's become a commonplace to observe that trading of this speculative kind is by definition a zero-sum sport. If I want to bet on a rise in the dollar, then I need to find some mug who wants to bet on a fall. We can't both be right. When those currency transactions, all

* To put that in slightly more tangible terms, the amount of foreign exchange being traded through London each day is nearly twice Britain's gross domestic product for the entire year. That's not quite the same as coming home to find that your mother has bet your salary on the horses, but it's not entirely different either.

the daily four trillion dollars' worth, are netted off at the Great Clearing House in the Sky, the final reconciliation of the final tally will end up with a big round zero. 'A tale, told by an idiot, full of sound and fury, signifying nothing.'

Yet something of the sort is *always* true of trading. Badgers used to speculate on movements in grain prices and didn't sow a single ear of wheat themselves. Their profit was someone else's loss. The Great Clearing House in the Sky always registers a zero, if you construe these things narrowly. But the narrow view is at best only half right. The half true bit is an accounting truth, which, if I sell you my sterling for your dollars, then my loss will be your gain, or vice versa, as the currencies move. But that ignores our motivations for engaging in the trade. Perhaps I was adding to my extensive collection of antique Navajo birthing mats, or perhaps I wanted to diversify my stock portfolio by adding some US stocks. Perhaps you also wanted to diversify your portfolio and were choosing to invest in some British government bonds, as a good solid way to do it. Neither of us was concerned much about currency positions. Both of us, in fact, have achieved our objectives and will remain happy with the transaction whatever, within reason, happens to those currencies.

What's more, the positive good that trading does is always hidden. The medieval regulators genuinely didn't know, didn't see and couldn't guess that speculators trading in English grain were bringing huge positive benefits to the country's poor. Badgers didn't sow wheat themselves, so they looked parasitic. Yet because, in effect, they guaranteed a reasonably steady price to farmers and to buyers, they made it safer for farmers to invest in improving their land and made it easier for poor families to budget their spending. As a result, badgers didn't merely help distribute a fixed stock of food more efficiently, they almost certainly enabled more food to be produced as well.

The same is true of modern badgers. In just the same way, the fact that it's hard to see the benefits of the foreign exchange markets shouldn't deceive us into thinking that they don't exist. For what it's worth, careful academic research has repeatedly demonstrated that the possession of sophisticated financial markets increases a nation's national income. Currency traders make us richer.

These reflections lead us towards the single most important thing about any market: namely, its price discovery function and the way that goods and resources flow in response to those prices. In a free market, with plenty of buyers and plenty of sellers (that is, without any monopolistic considerations to spoil things), then the price that clears the market will honestly reflect the sellers' costs and the buyers' desires. All kinds of games may be played along the way. Haggling, arguments, outright lying, open auctions, secret deals – you name it. If the market is working, however, the price will settle where sellers are happy to sell and buyers are happy to buy. Resources flow to where they're most needed, to where they most perfectly and most neatly satisfy consumers' wants, and no one can con anyone. Price, in this happy world, is Truth.

That Truth can do remarkable things. Yesterday, for example, I learned that my niece was coming to stay the night. She likes cornflakes for breakfast and I was all out of cornflakes – so I went out and bought some. The very first shop I went to had the item I wanted. I paid a small amount of money for my acquisition and went my merry way.

Now that's a remarkable story. Just because it's an ordinary one shouldn't stop us noticing the miracle. It's as though in a village just outside Oxford, a shopkeeper sat there and thought, 'Gosh, I wonder whether Harry's niece might just come along this weekend, because if she does, she'll certainly need some cornflakes – so I'd better get some in just in case.' But for that product to be available to the shopkeeper, the owner of some very large factory needed to think, 'I bet that little shop in Oxfordshire is going to need some cornflakes soon, so I better just go right ahead and press the button which sends my enormous production line clanking into gear, just so I can have some product ready the moment it's needed.' And for that factory owner to be in a position to set his production line a-clanking, some farmer on the American prairies needed to plant corn, someone else needed to make fertilizer, someone else needed to chop down trees, so that yet another set of people could turn them into cardboard packaging – and all these wonders just to feed my niece, who is not a particularly fussy girl and would probably have been perfectly happy with bread and butter in any case. That these miracles all work (and without my even needing to make a phone call, or register my desire for cornflakes, or book ahead for my place in the packet-cereals queue) is down to the miracles of markets, and the wonder of Price becoming Truth.

This truth is the lamp that burns at the heart of welfare economics, the reason why markets work, the reason why people in successful market economies are happier than people elsewhere. It's the reason why capitalism is the best economic system in the world and always will be.

It's also the lamp which keeps pro-market economists all fired up – and which sometimes burns so hot that it turns them a little nuts. Although markets are great, they operate in the manner of cranky computers running beta-release software. It works most of the time. Consider all the billions of computations that need to take place for anything at all to happen and the thought is gob-smacking. Things go well for a while and then you press the wrong button at the wrong time, or maybe the right button at the wrong time, or maybe it's nothing at all to do with what you press or when you press it, but the machine crashes, you lose critical data, those little pop-up dialogue boxes start going crazy with you, and you find yourself wanting to pour warm lighter fluid into the hard drive and threatening the damn thing with matches.

Markets work – and don't work – in much the same way. It's to those problems that we now turn, and the very first creature to catch our eye is a beast which free market economists universally revere but which they ought, if they were being strict with themselves, to hate. It's time now to look at the firm.

ELEVEN

The Firm

> A Russian scientist returned from Copenhagen and reported that economic conditions were very bad in Denmark. Surprised, one listener pointed out that Danish shop windows were full of goods. 'Oh. yes,' conceded the Russian, 'but the Danish people have no money to buy them. There were no lines in front of the stores.'
>
> – Joke adapted from Irving Levine, *Main Street, U.S.S.R.*

Only once in my life have I enjoyed paid employment as an economist. It was a year after the fall of the Berlin Wall. There was a new democratic government in Warsaw. Entire economies were throwing off years of state planning and wondering what to do next. I had no idea, of course. I was 23 years old and had never before converted a major socialist economy to free market ways. No matter. I teamed up with an Oxford don who knew rather more than I did (he's since helped steer British monetary policy, among other things) and off we went to Warsaw.

The person we were advising was Jerzy Osiatyński, the brand new Minister of Planning. Since the communist system had collapsed and the new economy didn't actually need a ministry of planning, no one was sure what it should now do for its living, but there was still a strangely large number of people rushing around its enormous corridors and crowding the canteen at lunchtime.

We gave the best advice we could. Everyone knew how little everyone knew. Those first Polish governments rose and fell quite quickly, but Osiatyński went on to have a decent career as Minister of Finance and member of parliament, so maybe our advice helped somewhere along the way. That wasn't, however, the last I saw of Warsaw or of the Ministry of Planning. After my stint as economic adviser, I worked in the newly set up European Bank for Reconstruction and Development, helping to fund the newly commercial companies of the old Eastern Bloc.

In those years I must have toured dozens of factories, in Poland and elsewhere. Most of them had conducted most of their external trade with Russia under the old, rotten Comecon system. When Comecon expired, so did the trade and plenty of companies faced shortfalls of 50 per cent and more in their sales. That would have been a challenge for any manager, anywhere, but for the managers of those factories the challenge was of an entirely unknown type. Communists always had a high regard for technical skills, so the factory directors we met tended to have excellent mechanical knowledge. If you'd asked one of them to quickly whip up a metal bike stand, say, or a cutlery drainer, they'd have been off to the lathe room, happy as a kid in a sweetshop. When it came to navigating the new commercial environment, however, their faces clouded over with worry. Because we had the word 'bank' on our business cards – and because we were Westerners to boot – they had this hopeless idea that we'd simply hurl money at them and life would be simple again. My boss, exasperated with one particularly stubborn Russian manager,* asked him if he even knew what a bank *did*. The Russian paused for a long, long moment then declared, 'A bank is there to supply money to the workers.'

* I don't mean stubborn for a Russian. Someone who was stubborn by Russian standards would be the stubbornest of the world's most stubborn things. A brick wall would be a pushover by comparison.

Needless to say, we didn't see our role in exactly the same way and getting to a plausible commercial funding arrangement was impossible in the huge majority of cases.

I did, however, get to see exactly what all those Osiatyński ministers of planning had been doing with their time. The Ministry of Planning had churned out regular five year plans, dictating inputs and outputs for all the factories under its purview. I bet those plans had looked just great. The ministry in the days that I worked there still had diligent staff and excellent data collection, and those things would have been even better in its days of glory. But the plans were works of fiction. If you were running a firm responsible for making, let's say, pumps suitable for domestic heating systems, then you'd need a whole host of inputs. Many of those inputs would need to be precisely specified. You wouldn't simply need bolts, for example, you'd need bolts of a certain length, width, strength, thread, head profile, and so on. The plan would probably allocate you enough of those bolts to make your pumps, but the bolts would most likely never arrive. Or if they did, they'd come too late. Or they'd be wrong in some entirely different way, a way that no Westerner would even be able to predict because they'd never have encountered so many possible varieties of wrongness in one small, simple thing.

As a result, most of the larger factories I saw were like little empires. One firm – not that huge in Western terms – owned its own pig farm, to make its own bacon, to send to its canteen, to feed its workers. It also, I kid you not, used to manufacture its screws and bolts itself, because that was simpler than trying to get them from the planned supplier. The technical aspect of that is incredible in itself. Handmaking a bolt so accurately that its thread will fit the intended part is a real feat of skill. I don't know how they did it. But the economic aspect is no less astonishing. How could these firms possibly carry out their core business successfully, when the best minds and hands in the factory were focused on creating something that you can pick up for just pennies in the West? They couldn't, of course, and the collapse of the whole system was the inevitable and unlamented result.

With hindsight, the really remarkable thing is that the system even lasted as long as it did. For a really gross example of its hopelessness, consider this. The Soviet Union's central planners were able to exploit the slave labour of prisoners in the Siberian gulag. The exploitation in terms of work hours and conditions was grotesque and, of course, the work went completely unpaid. And yet even so, *the camps lost money*. Western firms like to talk about 'value added', but in the bad old days of the East, entire industries could find themselves subtracting value. Getting iron ore out of the ground was a positive value-creating step but, often enough, every process thereafter actually turned the iron into something less valuable than it had been just one stage before. The system was so bad, you'd want to laugh, except that you can't help remembering that its foundations were packed with the bodies of the dead, so crying seems like the more appropriate response.

The point here is that central plans were disastrous. When things go wrong in a market economy, things quickly move to adjust: customers move elsewhere, firms sharpen up or close down. In a planned economy, each screw-up goes on rippling outwards for ever. I botch my consignment of bolts that I owe you. You need bolts, so you start to make yours by hand. Because you've hand-built your bolts, you then deliver pumps which arrive late at the boiler manufacturer's and which are prone to leaking because one in every twenty of your bolts has a sloppily cut thread. So in turn the boilers are rubbish, and so on. The ripples never stop. They finally built into a tsunami that knocked down the Berlin Wall and good riddance to all that fell down with it.

The conclusions here seem so obvious that you're probably already tapping your feet and flipping pages. Central planning is bad. Markets are good. But just stop for a moment and reflect. Large multinationals are famously bigger than small, or even medium-sized, countries. The US multinational, General Electric, has a turnover approaching $200 million which puts it in the same kind of league as the United Arab Emirates or Kazakhstan. WalMart is in the same league as Sweden or Venezuela.* These giant firms, as well as all their smaller brethren, *are* centrally planned. Literally. They have a chief executive and a finance officer and maybe a chief operating officer and quite possibly an executive whose job involves strategy and planning.

Naturally, wherever the firm touches the outside world, it'll interact in a market-mediated way. So when it takes on new employees, it'll advertise the qualifications required and the wage offered. It'll interview applicants, and hire the best of them. When it sells products, it sells them in an active, competitive market. When it raises capital, then it has to compete for investors to do so. But it only behaves like that where it touches the world outside. Within the firm itself, the system is a perfect little planned economy. Firms allocate capital according to the decisions made by senior management. Any interest charged has pretty much nothing to do with the rates that would be charged by commercial banks in the same situation. In the same way, job vacancies that fall open within the firm are nearly always filled by people within the firm. Pay is set according to the decisions of the good folk in human resources. Goods are moved around inside the firm according to in-house rules on transfer pricing, not by means of any open tender for those products. Entire new ventures are planned and implemented without recourse to market structures.

Many readers will be instinctively suspicious of this line of argument. It simply feels wrong to suggest that the most

---

* Sort of, at least. Corporate turnover and national GDP aren't strictly comparable and these analogies make companies look bigger than they really are.

successful capitalist firms on the planet operate through a system of central planning – but they do! The hubbub of price signals that indicates a real market is almost completely absent when it comes to intra-firm transactions. That's how it has to be. You can't have a market unless you have a plurality of buyers and sellers, and within a firm there may be different business units, but they all share a common owner and all bow to the same commands from on high. Modern management practice sometimes allows whispers of real market activity within a firm – forcing an intra-firm supplier to compete against an external supplier, for example – but these are croaky imitations of the real thing. Even Wojciech Jaruzelski's Poland had capitalist whispers that sounded louder than that.

Indeed, the more seriously you take markets, the less market-oriented the champions of capitalism seem to be. In the last chapter, I made a throwaway remark about how workers used to mob the gates of factories, looking for work. It's a scene we're familiar with from grainy black and white photos and the stereotypes echo on through our collective consciousness today: tough factory foremen, iron gates, a crowd of would-be workers with their dark jackets and pinched faces. Those images tell us what a 'proper' labour market ought to look like. In that era of Depression and joblessness, factories could hire labour by the day. The wage and number of hands employed often altered by the day. Those tough factory foremen would pick the men they thought would work hardest for the least amount. Workers took themselves off to wherever they thought they had the best chance of remunerative employment. Agreements were struck day by day or week by week, so they could respond to the conditions of the moment. That might not have been a fun environment in which to operate, but by golly it was a capitalist one.

By contrast, reflect, if you will, on how you yourself are employed today. No doubt you have some days, or even weeks, when work is pretty slack. Equally, there'll be times when you're rushed off your feet, when you could really use more help. Perhaps the firm even loses a little business because people are slow to return calls or handle business in those more frantic patches.

According to purists of the free market, both such times indicate market failures. When things are slack, the firm doesn't need you and it should lay you off for a few days and wait for business to pick up again. When things are busy, it should increase wage rates to the point at which it can attract enough talent to handle the extra work. As things return to normal, those new hands should be laid off. Or rather – our central planner-ish ways of thinking have a habit of persisting even here – the firm shouldn't lay off the *new* staff, it should organize a reverse auction for wages and keep those staff willing to work hardest for the smallest amount of money. These events – the layoffs, the wage negotiations, the new hires – shouldn't be exceptional responses to exceptional circumstances. They should be completely routine.

Nor should you think of yourself as being employed by a particular firm. Why should you be? You're an income-maximizing worker wanting to get the best remuneration for your time. You ought to be logging on to www.wherecanImakethemostdoughtoday.com as soon as you wake up in the morning and go wherever the market sends you. As a matter of fact, in free market heaven, the very concept of a firm would melt away. All transactions, every single one, should be mediated by the market. Since a firm is nothing but a legal wall built to shut the market out, then firms themselves would disappear completely.

All this is absurd, of course. Not merely absurd, but inhuman. No one would want to work like that; no employer would wish to run things that way. Sure enough, even in the midst of the Great Depression, the extreme free market for labour was in retreat. Increasingly, and led not by those socialist French but by red-blooded American capitalists, firms began to develop in-house personnel departments. Those departments represented the replacement of free market turbulence with careful central planning. In the modern guise of human resources departments, that planning is here to stay.

Although our modern way of running things may seem perfectly sensible, it poses a deep challenge to market purists. Price, remember, is Truth. Price signals ensure that resources are allocated where they're needed. Those who are best at producing a particular good or service will presumably already be doing just that. Entrepreneurs should simply contract out work to the best and cheapest contractor rather than taking the inherently inefficient step of hiring a worker. A whole mountain of economic papers exists to *prove* that market outcomes are always optimal. (Subject to certain assumptions, naturally, and to a restrictive definition of 'optimal'.) The fact that our entire capitalist world is made up of giant centrally planned firms bumping up against each other is perhaps the deepest paradox in economics.

The solution to this riddle was provided by the man who first noticed that there was a riddle there at all, a British economist named Ronald Coase who published an article, 'Nature of the Firm', in 1937, a feat which a mere fifty-four years later would help earn him a Nobel Prize.* Coase pointed out that all market transactions have a cost. If, for example, you want to buy a new laptop, you may well surf around online, checking out various deals, before choosing to buy one. Even when you've decided which one you want, you need to spend time filling out payment and delivery details. You'll either have to pay for shipping or arrange to go into the store yourself to pick it up. Simple

* He was also responsible for the aphorism: 'If you torture the data for long enough, it will confess.' Few economists are so honest.

as the internet has made these things, they take time and time is money.

In the labour market, transactions have costs too. Some of them are obvious. All that pushing and shoving at the factory gates required people to oversee the hiring, people to agree terms, people to handle payments at the day's end, and (presumably) some very strong gates. Those are the obvious costs, but there are other, bigger costs lurking around too. Workers who know the layout of a particular factory will be quicker and more productive than those who don't. Those who work as part of a team that they like and trust may be more inclined to put effort in. Those who believe they have an upward career path available to them may work harder and smarter than they otherwise would.

Similar considerations apply to the markets for capital and products as well. Applying for loans takes time and costs money – so why not just allocate funds centrally? Competitive tendering for goods and services is expensive and distracting – so why not just do the job in-house? Before long, an entrepreneur ends up walling off his firm from the market and enjoying his centrally planned paradise in the middle.

In short, using impeccably market-driven logic, we end up able to justify a world where hundreds of billions of dollars move around inside the centrally planned economies that are capitalism's proudest creations. Because firms in a capitalist system always operate via the market wherever they touch the outside world, they never completely lose touch with reality. The pump manufacturer which ends up running pig farms and handmaking screws just couldn't exist for long in the West.

The communist version of central planning defined the scope of the plan according to geography: from Vladivostok in the East to Szczecin in the West. Firms operating in the free market set their boundaries with much more care. There's no *geographical* limit at all. General Electric operates worldwide.

Richard Branson's Virgin group has set up a Virgin Galactic unit. On the other hand, if Western capitalists are more geographically greedy than even Stalin, they patrol the efficiency frontier all the time. Should catering be conducted in-house or by external caterers? No communist firm ever asked themselves that question. In the West, that question isn't merely routine, it's nearly always answered by an outsourcing contract. When the boundary around a planning unit is defined by cost and efficiency, there are limits on how badly wrong things can go. When you have clear objectives (making money) and furious engagement with the market all along the firm's boundary, then again catastrophes tend to be limited in scope.

Tend to be.

As I write, there is a furore in the United States over the $165 million in bonuses that is being paid to the financial products division of AIG, an insurance company. That $165 million is presumably being paid to reward performance – a performance which, so far, has forced the American taxpayer to cough up $173 billion in bailout funds. No one is remotely confident that the $173 billion will be sufficient. Another $30 billion is scheduled. More may yet follow. One is forced to wonder just how bad AIG's performance would need to have been for those bonuses to have been forfeited altogether.

Pretty clearly, the centrally planned behemoths of the capitalist system can go horribly wrong as well. In part, the reason why has already been addressed in this chapter: as soon as you exclude the market from anything, the scope for error increases. Very large capitalist firms exclude the market from their internal processes, so the scope for error becomes correspondingly large too. But that's not the whole story. Ronald Coase's account of the firm focused on the decisions that an entrepreneur has to make as she considers where to draw the boundary of the market. AIG, however, is not run by an entrepreneur. Nor is General Electric. Nor is WalMart. Nor is almost any very large company. Entrepreneurs create something, before, in the fullness of time, their creation is handed over to professional managers. These giant, centrally planned firms aren't run by owners, they're run by agents – and it's to the so-called 'agent–principal problem' that we turn next.

TWELVE

Agents

> The directors of such [joint-stock] companies, however, being the managers rather of other people's money than of their own, it cannot well be expected that they should watch over it with the same anxious vigilance with which the partners in a private copartnery frequently watch over their own … Negligence and profusion, therefore, must always prevail.
>
> – ADAM SMITH, *The Wealth of Nations*

In 1969, three men working for a small West Coast delivery company noticed a problem. Ships leaving San Francisco for Honolulu carried their documents on board. When they arrived in Hawaii, those documents needed to be processed and the ships were forced to idle around, doing nothing and wasting money. The solution was simple: the three budding entrepreneurs offered to fly the documents direct to Honolulu themselves so they could be processed ahead of the ships' arrival, saving money for the shippers and making money for the couriers. It was win-win, another of capitalism's little miracles.

The business took off. The service was much in demand and the three entrepreneurs started to rope in their friends to help. To begin with, there were only two qualifications needed for the job. Number one, you needed a car, so you could collect the documents from the sender. Number two, you needed to be ready to get on a plane at a moment's notice.

The early life of the company was both heady and chaotic. Heady, because it was growing fast. Chaotic, because – well, the three individuals concerned had many virtues, but organization may not have been absolutely at the top of the list. Aside from the company's founders, the first permanent employee was a chap called Max Kroll, a Honolulu resident, whose flat became a makeshift hostel for an ever-changing constellation of young couriers.

Now, one of the things about customers is that they have a habit of looking to you to solve their problems. If it was a good idea to send documents by courier between the West Coast and Hawaii, it was also a good idea to do the same between those places and Japan, Australia, the Philippines, Singapore, and elsewhere. The young company had a policy of always saying 'yes' to customers, so pretty soon it became a highly international affair. On top of the first two employment requirements – owning a car and being willing to jump on a plane at the drop of a surfboard – a third requirement emerged: you needed a passport too.

The company's hectic growth and relaxed attitude to organization didn't suit all three of its founders. After just a few months, Robert Lynn, then about 50 years old, decided that this game wasn't for him. He sold his shareholding back to the others and went off to do other things. In personal terms, you can understand his point of view. In financial terms, it proved to be an error. His two partners, the 20-something Larry Hillblom and the fifty-something Adrian Dalsey, were onto something. Before too long, the business's pellmell expansion took it to Hong Kong. There, they came across a Hong Kong Chinese, Po-Yang Chung. Chung saw more clearly than anyone else the extraordinary potential of the company's business model and understood that Asia, with its far-flung population centres and burgeoning trade, was the perfect place for it to take shape. He also possessed the gift for management and organization which the company so sorely needed. He acquired a shareholding and before too long, the company shifted its centre of gravity to Hong Kong. Though Lynn was now gone and Chung was now on board, the company retained its orginal name: DHL, named after the Mr D, Mr H, and Mr L of its foundation. The company continued to grow.

As it grew, customers came to rely on it. They didn't ask, 'Do you have an office in Vietnam/Burma/Bangladesh/Taiwan/South Korea/Macau/Malaysia?' They simply assumed that DHL could get any document to any location, and just asked how long the package would take to get there. In line with the original 'never say no' policy, DHL would accept the package and then figure out how to get it where it needed to go. A veteran DHL manager told me that in those early years, the company's regional offices were often started by a courier stepping off the plane with some documents in his backpack. He'd deliver the documents then find a place to stay. Where the courier unslung his backpack would become DHL's brand new country office.

In all this time, the company never once owned an aircraft. They owned transport all right. Way back at the start, the company's very first asset was a 1969 Plymouth Duster. Cars, vans, and motorbikes followed a-plenty. But not planes, never planes. It wasn't just that planes cost more than any car; it was that plane ownership flew in the face of everything the company had been built on. If you own a plane, you need to leave it waiting around on the tarmac until it's collected enough freight to be worth flying. If you're not encumbered in this way, you can just pay someone to nip down to the airport and put a package on the very next plane to be flying out. In effect, by not owning aircraft of its own, DHL possessed something even better: a fleet made up of every single aeroplane flying out of every single airport in Asia. As for customers, they didn't know whether DHL owned planes or not. They didn't care. Why would they? They only cared that their packages were delivered fast and reliably, and they always were. Before too long, the company expanded from Asia to Europe. It built up a US domestic business to complement its international business. It became one of the most global of the world's companies. For anyone based outside the United States, the word 'DHL' became a verb. If you wanted to send something urgently, you DHL-ed it.

But not in the United States. In America and Canada, an alternative verb began to emerge: you didn't courier something, you FedEx-ed it. Federal Express's founder, Fred Smith, was a former marine captain who'd served two tours of duty and flown on more than 200 combat missions in Vietnam. He received a Silver Star, a Bronze Star, and two Purple Hearts. He was also a Yale student and Skull & Bones society member who were friends with both George W. Bush and John Kerry. I suspect that if the young Fred Smith had met the young Larry Hillblom, Smith would have regarded Hillblom as a hippy and a waster, and Hillblom would have considered Smith an uptight square.

From the first, FedEx was similar to and different from DHL. It was similar in that it did the same thing: it delivered packages fast. But it was different in that it was conceived and operated *as an airline*. From all over the United States, flights would come into the hub at Memphis, Tennessee. The packages would be sorted overnight then flown immediately out again. Relying on commercial flights would have delayed the packages and ruined the business model. Smith's company made a loss in 1973, its first year of service. It made a loss in 1974. It made a loss in 1975. Smith himself had a relatively small ownership stake in the company, and some of his co-investors considered sacking him. But Smith's idea had always relied on scale. A small FedEx could never make money. Indeed, the company had acquired fourteen aircraft and almost 400 employees before earning its first dollar of revenue. All along, the idea had been to grow the system to a size where it would make money hand over fist. In 1976, the company turned its first profit. In 1977, that profit more than doubled. The idea was coming good.

Scroll forward a decade or so. FedEx was formidably successs-ful in the United States and was now keen to expand internationally. The undisputed heavyweight champion of the American market was coming to slug it out with DHL, the undisputed champion of the international one. What should FedEx do? It had two options. It could discard its US business model as inappropriate for the Asian and European markets, or it could stick with the model and to hell with the consequences. It chose the latter approach. It was an airline in the United States, so it would be an airline overseas as well. Asian airports started to get used to the sight of FedEx aircraft warming the tarmac. Baffled Asian customs officials started to receive lectures from FedEx staff telling them how to restructure their procedures to bring them into line with practice in the United States.

Between 1985 and 1989, the company lost $74 million in its overseas arm. In 1990, those operations lost $221 million. In 1991, they lost $419 million. In 1992, they lost an extraordinary $613 million. DHL, in the meantime, continued to grow and remained strongly profitable throughout.

In the wake of a financial crisis in which losses of tens of billions of dollars have come to be seen as routine, it's almost nostalgic to look back at the days when losing a few hundred million bucks felt painful, but in the climate of the early 1990s, losing over a billion dollars in the space of just three years got people genuinely riled. Folk were still old-fashioned that way. Fred Smith was still the chief executive and he was determined to make his Big Idea work in Asia, just as he'd once compelled it to work in the air over Memphis, Tennessee. But though Smith was chief executive and a shareholder, the company wasn't his property. It was the property of the stockholders and Smith was acting as an agent on their behalf.

Now if the company had had, let's say, just sixty or seventy owners and they had lived within wagon's distance of, say, Bugtussle Creek, Indiana, then presumably those sixty or seventy owners would have called a meeting in the Bugtussle town hall. Stormy words would have been spoken. Smith would have yelled. A couple of grizzled old backwoodsmen would have yelled. Outside the hall, a few young rips would have blazed off with a couple of blanks in their hunting rifles. The local pastor or perhaps the deputy sheriff would have called for calm. A vote would have been taken. And Smith would have been forced to back down. That's how the agent–principal agreement can work at its simplest. It's not necessarily ideal but, in a rough and ready way, you can see how it works.

That's not how it happened in the early 1990s. If you were employed in the early 1990s and if you were paying money into a corporate pension scheme, then quite likely you held an ownership interest in FedEx yourself. If so, the chain of ownership looked something like this:

1. You fill out a tedious form that you only half-read, but which signs you up to a corporate pension scheme. You go home and tell your partner that your joint futures are now secured.
2. Your employer deducts money from your monthly pay and passes it over to a pension trustee. In the UK, many trustees used to be ordinary company employees who worked on a voluntary or semi-voluntary basis. These days, trustees are required to have appropriate knowledge of pension and trustee issues, but the bar remains set fairly low. A proportion of all trustees are nominated by employees, and at some point you cast your vote in favour of Brian, because the job's notoriously dull and you think it'd be funny to make him suffer.
3. The pension trustees decide on a fund manager – not a person, but a company which takes a percentage fee for its services.

4. The fund manager splits the money across a number of different funds and investment instruments. One of those funds has a title like 'North American Growth' and invests in American and Canadian equities.
5. That fund is run by an experienced fund manager called Karen. She's a smart cookie. She enjoys a salary that's much bigger than yours and she'll supplement that with a bonus if she outperforms certain benchmarks. Karen invests some of your money in FedEx, not because she has a detailed view on the outlook for the next-day delivery market in Asia, but because FedEx is an S&P 500 company and the best way to make sure she doesn't wildly underperform the S&P 500 index is to buy shares in all of its constituents. By 'underweighting' or 'overweighting' a particular stock, Karen can try to get ahead of the index.
6. Karen reads a headline telling her that Fred Smith's FedEx has just lost over $600 million in its overseas operations. Domestic profits more than make up for those losses, but still, $600 million is $600 million. Reading financial headlines is her job and given that she has 500 companies to think about, she doesn't get too stressed about any one of them. She moves on to the next headline.
7. She receives a call from Merrill Sachs & Stearns, an investment bank. The caller is a salesman trying to get her to sell down her stake in FedEx. The salesman makes much of a recent MS&S research report which has complicated and well-informed things to say about the Asian next-day delivery market. Karen fiddles with the report as she talks to the salesman, but they don't only talk about financial reports. Karen is a tennis fan and the salesman knows this. The US Open at Flushing Meadow is a few weeks away. Tickets are mentioned. Pete Sampras's form is discussed. The phone call ends with Karen agreeing to sell down her stake in FedEx. She starts to think about what to wear to the tennis.

8. Because MS&S and other banks are making other calls to other fund managers and because, let's remember, FedEx is making a hash of things overseas, there are more people keen to sell FedEx shares than are keen to buy them. The share price falls.
9. The FedEx board meets. On the one hand, it is very conscious of the FedEx stock price and the red ink being spilled in international operations. On the other hand, most of the board members are personally loyal to Fred Smith. One of Smith's managers was reported as saying that, 'If Fred lined up all FedEx employees and told them to jump from a bridge, 99.9 per cent would jump.' That's remarkable testimony to Smith's leadership, but it makes it hard for the board to get genuinely tough with him. *In extremis*, the board could sack Smith but losing over a billion dollars doesn't strike anyone as an emergency that requires any such radical action. What's needed is a heated debate.

There are a number of ways you could look at all this. The first and most obvious one is that the connections between the principal (you) and your appointed agent (Smith) are so many and so weak and so riven by conflicts of interest, secondary motivations, personal loyalties, divided attentions, and inexpert or ill-informed decision-making that disaster is pretty much pre-programmed from the beginning. It would be hard even to compile a full list of the ways in which this chain of control looks deficient. Karen's motivations are driven to some extent by wanting to safeguard your money, but they're also driven by wanting to watch Pete Sampras at Flushing Meadow, by having regard for existing business relationships, by the need to ensure that her quarterly numbers look OK, by having to play office politics, by her bonus arrangements, by needing to get back home to look after her kids, and a host of other things too. In the United States, it used to be easy for a strong CEO to stock the board with personal supporters. That's got a little harder now but even so, Smith is certain to be the most powerful presence in the room. Karen isn't even there, still less you or your fellow owners. In any case, you and Karen and all the rest of you know far less about the business than do Smith and his fellow executives. Your arguments may be right or they may be wrong, but either way Smith is going to be able to swat you away with a barrage of detail. Realistically, Karen's never even going to have that fight, she'll just sell down her shares, because it's easier to walk away than to initiate change.* The investment banks which pollinate the whole share trading industry have multiple conflicts of their own – MS&S, for example, would quite likely not be telling Karen to sell down her shares if the bank was hoping to get any business from FedEx any time soon. And so on.

If the chain of control above concerns not FedEx but a financial institution, then the nest of agent–principal issues becomes vastly, vastly more complicated. Because a bank's balance sheet is made up of financial assets, and because those financial assets are each claims on some other company or financial institution, and because all those other companies and financial institutions are involved in complicated chains of control themselves, then the issues involved in the world of finance are massively more convoluted still. That's not a polite way to say that all bankers are conniving crooks. Some are, most aren't. It's just that if you're going to have banks at all, then you've already signed up to a whole new order of magnitude of agent–principal complexity. Seen like this, these chains of control look about as strong as wet spaghetti; the poor old principals seem about as able to force change as a litter of kittens mewing for milk.

That's one way to look at the whole business. It's a perfectly valid one, more right than wrong. It's not too much to say that

* According to *The Economist*, the average American share now changes hands every ten months or so, down from around three years in the 1980s.

by far the hardest problem in financial regulation is how to address issues of this kind. It's not just government regulators that have this problem, it's all the private sector players too. How should Karen's contract be written to get her to act as energetically as possible on your behalf? What should the contract look like between your employer and its pension trustees? Between those trustees and the fund manager? Between FedEx and its board members? Between FedEx and Smith? These are fabulously knotty problems. The 'fat cats are bad, stupid, and greedy' slogan-mongers are only able to distill these issues down as pithily as they do because they've never actually had to grapple with them.

The other way to look at things is that, give or take, the system works. FedEx's stock price plunged. The company slashed its overseas aircraft fleet and made thousands redundant. FedEx didn't give up on its aircraft altogether. DHL, not wanting to look underpowered, bought some of its own. (In Asia, that is. It had been operating aircraft in Europe for some time already.) DHL made money. FedEx made money. Your distantly owned shares in FedEx began to recover their value and would go on to contribute very nicely to that prosperous future you once promised your partner.

Indeed, if there's a moral in all this, it's certainly not that the whole stock market system of ownership is inherently awful. The third great behemoth of American and (later) international logistics is UPS. Until 1999, the company was owned by its employees. It was, indeed, a worker owned cooperative, if you want to call it that.* Now like FedEx, UPS had a very widely distributed ownership, but those owners actually pulled on the uniform every morning when they tootled off to work. Their

* Many Wall Street firms used to be partnerships – which is really just a fancy way to say that they were worker-owned cooperatives too. I doubt if that's how partners at Goldman Sachs used to see themselves, however.

relationship with the company couldn't possibly have been closer.

And what happened? When UPS decided to expand overseas, it lost money. Huge amounts. FedEx-sized amounts. Of the three companies, the one that most successfully avoided disaster was the one managed by a tightly restricted group of owner-managers. The two that walked into trouble and then chose to stay there both had widely dispersed ownership and the problems consequent on a diffusion of responsibility. Naturally, entrepreneur-owned companies can get into messes as well. There's no simple formula for avoiding messes in life. But at least when an entrepreneur-owned company starts to lose money, then there's a completely direct relationship between what the owner wants and what the senior manager does, because it's one and the same person. As soon as ownership is dispersed, the room for catastrophic misjudgements multiplies at remarkable speed.

Nor should you allow yourself be fooled into thinking that there's something uniquely dumb about international logistics companies. There isn't. The agent–principal problem affects every organization with numerous, widely dispersed owners.

For example, until its recent collapse, General Motors owned part or the entire Swedish car manufacturer, Saab, for twenty years. You want to guess how often Saab turned a profit in that time? The answer is once. The total cost to GM has been about $5 billion, and that for a car-maker which builds just over a hundred thousand cars a year. At a rough guess, each Saab sold in the United States cost GM $5,000. The former GM vice-chairman, Bob Lutz, was quoted as saying that the reason why they persisted with Saab for as long as they did was because they loved the marque and the cars it made. Which is nice, but he was paid to look after the money of his stockholders, not to collect quirky and unprofitable Scandinavian car companies.

Or, since we've got a bit of a transportation theme going, would you care to guess which of the following has generated greater profits over the course of their histories:

A The literary consultancy business which I run from my attic with the help of one full-time employee and a few dozen freelancers; or
B The global airline industry?

Anyone who guessed (B) should go to the back of the class and get stuck into some remedial homework. The airline industry as a whole has made a loss over its history. In 2008 alone, it lost $8 or $9 billion. In 2009, it lost about the same amount.

The previous chapter pointed out that firms themselves are strange creatures. They've been created by market forces, but they themselves are creatures formed by central planning and top-down control. As firms grow ever larger, their remoteness from market forces increases too. A small FedEx or a small UPS could never have lost billions of dollars in expanding overseas. If Saab had been left to thrive or fail on its own, it would have thrived or it would have failed but it would not still be costing its owners $5,000 every time they sold a car in the United States.

This chapter has followed a closely allied theme: namely the feebleness of the chain of control that links owners on the one hand to those paid to look after their property on the other. It's not that rich people are in some giant conspiracy against the rest of us. It's just that it's genuinely difficult to create a system of corporate governance which is tough enough and flexible enough; which motivates in the right ways but never in the wrong ones. Indeed, the capitalist world only works as well as it does, precisely because most people go into work wanting to do a good, honest, decent job to the very best of their abilities.

Nevertheless, when economists talk about the free market's ability to grope towards optimal outcomes, we need to remember to take it with a hefty pinch of salt. As a rough guide to estimating the size of that pinch, I'd suggest the following procedure. Take one of the world's most entrepreneurial and best-managed companies: I'd suggest FedEx. Look at that company's worst screw-up: I'd suggest its botched international expansion. Take a rough estimate of the total costs involved: let's say around $1.5 billion. Scale that up to take account of the larger world economy of today: $3 billion should cover it. Take into account that FedEx is not, in fact, a terribly large company by the standards of terribly large companies: so let's treble that $3 billion to get a figure of $9 billion and that is a rough measure of how big a pinch of salt you need ...

... assuming that we're talking about industrial companies. With financial companies, because of their humungous balance sheets and the extreme complexity of those agent–principal interactions, the pinch of salt needs to be far, far greater. Estimates of the cost of the 2008 financial crisis are still being worked out now and will go on being worked out for years to come, but $3 or $4 trillion should cover it nicely. That's a lot of salt.

Economists, of course, are well aware of agent–principal problems – it was economists who first named and investigated the issue and, indeed, it was one of Adam Smith's major themes in his *Wealth of Nations.* Yet economists and politicians and pundits with views that favour the free market can find themselves so mesmerized by the big point – markets work! markets are great! – that they can completely forget about the giant caveats that gallop along just a few inches behind: markets are made up of firms. Firms are run by people. People can screw up. Big firms can screw up big time. Mega-banks can screw up mega-big time.

It is time to leave these thoughts, but a few last reflections before we do.

First of all, Larry Hillblom. In 1995, he died in a seaplane crash. The bodies of the pilot and a fellow passenger were recovered. Hillblom's corpse was never found. His will left his fortune of $500 or $600 million dollars to medical research – a worthy intention – but Hillblom was resident in Saipan in the Marianas Islands when he died and, under Saipan law, illegitimate children born after a will is drawn up are entitled to claim against the estate. Before too long, a host of women came forward complete with babies and stories of how Hillblom used to visit bars in Micronesia and the Philippines offering teenage girls money in exchange for sex.

The obvious thing to do was to establish paternity, yet when investigators came to search Hillblom's home, they discovered that it had been wiped clean. Sinks had reportedly been scrubbed with muriatic acid, a powerful cleaning agent. Combs, toothbrushes, and clothes had been destroyed or buried, rendering any DNA they contained useless. Hillblom had once had a facial mole removed at a University of California hospital and it was thought that the mole was still kept in storage. Even though the University stood to gain enormously from Hillblom's bequest, it generously decided to release the mole. Alas, further investigation revealed that whoever the mole belonged to, it didn't belong to Hillblom and the investigation was back to square one.

Hillblom did, however, have a mother. She was persuaded to give up a sample of her DNA in return for $1 million and a very nice house in France. The paternities of the various litigating children could then be assessed and one Vietnamese child, two Filipinos, and a child from Palau were determined to be Hillblom's. They were awarded $90 million each which, after lawyers' fees and taxes had been deducted, left them with a paternal gift of some $50 million. The medical research charities received around $240 million.

I'm more familiar with this story than you might think because, in the twilight of my banking days, I had a tangential involvement with all this. Hillblom's shares in DHL were subject to various clauses in a private shareholder agreement, which permitted the company's existing shareholders to have first bite at purchasing those shares in the event of Hillblom's death. The mechanism involved required fair value for the shares to be determined and my investment bank was one of those asked to give its views. I led that valuation team and flew out to Hong Kong, Singapore, and Brussels to interview senior operating management and get to grips with the company's finances and operations. I signed a confidentiality agreement at the time, so I can't say much in detail – but I will say that DHL was the most impressive company I encountered in my ten years of investment banking.

Secondly, Fred Smith. He is, at time of writing, still FedEx's boss. He is also, and deservedly, one of the most admired CEOs in the United States. Screwing up an overseas expansion doesn't make you stupid; it makes you human. In its most recent financial year, FedEx earned an operating profit of $2 billion on revenues of nearly $40 billion. It too is quite a company.

And last, Robert Lynn. The 'L' in DHL and the guy who sold out after a few months' ownership died in 1998 after a short illness. He was the last survivor of the entrepreneurial threesome. A brief obituary, printed in *Air Cargo World*, recapitulated the few public facts about Lynn's early involvement with the company and ended thus: 'Years later, a DHL spokesman said the company had only a single, indirect contact with Lynn over the years: a small transport company in Seattle called to confirm a curious item on a resumé from a job applicant, Robert Lynn, who claimed that he had founded DHL Worldwide Express.'

THIRTEEN

Psychopaths

> The corporation is an externalizing machine, in the same way that a shark is a killing machine.
>
> – ROBERT MONKS, corporate governance activist

This section of the book has been a story of disappointment. We began bright with hope at the wonder of markets then discovered the extent to which firms themselves aren't creatures of the market, and then saw how feeble is the chain of control which links owner to manager, thereby further weakening the flag-bearers of capitalism. We now come to a still more sombre accusation: the claim that firms aren't merely capable of ineptitude and failure but that they are, in the most literal possible way, psychopaths. Creatures motivated only by profit, willing to murder, maim, or poison if it advances their interests, incapable of remorse, incapable of ordinary fellow feeling.

The argument has its roots in the history-making legal case of *Hutton* v. *West Cork Railway Company*, a dispute brought before the English high court in 1883. One railway company, Bandon, had just purchased another, West Cork, but immediately prior to the conclusion of the transaction, West Cork had announced a jumbo cash payout to its directors. At this point, Bandon sued, arguing that the money wasn't West Cork's to give. In effect, the issue at stake was this: could a company spend its money for any purpose other than the maximization of profits? Was a company, in fact, *allowed* to be kind?

The court considered the issues and came to its verdict. The answer was that yes, some corporate generosity was just fine. In the words of the judge:

> Take this sort of instance. A railway company, or the directors of a company, might send down all the porters at a railway station to have tea in the country at the expense of the company. Why should they not? ... A company which always treated its employés with Draconian severity ... would soon find itself deserted.

There was, however, a 'but'. Generosity for an ulterior motive was fine. Generosity for its own sake was definitely not. 'The law does not say that there are to be no cakes and ale,' intoned the judge, sticking closely to his culinary theme, 'but there are to be no cakes and ale *except such as are required for the benefit of the company*.' (Italics added.) Real charity, the milk of human kindness, the overflow of one person's tenderheartedness towards another was illegal. The only kind of charity that was permitted was an impostor, a legally sanctioned hypocrite. To quote the good judge again: 'There is, however, a kind of charitable dealing which is for the interest of those who practise it, and to that extent and in that garb (I admit not a very philanthropic garb) charity may sit at the board [of directors], but for no other purpose.'

The judgment put an end to the matter in dispute. Bandon won. West Cork lost. The directors had to repay their looted cash. Life moved on. Yet the judgment was and has remained one of the most significant milestones in corporate law. Any corporation, from a corner grocery shop to a $200 billion multinational, is *prohibited* from doing good for the sake of doing good. If charitable sentiments are aired in the boardroom, they are either hypocritical or illegal; there is no other option.

If this sounds singularly self-interested – well, singular self-interest is one of the traits used in the diagnosis of psychopathy. Other such traits include a grandiose sense of self-worth, pathological lying, lack of remorse, manipulativeness, lack of empathy, and a failure to accept responsibility. That might seem a harsh description of your average corporation, until you start to consider how happy some companies are to target advertising at pre-schoolers. If that's not manipulative, what is? As for the other items on the checklist, there are almost too many examples to choose from. Pathological lying – hello Big Tobacco. Lack of empathy – yoo-hoo, Big Pharma. Lack of remorse and failure to accept responsibility – here's looking at you, Wall Street.

As for grandiose self-worth, no one with a Napoleon complex has even got close to the self-importance of the average multinational. One of the biggest delights of the credit crunch was watching how some of those corporate self-images imploded as they encountered reality. One particular favourite of mine is AIG's gloriously inept 'The Strength to Be There' motto – a nice one to have on your office stationery as the government is bailing you out to the tune of $173 billion. You've also, though, got to admire the mottos of Lehman 'Where Vision Gets Built' Brothers and Northern 'If You Need Some Cash, You've Got It' Rock. Or maybe you prefer the Belgian bank, Dexia's, alarmingly honest, 'The Short Term Has No Future'. Too right. Perhaps all the failed institutions should have been forced to rebrand themselves with a new slogan for the new era: 'Because We're Worthless'.

Outside the financial world, things aren't much better. Carlsberg's pseudo-modest 'Probably the Best Lager in the World' at least makes a show of trying not to sound off too much, which is more than can be said for many. For sheer gall, Gillette takes some beating. 'The Best a Man Can Get'. It's a razor, for crying out loud. It shares shelf-space with dental floss. Gillette may just about hope to be the best thing a man can get *in a standard bathroom cabinet*, but their marketing executives somehow managed to miss off that not insignificant qualification.

More seriously and more disturbingly, there appear to be no limits on how far the market will be prepared to take things. If the law said that it was OK to use child labour, then the market would get to work establishing a price for 12-year-old coal miners. If the law said it was OK for poor people to sell their organs, then webuyyourorgansforcash.com would soon become a valuable online property. These aren't the speculative assertions of some socialist nutcase. When it was legal for firms to employ children, then children were duly employed. In countries where it's legal to employ children today, then guess what? Children are legally employed. In Iran, kidney sales are legal and there's a thriving market in them. In other countries, it's not legal but neither is it effectively prohibited and there's a thriving market there too. You can pick up a decent Iranian kidney for about $3,000, a semi-legal Pakistani one for $2,500, or a cheaper Indian one for $2,000. In the wake of the 2004 Indian Ocean tsunami, the price of Indian kidneys plummeted to as little as $900 because poor fishermen were desperate for capital to rebuild their businesses. The laws of supply and demand don't go soppy just because of human tragedy.

That quotation at the head of this chapter – the one about corporations and killing machines – wasn't intended by Robert Monks as crude invective, but as an accurate statement of how things are. Firms, inevitably, cause harm as they go about their daily business. Oil companies pollute. Mining companies affect landscapes. Airlines create noise. Confectionery companies encourage poor eating habits. And so on. If any one firm in these industries tried to act with puritanical rectitude, picking up the tab for the costs it was creating, that firm's business model would instantly implode. Competition is tough enough without having to bear the weight of finicky morals too. Firms make money by finding ways to charge for the benefits they create, but ducking away from the penumbra of 'negative externalities', or extraneous social and environmental costs, that they cannot help but generate at the same time.

You don't have to spend long on reflections like these before you start to feel a little crazy yourself, and maybe the best way to get deal with that craziness is to remind ourselves of some basic principles. First, the best response to anyone telling us that the corporation is a psychopath is roughly: what on earth did you think it was? The revelation is about as surprising as the discovery that a railway company is obsessed by trains or that an army is constantly training people to kill. Corporations are there to sell goods and services and make a profit from doing so. It's what they do.

Naturally, a decently run corporation will obey the law 99.9 per cent of the time, but corporations face two challenges in dealing with that last 0.1 per cent: they're run by humans and the clarity of law has a tendency to dissolve as it comes into contact with real life. Take health and safety as an example. Clearly manufacturers can't recklessly endanger life, either among their workers or among their customers. But what's reckless and what isn't? A really safe car would be crowded with airbags, be speed-limited, have a super-strong steel impact protection system, maybe a defibrillator or two, a fridge stocked with bags of blood matched to the driver's blood type … and would cost about a million pounds and look something like a slow-moving brick.* Clearly there's a need for compromise. Sometimes – most of the time – corporations take a perfectly

* The US President's Cadillac One does have bags containing the Presidential blood. It also has shotguns, tear gas, and night vision cameras. It does eight miles to the gallon.

decent shot at that compromise. Occasionally, they screw up and it's often possible to detect the hidden hand of the cost-cutting accountant when they do.

In one notorious case, Ford chose not to redesign to its 1971 Pinto model, despite knowing that the fuel-tank had a tendency to catch fire in rear-end collisions. Sure enough, when the car was launched, accidents happened. Some of those were rear-end collisions and because the fuel-tank was dangerously exposed, many of those collisions resulted in fires that killed or seriously injured the people inside. When the resulting injury suits came to court, it came to light that Ford had calculated the cost of strengthening the rear-end on the one hand and the cost of paying out damages to the relatives of the deceased on the other. The cost–benefit analysis indicated that it would be cheaper to leave the car as it was, and Ford's engineers had run with cost, not safety. The court process made it possible to document Ford's precise thought process through this episode, but there's no question that countless other such decisions have been and are being made by countless other corporations.

It's not totally clear, however, whether Ford's actions constitute corporate psychopathy or the careful evolution of a rationally desirable outcome. It's certainly easier to argue the former. Ford's engineers could have saved lives and chose not to! They're cold-blooded killers! They killed for money! Well, true, true, and true. The legal prohibition on corporate charity seems very much in evidence here.

Yet it's worth retaining a dose of common sense. Ford manufactures large chunks of metal that travel along at high speeds and are driven by people like your Auntie Edna who quite frankly shouldn't be allowed behind the controls of a coffee machine, let alone those of a car. Casualties are inevitable; the real wonder is that our roads aren't strewn with corpses and burning wrecks. The reason they're not is that car-makers have been rather good at improving their products, with Ford playing a leading role in that improvement. Prior to the Pinto debacle, it was Ford who had pioneered the introduction of safety belts in cars and it only knew about the rear-end collision issue because it had conducted tests that most car-makers back then didn't bother with and which federal safety standards didn't require.

Even in the Pinto case, what *should* Ford have done? It was pioneering a new, cheap, affordable car. The car met every single federal safety standard. At the same time, and inevitably, every aspect of the design reflected a compromise as against more expensive models. It wasn't just safety; it was styling, spaciousness, speed, and everything else. On every front, quality fought with cost. Those fights are an elementary part of design; they're why we have engineers. In this particular case, Ford accurately identified a problem, worked out the costs of putting it right, and weighed those costs against (i) the number of expected fatalities and (ii) the court-determined value attached to each of those lost lives. In effect, it was looking to the courts of the United States to determine the value of a human life and was applying those values in its own calculations. Unless you take the view that it is wrong ever to place a monetary value on human life, then Ford's thinking arguably reflected the best possible way to approach these issues.

And the bald fact is that all of us place an implicit monetary value on our life. True, we're seldom put in a situation where we start auctioning our life off on eBay,* but we face a similar calculation each time we decide whether or not we want to pay extra for a certain safety feature, or whether or not a lucrative-but-dangerous job is worth the risk. Economists – cold-blooded reptiles as they are – have explored these implicit

* Ian Usher, a Brit who emigrated to Australia, did sell his life on eBay. The bidding opened at A$1 and shot up to a sum equivalent to £192,000. The buyer never paid up.

calculations and calculated the value that we ourselves place on our own lives. The answers aren't exact, and all kinds of methodological issues bedevil the mathematics, but for a round answer then $10,000,000 is approximately right. Our own internal calculators are doing precisely what Ford's 1970s era engineers did, only they did their work with precision and care, while we do ours in a slapdash way, while mostly worrying about how many cup-holders we can find and how to use the CD-changer.

In fact, though, Ford and its engineers did learn a lesson from the Pinto affair. Although the firm made a reasonably prescient estimate of deaths and costs, it failed to factor in another, larger cost: reputation. Needless to say, newspaper headlines of the 1970s didn't choose to report, 'Auto Manufacturer Vindicated as Victim Tally Reaches Predicted Totals' or 'National Motor Show Honors Ford Death Count Estimate Heroes'. On the contrary, headline writers took huge delight in exposing Ford's supposed psychopathic tendencies and the company's carefully nurtured reputation for safety began to go up in the smoke of all those blazing fuel-tanks. So it withdrew the car, fixed the issue, moved on. Market forces combined with media campaigning and government pressure solved the problem.

This triumvirate didn't just fix a problem with the fuel-tank protection on one car. Over the last century, the same three forces have brought about a stunning improvement in the safety of our lives. It's hard to find data which is strictly comparable from one end of the century to the next, but a few examples make the point. In Britain, accident statistics compiled by J. J. Leeming, a road engineer, suggested that in the mid-Victorian period, transport-related fatalities were about 50 per cent greater, per head of the population, than they would be a hundred years later – and that was despite the massive increase in passenger-miles travelled. In 1906/7, in Allegheny County, Pennsylvania, there were a total of 526 workplace fatalities, of which 195 were suffered by steelworkers. A hundred years later and the steel industry across the entire United States reported just seventeen fatalities. Infinitely more steel was being produced, and yet the death toll across the whole country had fallen to less than a tenth of what it had been in just one county.* In the Western world, one could multiply these examples almost infinitely. Deaths from dodgy food have declined. Contaminated drinking water is all but unheard of. Buildings don't collapse. Planes don't fall out of the sky. Rear-end collisions don't fry those who are hit. There are exceptions to every rule, of course, but the exceptions become ever fewer.

These improvements haven't come about *despite* all those corporate psychopaths, legally prohibited from engaging in charitable behaviour. It's come about *because of* them. I am personally a very trusting type. I'm the sort that doesn't research vehicle safety before I buy a car; I don't check crash statistics before booking a flight; I'll buy a central heating system with the happy-go-lucky confidence that it's not going to incinerate me and my family as we sleep.

On the other hand, although I'm trusting, I'm not an idiot. My car is a Volkswagen Passat, made by Europe's biggest car manufacturer. Although I don't check safety statistics myself, I know that there are plenty of others who do, not to mention a host of media outlets ready to scream loudly if there were serious lapses in VW's safety standards. I also know that there's a lot at stake. VW sells a few million cars a year and its market capitalization knocks around the €80 billion level. If it starts to

* Currently the most dangerous occupation in the US is that of lumberjack, with 118 fatalities per 100,000 worker-years. Most of the other top ten danger jobs are fairly predictable – pilot, fisherman, structural metal worker – but you'd never guess that pizza delivery was a more lethal occupation than roofing. It is, though; it has 38 fatalities per 100,000 taking it into fifth place in the Ultimate Danger League, just ahead of roofing with 37. Next time tip the delivery boy, OK? It may be his last.

kill people because of sloppiness over safety, then it stands to lose tens of billions of euros and a potentially huge volume of car sales. That's enough for me. I'm pretty damn sure that if a bunch of capable people stand to lose tens of billions of euros if they kill me, then they're going to try quite hard not to. It's the same thing with airlines. The same thing with heating systems. The more corporate a brand name is, the more scrutiny I know it's under. I take a free ride on the scrutiny of others more suspicious than myself.

So powerful are these forces, that I can even trust them when I know nothing about the corporations in question. When I step inside a large building, for example, I do so without knowing which construction company put it together or what the reputation of that company might be. Yet I (and you and all of us) step trustingly inside large and potentially dangerous structures without a second thought for the tonnage of masonry above our heads. We do so, because we trust that the whole system – the architects, engineers, government inspectors, the building owner, the finance company, and the rest – does what it needs to do. In part, we're trusting the good folk from the government with their bookfuls of regulations and their pernickety attention to detail, but in part we're also trusting that good architects don't commission dodgy engineers, that sane building owners don't go to reckless architects, and so on. Even when we don't know anything about the web of relationships that have created a structure, we're happy to trust that others do know and that the importance of reputation will always be decisive.

My cheerful trust in the world around me starts to wane as soon as I enter areas where reputation is less likely to produce desirable outcomes. Buying a new car from Volkswagen is one thing; buying a second-hand VW from a classified ad is a totally different matter. According to the theory which says 'corporations are psychopaths, only individuals can act morally', I should be much happier to trust the individual seller. I can look her in the eye, grasp her hand, and remember that 200,000 years of shared evolutionary history has given my fellow human being a conscience not totally unlike my own.

Alas for the theory; we all know that buying second-hand cars is a notoriously perilous business. The seller probably has little or no track record in selling cars and, in any case, I have no way of checking it if she has. The car may be fine. It may be lousy. I know that in a similar situation I tend to be pretty honest, but not always completely candid. If all other things were equal, I'd sooner buy my car off a corporate psychopath than buy one from a clone of myself. The critical thing here isn't whether the seller is human or corporate; it's whether the seller has to care about their reputation with customers. Most of us only sell a few cars in a lifetime. When we do, we're unlikely ever to encounter the buyer again in any other context. Although most of us would choose not to rip off our buyers, we also know that it doesn't much matter if we do.

Anyone who sets themselves up as a car dealer, however, does have to start caring. A bloke with a corner garage in an urban area may still not care very much. Perhaps he can rip off a few customers and just hope that the throng of people in his catchment area won't for the most part ever learn of his roguery. On the other hand, even then, he makes his money by selling cars. The more happy customers he has, the more those happy customers are likely to recommend him and the more his business is likely to expand. As soon as he starts to set his sights higher – a chain of salesrooms, a giant car supermarket, a national brand – reputation starts to become all important.

The paradox we're left with is strange enough that it's worth spelling it out in full. A corporation *cannot* seek to act morally. It's not allowed to do so. The courts won't let it. The board of directors, the senior management, the operating procedures, the financial accounts, everything drives at avoiding moral behaviour for the sake of it. A person, on the other hand, may be a messy old bunch of contradictions, but they're very seldom psychopathic. They'll have some selfish motivations, some moral ones, but it's rare that someone truly doesn't give a damn about those they come into contact with. Yet it's the psychopath, not the human, which we end up trusting.

FOURTEEN

Generation Bollywood

I dream of India becoming a great economic superpower.

– DHIRUBHAI AMBANI, founder of Reliance, the first Indian company to feature in the Forbes Global 500

Take, if you would, an ordinary drinking glass – and I do mean stand up, dig out a glass, and come back with it. Not one of your fancy cut glass, lead crystal, handcrafted-by-twinkly-eyed-craftsmen-in-Donegal affairs, but the very cheapest tumbler you've got. As a matter of fact, two or three tumblers would be even better, ideally of slightly different manufacture. A cheap wine or beer glass would also be fine.

Good. You have in front of you two or three glasses. Examine them carefully. Run your finger carefully around the rim. There's quite likely to be a lip on at least one of them. On that lip, you'll probably find a spot where the glass fattens slightly. You can both feel it with a finger and see it as you hold the glass to the light.

Now examine the base of the tumbler. If your tumbler did have that characteristic fattening on the lip, then the base of the tumbler will be a little uneven. Two glasses from the same batch won't have the base in exactly the same place. There's likely to be some minor asymmetry in the way the glass gathers at the base. If you run your finger over the bottom of the glass, you'll find that it's not perfectly smooth or even. If you rotate the base against the light, you'll notice a host of small irregularities and imperfections.

What you have in your hand now may be cheap, but it's entirely handmade. One man (it'll certainly have been a man) will have dipped something like a large honey-stirrer into a pot of molten glass and lifted it up and out. A second man was there waiting for the liquid glass to start dripping from the stirrer, and he'll have 'snipped' the dripping glass off at just the point when there was a roughly tumbler-sized amount. A third man will have caught that dripping glass and directed it into a mould, while a fourth man will be responsible for blowing the glass – literally blowing through a hollow tube – out against the walls of the mould and down into the base. The glass then needs to be cut around the top to produce a nice even finish but as the cutting tool is pulled away, the molten glass clings to the tool in exactly the same way that mozzarella clings to the pizza knife. It's that mozzarella-ish tail which shrinks back to form the slight fattening on the lip that first caught our attention. The different thickness of glass you get in the bottom of the tumbler is accounted for by the imprecision of the process by which the initial blob of glass was snipped from the honey-stirrer.

Though you may be pleased to discover that your dirt-cheap tumbler has been made by hand, you shouldn't be too pleased. A team of six workers can produce about 1,000 glasses in an hour, 8,000 in a working day. Your glass may be handmade, but it's hardly special. Because wage rates in China, India, and their peers are so low, no volume manufacturer in the West can possibly compete. That's why those few glass manufacturers left in the West rely on selling expensive lead-crystal items, marketed using the supposed prestige of all those twinkly-eyed Donegal craftsmen.

I always knew that if I were to write a book about global wealth creation, I'd need to explore beyond my own Anglo-American-European comfort zone. In particular, I'd need to deal with the emerging giants of the world economy, notably China and India. China was, in a way, the more obvious choice for investigation. It's bigger. It's growing faster. Its manufacturing prowess is apparent in our shopping baskets, where India's much more broadly based success is more concealed from view. But China was the wrong focus for my investigation all the same.

For one thing, it's both communist and capitalist. Its growth rates reflect the creative energy of capitalism and the coercive power of a fully fledged police state. In China, if the state wants to create an airport, build a power plant, bulldoze a slum, it'll go ahead and do it. If anyone objects, there'll be some nice young men with big sticks and loaded guns inviting protesters to think again. China has certainly executed its strategy with remarkable skill, but Stalin too succeeded in industrializing Russia at a speed which shocked all Western onlookers. The success of a coercive state may be dazzling, but it offers few lessons for those who believe that freedom matters more than money.

Furthermore, China's success tells us nothing about our own past. When Britain gave birth to the Industrial Revolution in the last third of the eighteenth century, it did so without a coercive state or huge public infrastructure spend. When America leaped into the industrial lead following the Civil War, it too did so democratically and with modest outlays from the public purse. In the histories of continental Europe and Japan, democracy has been too often absent, but the great post-war economic miracle happened under firm democratic control. China, therefore, has little to teach us about our own pasts, whereas India, for all its differences, abounds in parallels. By examining India today, we are reaching back in time to our own pasts, in much the same way that astronomers reach back in time when they point their telescopes at light from the most distant stars.

And, finally, there was for me a factor that clinched it. I didn't just want to go out to China or India to talk to people about how they did business. I wanted to go out there with someone actually *doing* business. Fortunately, a friend of mine, James, owns and runs a glass manufacturer in the UK. Not a maker of humble tableware – those businesses no longer exist in Britain – but a maker of specialist scientific glassware, of the sort that you'll find in any laboratory anywhere in the world. In line with the modern way of things, James's factory specializes in low-volume production runs and custom-builds for Western clients. If you want a fancy bit of scientific glassware, then James's company can almost certainly make it for you. If you want a slightly less fancy bit of glassware, then you'll find it in James's catalogue all right, but increasingly those other bits and pieces come from abroad. They don't, however, simply appear by magic. They come because James gets on a plane, goes to India, and makes it happen.

Which was how I ended up in the offices of ASGI, a glass manufacturing company in Agra, sipping ginger-infused tea* and examining a table full of samples and spec-sheets. Laboratory glass is a lot more intricate than a water tumbler and at the same time, it needs to be made to demanding standards of quality and accuracy. It is still, nevertheless, made almost entirely by hand. Take, for example, a five-litre volumetric flask (which looks like a glass balloon with a long glass neck). To make that, you need to take a length of glass tubing, pop it into a lathe to keep it turning, melt a section of tube and pinch it until you can nudge the ends into meeting. From there, you simultaneously heat the tube and blow into it in order to make the glass balloon out into your desired shape. You have a template to indicate the form you're seeking to achieve, but the work is done by hand and eye. There simply aren't enough five-litre volumetric flasks in the world to be worth the expense of

* Ginger-infused, our host explained, because it was January and the warmth of the ginger would help keep the cold away. It was 24°C outside.

automating the process. Once you've blown out the flask, you need to flatten the base, form the neck, bore it to take a stopper, and then calibrate it so that the flask is accurate to within plus or minus 2.4 millilitres, or about five-hundreths of 1 per cent. If the flask achieves an accuracy no better than 2.5 millilitres, then it's of no value and will need to be discarded. And a volumetric flask is a fairly simple item. Scientific laboratories use much more weird and wonderful things than that and each item, no matter how weird and wonderful, needs to meet the highest possible standards of accuracy and manufacture.

It was a surprise, then, for me to see how entirely craft-based the industry is. At the heart of the Agra factory is a large hall containing about about ten workstations, equipped with propane burners and, in most cases, lathes. At each station, a worker sat steadily transforming their raw materials – essentially vast quantities of glass tubes imported from China – into finished glassware. The hall was noisy, because of the rush of the burners, and with about ten propane flames continuously burning, also hot. In other parts of the factory, there was a place where necks are bored. Neck-boring may sound easy, but you can't just make one neck so that it fits the stopper for that particular bottle, you have to ensure complete interchangeability of parts, so that any neck can take any stopper. The steel templates which deliver that kind of accuracy wear out after about twenty uses, so the factory also needed a metal-working lathe able to manufacture further templates on demand.

The next critical element in the factory was the calibration room, where flasks and pipettes and everything else are calibrated by hand. The process involves pouring a measured amount of water into the vessel, adjusting for temperature changes (because the water changes volume according to the temperature in the room), and marking off the appropriate levels accordingly. Once this is done, the glass may be printed on or transfers applied. Products are then baked at a few hundred degrees Centigrade to even out any stresses that may be in the glass after the glassblowing process. Once cool, the glass is packed and ready to sell.

It's a little hard to know how to convey the impression that all this made. On the one hand, although there wasn't much high technology in evidence here, it was equally clear that not much was needed. James himself said that although his own factory was better equipped, the differences weren't vast. In many cases, the additional machinery available to James's own workers had been put together by the factory engineer from easily available parts. On a purely technological level, James's factory – which is as well equipped and well run as any of its Western competitors – was not hugely different from the Indian one.

At the same time, no one could step into the factory at Agra and not identify it instantly as non-Western. Take, for example, the fairly elementary matter of light fittings. The operator of the metal-working lathe needed to see what he was doing. Since the metal-working lathe was in a windowless bay off the main factory hall, he needed lighting. The British – or American or German or Japanese – solution would have been bright white walls, strong overhead lighting and perhaps a lamp on a flexible arm for detailed work. But this was India. In one hotel I stayed in – not a tourist hotel, but nevertheless the best one anywhere in this prosperous north Indian town – there was a leak from the bathroom ceiling that dripped on me when I brushed my teeth or went to the loo. I couldn't escape that leak by retreating to the bedroom, because a second leak in the ceiling there dripped directly onto the bed once every minute or so throughout my stay. By shoving my bed to one side, I was able to clear a patch dry enough for me to sleep on, but I knew perfectly well that the chance of finding someone to fix the leak was roughly zero. To judge by the huge damp stain in the ceiling and the lumps of missing plaster, the problem had been continuing for weeks or months, not hours or days.

Or another example: Indian roads. In the tediously rule-inclined country of my birth, we drive on one side of the road only. We use our indicators to show an intention to manouevre then execute that manouevre as signalled. We use our horns very seldom, in my case mostly to warn pheasants away from my car's front bumper. We also, as it happens, expect our cars to be almost or completely free of scrapes, dings, and dents in their bodywork.

In India – well, things are more interesting. For one thing, there's the multi-media aspect of the whole road experience. There aren't just cars, buses, and lorries to deal with, there are cycles and motorbikes, rickshaws both motorized and pedal-powered, plenty of tractors, a strange and varied host of horse-carts, hand-carts, bullock-carts, and camel-carts – and then the animals, a cornucopia of sauntering dogs, complacent cows, rooting pigs, wandering buffalo, the occasional monkey, and (once) an elephant. That's not even to start listing the strange and wonderful variety of inanimate objects to be found on major roadways. If, for example, you're an Indian builder, then where better to deposit a huge pile of cement powder (or sand, or bricks, or timber) than right there on the road? Once we came across a pile of cement so large that we were obliged to mount it with our right-side wheels, while trying to keep the left-side wheels from slithering sideways into the open sewer that ran along the road. We succeeded, but it was touch and go.

Traffic priorities and conventions of the road are almost completely invisible on anything but the most major routes, but even on major highways, conventions are soft- rather than hard-edged. Once, our driver swerved out of the way of a large obstacle in the road – I forget now whether it was an unmarked road repair, or a fallen pipe, or just a slow moving tractor – and found himself driving at full speed down the wrong side of a dual carriageway. In Britain, if you found yourself in that kind of situation, your heart would be in your mouth. Panic would fill the car. If you survived the situation (no doubt by manouevring carefully to a place of safety and then phoning for help) you'd be dining out on the incident for days. In India – well, I did notice the driver tut slightly to himself and I saw him drum on the steering wheel with his thumbs. But despite his moment of being disconcerted, he knew exactly what to do. He honked his horn loudly in the hope of dematerializing any advancing chunks of metal, kept his foot on the accelerator, and about a minute or so later swerved back onto the proper side of the carriageway. He wouldn't even have been thinking about the incident thirty seconds later. Needless to say, outside the hallowed precincts of New Delhi, it's all but impossible to find a single vehicle without a scratch. Most cars are dinged, dented, and scratched all over.

Now if all this strikes you as a mere digression – we were, if you recall, considering the business of lighting for ASGI's metal-working bay – then nothing could be further from the truth. This was India and the lighting in that bay was not Western but Indian. The walls were rendered in a dark cement mortar. The only lighting came from a low-wattage incandescent bulb that dangled precariously from a length of flex that dangled from some other flex which was in turn connected to Agra's only intermittently effective power grid. I wouldn't say that the lighting was too dark to operate by, but it was put together by an electrician operating to a set of rules and expectations utterly different from our own. Quality, reliability, tidiness, safety – it's not that Indians lack norms for these things, but they live in a culture where it's just fine to leave mounds of loose cement in a busy city street and where the phrase 'dual carriageway' is used to imply a choice of options, not a set of rules. The cluster of norms to which that Indian electrician worked was simply different from yours or mine. Equally, the person who employed him to do the job presumably looked at the dangling flex, the hanging bulb, the dull sheen of exposed copper wire, and commended the workman for a good job well done.

These cultural norms lie at the very heart of what has made the poor world poor and the rich world rich. For sure, Western factories generally have a load more technology in them than do Indian or Chinese ones, but to focus on the technology is to miss the point. For one thing, there are plenty of areas – such as scientific glassware – where the technological differences aren't huge. For another thing, technology is freely available. You can simply go and buy it. If an Indian company wants a factory full of lots of shiny new machine tools, then it only has to get out its chequebook. Machine tool manufacturers and the like make their living by selling their kit to all comers. If a manufacturer needs help in designing its production system, then there are plenty of consulting engineers who'd be only too pleased to assist. The German economy, indeed, is founded on the export of just such goods and and the services that go along with them.

Last but not least, the shiny new technology in Western factories is very often a sign of weakness not strength. Western manufacturers have been forced into a very high degree of automation, because their labour costs have become almost lethally high. Manufacturers in the emerging markets can automate if it makes sense, not if it doesn't. In other words, the high level of machinery in most Western plants often reflects the narrowness of their strategic options not the scale of their advantage.

For most industries, therefore, it's not technology that lies at the heart of the rich world/poor world difference, but culture. The Agra-based manufacturer was probably the best run company James and I visited on our tour of Indian glassworks, and we saw perhaps a dozen glassworks altogether. The company is run by a father-son team, where the older man is the more technically skilled of the two. He understands the details of the production process. In order to illustrate a particular technique of value in a specific aspect of glass manufacture, James had brought with him some video material showing one of his workers carrying out the technique. Where the son sat back, knowing his own limitations, the father craned forward to catch the method in detail, nodding his understanding and approval.

But if the son brought little technical skill to bear, he brought an entirely new cultural approach. He is an excellent English speaker. He has an MBA from a top Indian school. (His wife also speaks perfect English and also has an MBA, indicating a seismic shift in Indian cultural expectations about gender.) He also knows that while he could perfectly well make decent money from serving the Indian market alone, the real jackpot is to be won by breaking into the Western one. He's aware that that means meeting the expectations of customers like James, and he's perfectly prepared to overturn generations of past practice in order to create the right result.

James had last been to see this company two years before. At the time the factory had been unremittingly dark, even in the calibration room. James had pointed out that glassblowers could hardly work in near-darkness and that calibration in particular needed strong bright reliable light. Most Indian manufacturers would have heard those words and ignored them. We visited other glassmakers to whom James had also given the same sage advice and whose workers still laboured in near-darkness. But this outfit was smarter than that. They understood that there was an issue here, and that quality was affected.

They had also come to learn of the weirdly high importance placed by Westerners on the right quality standards. At a fairly early stage in their relationship, James had taken a delivery of glassware from Agra that was of poor quality, had numerous breakages, and that had been heavily infiltrated by rats. In India such problems would have been shrugged off, part of the natural order of things. But to a British manufacturer which earns its crust by selling glassware to some of the most advanced pharmaceutical laboratories in the world, such quality problems would have been catastrophic. James had to ditch most of the order and his email to India contained some very strong messages indeed. And the young entrepreneur now in charge of things understood. If he was to succeed in cracking Western markets, he had to deliver goods to Western standards. In turn, that meant that when an intelligent English glassmaker offered advice on production methods, it was probably wise to follow that advice to the letter. After all, those Western production methods have been honed to deliver goods to the proper standard.

And lo and behold, when we toured the site, the main hall of the factory was tiled in large white tiles. The calibration room was tiled too, and a large neon tube hung right above the workbench. Because calibration is affected by variable temperatures and because the temperature in Agra before the onset of the monsoon can easily reach 44°C, the calibration room had been moved away from the main factory hall and air conditioning had been installed. I don't know why the metal-working bay hadn't received similar treatment, but perhaps the lathe operator simply didn't need the extra light for his relatively simple machining operation.

The company's achievement here had relatively little to do with spending money and just about nothing to do with technology as normally understood. It did, however, have everything to do with ditching one set of cultural norms and starting to embrace another. Because those cultural differences reside in a huge accumulation of details, it's not a process that can happen overnight. Still less is it something that you can just buy off the shelf from some European or North American vendor.

Quality is what dominated every conversation I heard between James and his Indian counterparts. Not once – not once in a dozen site visits – was price even discussed. James knew, everyone knew, that if Indian suppliers could make products of the right quality, then it would be a simple matter to negotiate a price that left a fatter than normal margin for the Indian company and a fatter than normal profit for James. That situation isn't unique to the glass industry. It's common to pretty much every area where East meets West.

Also universal is the broader dynamic underlying that exchange. James isn't some kind of cultural emissary working for the good of Indian development. He's there to make money. Having first-rate suppliers in the emerging markets is a major competitive advantage for James. Like any other competitive advantage, that edge doesn't come by chance; it's the product of careful effort sustained over a period of years. It's something that helps him stay ahead of his European rivals. At the same time, James knows that every time he helps an Indian supplier, he's helping to nurture a future rival – and a rival that he'll never, ever be able to beat on cost. The very process that allows James to maintain his success today simultaneously ensures the advent of a new and invincible wave of competitors in the future. As it happens, James's business has a rosy long-term future, because it specializes in short-run, high-quality glassware of the sort where price competition is relatively unimportant, but there are plenty of British, American, and European manufacturers for whom that isn't the case.

These developments are wonderful news. The Agra manufacturer pays its workers about US$10 a day, or about the amount that James's least well-paid worker collects per hour. The same resistless tide that pushes volume manufacturing to India and other emerging markets is the same tide that raises wages there, lifting workers and their families from poverty into prosperity. The process that I watched at work in India – driven on both sides by good old-fashioned self-interest – is the single thing most likely to banish the spectre of global poverty for ever.

All this perhaps sounds a little too optimistic, a little too inevitable. That's true. On the one hand, the India I saw in 2009 was vastly different from the one I'd seen almost a quarter of a century before when I spent six months travelling there as a student. There were fewer signs of extreme poverty, many more signs of comfortable prosperity. The younger generation of businessmen we met, with their international outlook and confident English, were clearly destined to reshape their businesses and make a vibrant impact on world markets.

On the other hand, cultural change is something that can't successfully take place in a handful of fast modernizing firms alone. Those firms need local suppliers. They need local transportation and logistics. They need banks and insurers and access to equity markets. They also need government to do its bit. One businessman we met in India made his money by selling American-branded diesel generators to Indian businesses. In Britain or Europe, that kind of business would find its customers among firms that needed mobile power sources, or ones whose businesses couldn't afford even a moment's interruption. In India, potential customers for diesel generators are everywhere. Power cuts happened all the time. I don't think I once heard an Indian even pass comment when the lights died. Why would they? It was part of life. Someone somewhere would just get the generator powered up and the lights would come back on.

Failing lights are a highly visible sign of government failure, but the problem extends much more widely than that. Crazy labour laws deter manufacturers from expanding. Lunatic import duties make it hard for exporters to buy raw materials from overseas. Abysmal infrastructure spending makes transport hazardous and slow. Corrupt tax inspectors force businesses into costly, pointless business arrangements.* These problems arise in part because of democracy. In a poor country, it's tough for elected politicians to argue in favour of loosening labour laws. It's difficult to pay tax officials well enough that bribe-seeking isn't temptingly attractive. But democracy isn't the root cause. Culture is. And because culture has its roots in individuals, in their attitudes and beliefs, change tends to come hard and slow.

One Western businessman I spoke to told me that he had been engaged in a major project to build a power plant in a part of India that was desperately short of power. The Indian government had passed an act specifically intended to enable a fast-track approvals process for such projects and in a crucial clause of the act, the law created powers for regional bureaucrats to give certain essential approvals. When the businessman concerned went to the designated regional bureaucrat to seek the necessary approval, the bureaucrat pointed out that technically speaking he was in charge of a district, not a region, so the law did not apply. Since all bureaucrats at this level were technically in charge of districts, not regions, the argument voided the law of any force at all. The bureaucrat's resistance ran directly counter to the clear purpose of the national legislature, to the government's drive to improve infrastructure – and to the state government's own desperate need for power, and for the jobs that could be created. Yet from the bureaucrat's point of view, actually *doing* something meant risk, and if a specious legal argument could avoid that risk, then he'd argue speciously until the goddess Kali came to lead him to the great paper shuffle in the sky.

---

* On the plus side, though, all these challenges produce typically colourful Indian responses. One town tried to tame its chaotic roads with signs that read, 'Don't be Rash and End in Crash.' One firm we visited was so fed up with corrupt officials that its plant sported a massive sign outside the front entrance saying, 'Corruption Free Zone. Bribe Takers Be Warned.' If only things were so simple.

Short of writing laws so tight that no ingenious bureaucrat could find a way to avoid their intent, the Indian government couldn't have done more here to engender the desired outcome, yet change may need to wait until the older generation of bureaucrats, with their entrenched views and attitudes, makes way for a younger, more outward-looking crew. This change is happening – I saw it – but it's evolutionary, not revolutionary. If that sounds like a negative summary of the Indian experience, then it certainly shouldn't. The economy has been galloping forwards at rates of 8 or 9 per cent every year. That's a little less than the coercive growth of China, but it's stunning all the same. By comparison, for example, Britain achieved a growth rate of around 2 per cent in the white heat of its own industrial revolution. The United States achieved about 4 per cent in its. Post-war Germany achieved a growth rate of just under 6 per cent.

Three last thoughts to finish on.

First, the economics and business press likes to focus on tangible things: import tariffs, educational attainments, the price of iron ore, wage rates. These things matter tremendously, of course. You can't do serious business at any level without getting very involved in such things. Yet culture matters. It matters at least as much as all those things put together. That Agra entrepreneur couldn't force a revolution in the price of his inputs, in the wages paid to his workforce, in the intermittent Uttar Pradesh power supply, or in any of those other things that the business pages talk about incessantly. But he could change the culture. He could change the company's mindset from something that was emphatically Indian to one that was outward-looking and modern, and that cultural shift is the most important single element in India's contemporary success.

Secondly, we shouldn't make the mistake of thinking that culture only matters in the emerging markets. Virtually every entrepreneur I spoke to, directly or indirectly, spoke about the importance of culture. Alan Bond, the rocket scientist, told me that engineering excellence is 50 per cent about culture, and only 50 per cent about expensive technologies and fancy hardware. A good corporate culture is hard to create and delicate to sustain. These things are highly obvious in India, where the disparities between our Western expectations and theirs are so glaring, but they're true always, everywhere. The difference between the banks that failed and the banks that thrived has vastly more to do with culture than any difference in, say, bonus arrangements or risk management technology. If politicians and economists focus only on regulating bonuses or adjusting the arcana of risk management, then they'll have missed the elephant in the room, the only thing that really matters.

Finally, you sometimes hear people worrying about the homogenizing effect of economic growth. The idea is that if McDonald's and Starbucks can open up in Delhi and Bangalore, then diversity and vitality has been lost for ever. That's tripe, and there's no better place than India to see its tripeishness. On my last day in India, I was speeding by first class train back to Delhi. The seats were generous, the carriage was air-conditioned, and the train was perfectly on time. A uniformed waiter brought a delicious hot breakfast on an aeroplane-style tray. A second attendant offered me a choice of newspaper. Remembering the days when, as a student travelling in India, I'd have been grateful to find an empty luggage rack to sleep on, I was musing on how far and fast the country has moved. As I mused, I glanced out of the window. The train was coming into Delhi. Perhaps eight or ten tracks lay side by side, and were in busy use. Then, from the streets lying at the edge of the track, a man strolled out into the middle of the railway lines. He was barefoot and wore nothing more than a dhoti, or loincloth. He carried a mug in one hand and a toothbrush in the other. And there, as my train swept past in its regal, air-conditioned luxury, he proceeded slowly and contemplatively to do his teeth, brushing and spitting and rinsing as though there were no better place on God's earth to do his teeth than the mainline railway track connecting Delhi to the north.

Much will change. Some of it already is changing; still more change needs to happen and happen as fast as it can. But India will always be India, and a truly modern India will be a delight to behold.

PART FOUR

Into Our Heads

FIFTEEN

Morons

The consumer is not a moron, she is your wife.

– DAVID OGILVY

In 1933, alarmed by the upsurge of untested consumer products and the huge increase in advertising, a couple of engineers, Arthur Kallet and Frederick Schlink, published a book entitled, *100,000,000 Guinea Pigs: Dangers in Everyday Foods, Drugs and Cosmetics*. Given US census data of the time, the good scientists could be accused of understating the number of involuntary guinea pigs by some 25,000,000, but they were onto an important point nonetheless. The pair moved their nascent consumer testing organization out to rural New Jersey, there to bring the Sword of Truth into battle against the Blade of Deceit.

Alas, the first major battle which the organization faced was with its own employees. Most of those employed had come from New York City and they liked neither the rural setting nor the long hours or the miserable pay. A labour conflict ensued. Schlink accused his workforce of being closet communists – a convenient term of abuse for anyone wanting a raise – and used armed policemen to help break a strike. Schlink won that battle, but lost the war. His employees deserted him and set up an outfit called the Consumers' Union, not quite the first consumer protection pressure group in the world, but certainly the most influential. Similar organizations would in time spring up in every other country where capitalism brought the thrill of choice to the masses. The British equivalent, the Consumers' Association (which now trades, in a snappy twenty-first-century way, simply as Which?) has just celebrated its fiftieth anniversary. Other Western European countries have comparable organizations of similar vintage.

The 100,000,000 guinea pigs of the Kallet-Schlink era have become 300,000,000 today and it seems fair to ask whether consumers now are any better protected than they were. Over seventy years on, has the Sword of Truth proved triumphant or has the Blade of Deceit emerged victorious?

Perhaps the first point to be made is that health and safety legislation, for all that it's fashionable to moan about it today, has made a radical difference to product safety. It's quite hard now to find a foodstuff that will kill you, a toy that will murder your child, an outfit that will go up like a torch if touched by a cigarette end, or a cosmetic product that will poison you. The media still like to report scare stories as often and as shrilly as ever they did, but the stories aren't what they used to be. A recent consumer scare in the United States reported that some commercially available lipsticks contain lead. That's true. Independent tests suggest that while about 40 per cent of lipsticks may be lead-free, the remaining 60 per cent contain lead in the ratio of between 0.03 and 0.65 parts to a million, with most clustering at the lower end of that range.

Now I accept the verdict of toxicologists that any lead at all is a bad thing, that there is no such thing as a safe level of exposure to the stuff. There may be other more important health issues than the lead content, in any case. If you're on the point of sending me a letter to tell me a hundred terrible things I never knew about lipstick, then please don't bother – I accept every single one of your points in advance. All the same, the risk of a modern lipstick is, I would humbly aver, as nothing compared to the *tiro* make-up of the old-style Japanese geisha. That make-up, a thick white paste applied to face and neck, was traditionally made out of white lead. The lead didn't constitute one part in 33 million; the lead *was* the make-up and would have killed or sickened a very large proportion of the women who wore it. The plain truth of the matter is that the world of the Western consumer has become substantially safer, its guinea pigs infinitely better protected than once they were.

But safety isn't everything. Part of the reason that advertising has a bad name is that anyone can advertise anything, as long as a few basic rules are followed. A product doesn't have to be better or newer or cleverer or more inventive. It doesn't have to wash whiter, shine brighter, feel softer, or taste better. In a world where anyone can advertise, good ads have often sold bad products and bad ads have seldom sold good ones. As consumers ourselves, we tend to suspect that we're being conned.

Fortunately, one of the legacies of Kallet and Schlink is that we now have the data to find out. The Consumers' Union in the United States and its sister organizations in Europe have run countless product tests in countless consumer areas. The tests are conducted with impeccable regard for scientific objectivity. Trials typically include lab testing, controlled-use tests, and expert appraisals. All the consumers' organizations involved are entirely free from both political parties and commercial interests. A recent mammoth study looked at 616 different tests conducted in five different countries on a total of over 15,000 different consumer products.

The results make sobering reading. Although price and quality are correlated – that is, higher priced goods do tend to be better – the relationship is extraordinarily weak. To put it in statistical terms, price differentials are able to explain less than 2 per cent of all variation in quality. That's a correlation so low, you can pretty much forget about it.* This finding should be disconcerting to anyone at all who buys branded products. Faced with studies like this, perhaps David Ogilvy, one of the giants of post-war advertising, would need to revise the dictum that stands at the head of this chapter, 'The consumer is not a moron, she is your wife.' The second half of that aphorism may still be true; the first part is looking decidedly dodgy.

Perhaps, however, there's more going on than meets the eye. For one thing, most of the decisions we make in a grocery store are made very rapidly. Modern 'buyologists' estimate the average purchasing decision as taking just 2.5 seconds to make. That's a time period so small that we can't make any sensible purchasing choice. We can't read the back of the packet, compare ingredients, evaluate claims – or, indeed, do anything much, beyond reaching for the product and hurling it into our shopping trolley.

When we are making a major buying decision – white goods, perhaps, or a car – our buying decisions take longer. We'll talk with our partners, discuss our wants, talk with friends, check online reviews, and so on. We'll also store brand information for the future. If I happen to come across a statistic that ranks Toyota high for build quality, or Volvo high for safety (and all-round Swedishness), then those stats will likely be lodged somewhere for future recall, the next time I come to buy a car. Sure enough, when it comes to durable consumer goods, the price to quality relationship is signficantly higher than with grocery-type purchases. It's still not good, but it's no longer awful. Perhaps we're not morons; perhaps we're just averagely dumb people in a rush.

---

* This leads to a couple of conclusions, by the way. If you're so rich that money means nothing to you, then you should always buy the most expensive version of everything, because you will end up with a very slightly better portofolio of goods in your kitchen and your bathroom. If you are anyone else, then you should buy the very cheapest products available, because the difference in quality will be too small to be worth worrying about.

That might sound like a perfectly sensible conclusion to draw, except for a faint alarm bell which may just have rung when you read the first paragraph of this chapter. Kallet and Schlink were *engineers*. Both the Consumers' Union and its fellow pressure groups elsewhere, have adopted a basically engineering type approach to quality problems: lab tests, checklists, expert appraisals, and all the rest of it. Now engineers may be good at building cars. They may possibly also be good at evaluating just how white a particular laundry product can get your whites. They are not, however, famous for their all-round touchy-feely human empathy and understanding. Just possibly, when we buy a laundry product, we don't really care which one washes whiter. Just possibly, when men buy a razor that boasts 'five blade shaving surface technology' with 'fifteen microfins', they aren't expecting a shave any different from a razor with three blades and ten microfins – or even two blades and no microfins at all. It's also possible that when women buy a mascara, they know perfectly well that the 'new collagen enriched formula' with the new 'oversized megabrush' will probably not achieve up to 'seven times more volume!' than can be achieved with any mascara bought from any discount outlet.

The simple truth is that human consumer technology has reached a comfortable middle age. All the easy challenges – cleaning clothes, shaving chins, canning beans – have long since been met. All the impossible challenges – such as halting the ageing process, eliminating, illness or reversing time – still lie a little way in the future. We know this. We know it better than the good folk from all those consumer pressure groups, who seem weirdly obsessed with trying to determine precisely which brand of washing powder is best with dried-on gravy stains. They're *all* good. And if the T-shirt is stained beyond repair, then chuck it. It only cost a few pounds.

This explanation solves half the riddle, but no more. If we simply don't mind too much about whatever quality differences do exist, then it would surely be logical just to buy the cheapest version of everything. Since we clearly don't do that, there's more to understand yet.

The next clue is to be found in one of the weirdest market research experiments ever undertaken. The experiment involved a few dozen smokers, a number of smoking-related images, and a large fMRI scanner. The scanner is a device that allows scientists to identify activity in the brain as it is happening. The images produced are so precise that the location of brain activity can be sited to the nearest millimetre or so. Since neuroscientists have a good idea of what bit of the brain is used for what, it's possible to research not what we *think* we think of products, but to go straight to how the brain actually reacts.

In one experiment, smokers were shown three different groups of images:

1. The logos of major cigarette brands and/or pictures of packets of cigarettes themselves;
2. Cigarette adverts, like the 'Marlboro man' poster ads, for example; and
3. Images that had nothing to do with cigarettes at all, but which recalled the look and mood of well-known ad campaigns. Thus the Marlboro man campaign was echoed by such things as pictures of cowboys, landscapes of the American West, bright red sunsets, parched deserts, and the like.

Given that the experimental subjects were asked to refrain from smoking for two hours before they were tested, it's not surprising that all these images aroused feelings of craving in the volunteers – feelings that could be precisely monitored and measured by the fMRI scanner. But which set of images do you think produced the strongest response? The answer is that it was the last group of images, *ones that had no explicit relation-*

ship to cigarettes at all, which had subjects most strongly craving their smokes.

If that's not quite weird enough for you, then try this. When you ask smokers whether they are deterred from smoking by the warnings now printed on cigarette packets, they generally say yes. That's hardly surprising. Warnings just don't get more explicit than the anti-smoking messages.

Yet asking people what they think is a mug's game. We often don't know what we think. An fMRI scanner gets a whole lot closer. And when a whole group of smokers were exposed to images of cigarette warning messages while their brains were being scanned, the results were stark. Warning messages actually *increase* smokers' tobacco cravings. Smokers associate those messages with the feel of a crisp new cigarette packet, the foil wrapping, the smell of tobacco, the glide of a cigarette as it slips out of the box. The content of the message has been registered long ago. It's hardly even read, let alone weighed up and pondered. All that matters is that you only find such messages on those lovely, lovely cigarette packets, so the warnings themselves become part of the whole addictive experience.

These experiments clearly call into question the entire thrust of governmental anti-tobacco campaigns. (Although it's not quite clear what to do instead. Taking health warnings *off* cigarette packets hardly seems like a step forward.) More to the point, though, they make it clear that consumer products amount to much more than simply a way to solve a particular problem or satisfy a particular want. Humans just don't work the way that engineers might want us to. Our decision-making processes are associative, non-rational, metaphorical, emotional. Consequently, no product can be understood simply as a particular technical solution to a particular household problem. On the contrary, a whole bundle of associations, feelings, connections, and reactions come skipping along for the ride.

This fact may be distressing to the descendants of Messrs Kallet and Schlink in the product testing labs, but it's a fact nonetheless. What's more, it's a fact that can be proven in the most literal way possible – in the product testing lab. If you give a drink of distilled water to a group of volunteers, and tell one-third of them that it's distilled water, one-third that it's tap water, and the last third that it's a new French mineral water being trialled for the international market, you will get three utterly different responses. The first group will say that the water tastes of little or nothing, or perhaps that it seems very pure. The middle group will quite likely react negatively to the flavour of chlorine. The last group will tend to praise the delicate, sophisticated flavour. These people aren't making things up. As humans, we taste an *image* every bit as much as we taste a *flavour*.

When subjects are given somes wines to taste, they will enjoy a particular bottle of wine much more if they're told that it's an expensive bottle than if they're told it's a cheap one. You can give the exact same wine to the exact same volunteer a few minutes apart and, if you give that person different information about the cost of the wine, then he or she will have a different reaction to it. It's not just that they say they have a different reaction, perhaps out of a desire to look clever or to tell the experimenter what they want to hear. Those trusty fMRI scanners pick up different brain activity. The brain itself enjoys an 'expensive' wine more than the same wine when it's 'cheap'. Although the language of science insists that we talk about lab subjects and *their* experiences, it would be more accurate to personalize these results. You and I work the same way as those volunteers. *I* taste an image and a price, as much as any flavour. So do you.

Needless to say, marketers know this too. They know that our experience of a product is a holistic one, in which every tiny element plays its part. I don't know whether you drink instant coffee, but if you do then you probably enjoy the moment of opening a new jar of the stuff. There's that enticing silver foil beneath the lid. When you pop that foil with a spoon, it rips apart in a deliciously satisfying way. It's an experience that combines a hint of sexual excitement (ripping open that shirt) with something like the satisfying technical *thunk* you get from closing the door on an expensive German car. Now there's nothing coincidental about that pleasure. Sealing a jar is easy. It can be done without bodice ripping or car door thunking. Yet the good folk from Nescafé know that you will enjoy your coffee more if the foil rips apart in an enjoyable way, so they've put plenty of R&D cash into engineering a satisfying foil.

If you doubt me, then consider this. What do you associate with the moment immediately after that foil has ripped open? You surely think of the lovely coffee aroma wafting out of the jar. An aroma that makes you want to go straight to the kettle to enjoy that flavour fresh. Of course that's what you think – everyone does – but here's the thing. Freeze-dried coffee doesn't smell, or at least nowhere near enough to generate that aroma. The aroma has been put into the jar quite separately; it has nothing to do with the desiccated little granules that fill the jar.

On the other hand, the aroma has everything to do with your choice of coffee brand. Imagine how joyless that coffee would be if it came without the smell and the fancy packaging. Those things are there to enrich and maintain the whole nest of associations you have around Nescafé. Those things are the reason why, in all your years of coffee drinking, it has never once occurred to you that freeze-dried coffee doesn't smell.

It's also why lab testing will never properly understand our purchasing decisions. When, in our 2.5 second pause in front of the soap counter, we choose to reach for a bar of Dove soap, our decision-making process would, if fully unpacked, probably run something like this. 'Well, that is an awful lot of soap to choose from and, really, I'm a busy person with very many better things to do than think about soap. After all they all clean you, don't they? But I like Dove. I associate Dove soap with moisturizer and soft skin. And I love that campaign for real beauty thing they do. And it's got a nice smell, sort of soapy, but milky as well. I'm going to buy Dove.'

To look at this sequence of thoughts in a Kallet-Schlink way rather misses the point. The cleaning power of the soap comes into it, but only to be rather rapidly (and appropriately) dismissed. Every single bar of soap sold by every single grocery store in the Western world will wash you. The sane consumer doesn't spend much time worrying about the functional aspect of soap. The rest of our rapid-fire decision-making process assesses all the other things that a product testing lab can never get close to: our feelings and associations that can make the same bottle of wine taste good or bad, depending on what we believe about it; that can turn a beaker of distilled water into the essence of purity, a mouthful of chlorine, or the epitome of French sophistication.

In fact, if we wanted to obtain an accurate measure of the ratio between price and quality, there's really only one way to do it. Quality would need to be measured holistically, with due weight given to how our brains light up when choosing various different products. If Dove happens to fire up our pleasure circuits more than another brand of soap, then for us Dove simply *does* give more pleasure. It's plain silly for a product-tester to try to deny it. That holistic price–quality experiment has never been conducted, at least not as far as I know. But here's my prediction. That price and quality, when measured in a holistic, associative, brain-firing-up sort of way, will prove to be very strongly correlated indeed. To paraphrase David Ogilvy, the consumer is not a moron, she is your brain.

Ever since the dawn of advertising in the late nineteenth and early twentieth centuries, there's been a debate fought out between the puritans and the realists. The puritans have disliked the sheer detachment of advertising claim from product reality, a detachment that has existed ever since Gerry Lambert discovered that he could sell Listerine by inventing a disease for it to cure. The puritans don't just come armed with a sense of distaste. They have a solid intellectual case to make besides. Economists see any economic system as a means of allocating scarce resources (labour, capital, land, raw materials) to meet material wants. The capitalist economies of the Western world have, it would seem, generally done that job in a pretty efficient and innovative way. Yet where does advertising fit in? Its job is to create wants where none previously existed, and to inflame desires and arouse fears that had been happily dormant beforehand. It's as though capitalism is superbly adept at creating a world of plenty – and equally adept at generating dissatisfaction with the plenty it's worked so hard to create. The whole exercise can seem like an illusionist's banquet, dazzling but empty.

J. K. Galbraith, the economist who argued most impassionedly against advertising, wanted a tax on all consumption to counterbalance the gravitational pull of intense marketing. In the United States, no such tax was ever imposed and sure enough US savings ratios have ploughed ever lower since Galbraith first started writing about the issue. It's not difficult to argue that the collapse in those savings ratios was one of the prime causes of the 2008/9 credit crunch, nor is it hard to argue that the 'Buy now, buy more, buy bigger' message of countless billions of marketing spend was a critical factor behind the change in American and British habits of saving and spending.

The realists don't really seek to counter that logic. The realist view of advertising is marked by a kind of weary acceptance. Yes, it's cynical. Yes, it promotes consumerism. Yes, most of these products are all much the same. But what is the alternative? Life goes on. That is probably the view of most consumers and most advertising executives. Free market economists, however, go further (as they always do). There's no point in doing the hard graft of entrepreneurship – designing the product, manufacturing it, arranging finance and distribution – and then not seeing any sales. Advertising is petrol hurled onto the dull embers of innovation; advertising is what allows competition to catch light and burn hard. In the words of Ludwig von Mises, a leading Austrian economist:

> Business propaganda must be obtrusive and blatant. It is its aim to attract the attention of slow people, to rouse latent wishes, to entice men to substitute innovation for inert clinging to traditional routine. In order to succeed, advertising must be adjusted to the mentality of the people courted ... Like all things designed to suit the taste of the masses, advertising is repellent to people of delicate feeling.

Not a man to mince his words, von Mises.

One possible response to these controversies is a kind of shoulder shrug. The intellectual battles between realists and puritans don't ultimately matter too much, because the realists will always win out in the end. In societies built around individual choice and freedom of expression, it's hard (and dangerous) for a state to restrict much of either. When it comes to more specific regulation, the sheer difficulty in drawing a useful distinction between 'good' ads (those that inform and advise) and 'bad' ads (those which inflame and arouse) means that the easiest action will usually be no action.

Personally, I subscribe to a less weary, more optimistic view. This chapter has argued that the purely technical characteristics of a product play a relatively small part in whether we choose to buy it and in whether it pleases us when we do. The technical aspect of things is greater when it comes to bigger-ticket, more inherently technical items like cars and washing machines. It's vanishingly small when it comes to toilet cleaners and fizzy drinks. Advertising (and all the ancillary marketing gimmicks that go along with it) shouldn't be understood simply as a way to *sell* a product. It's also there to *create* a product. Would Dove soap *be* Dove soap if the product had never been advertised? Kallet and Schlink would say yes, arguing that the product is the product is the product. Its performance characteristics can't possibly be affected by an advertising slogan or some appealing packaging.

Yet consumers don't think anything of the sort. We don't even think distilled water is distilled water, unless we're directed to think that way. What matters about any product is whether it makes us happier or not, and happiness has far more to do with advertising and packaging and pricing than with the material properties of the underlying product. There's no point in lamenting that fact, wishing to change it, or raging against it – or rather, if you do, then you are lamenting, wishing to change, or raging against our humanity itself.

My optimistic view of things does not, however, mean that there are no ethical issues involved in advertising. On the contrary, one of the major themes of this book is that there are no simple answers to anything. Simple is always wrong. It's too simple to say that Advertising is Bad and should be restricted (à la Galbraith). It's too simple to say (à la von Mises) that Advertising is Freedom and freedom should never be restricted. The facts are just more complicated. If advertising is part of what creates a product, and part of what creates satisfaction and pleasure in a product, then you'd be daft to get rid of it. Part of what advertising does is to create joy and we should relish that.

On the other hand, it is difficult to think that, for example, there is no ethical issue with tobacco advertising, or with advertising junk food to young children, or with erecting billboards in places of beauty and tranquillity. And those are among the simpler ethical concerns one could think of. I can't quite think where the nearest advertising hoarding is to where I live in the countryside, but it's certainly a good long way from my front door. The nearest advertising site of any importance is the front window of the village shop, a mile or so from my house, where a series of mostly handwritten index cards tell me who's selling which bit of furniture, or what number to call if I want my hedges trimmed or my boiler serviced.

When I go into London, however, I'm taken aback by the sheer density of advertising material launched in my direction. Buses, billboards, taxis, Underground posters, notices illegally clipped to lamp posts, neon signs, moving digital displays, shop windows, people handing out fliers, people encased in sandwich boards and holding signs. I find the deluge almost overwhelming. My eyes and brain are constantly being sought out and told stuff that I really, really don't need to know. Most people do live in cities. Most people (especially in the United States) are exposed to far more TV and radio advertising than I am. What does this deluge do to the brain? Do we successfully filter it all out, so that we only take in the messages that we actually care about? Or are we transformed over time into the unwitting drones of the admen?

I don't know. No one does. I'm sure, however, that the answer lies in between these two extremes. I think there is an issue with the noise generated by advertising excess, but I don't think that we've been turned into the hypnotized drones of some sci-fi movie. Simple is always wrong. Complicated answers have the serious disadvantage of being complicated, but just possibly true. That's a hard pitch to sell, but the only sane path to follow.

SIXTEEN

Happiness

> Salud, amor, dinero y el tiempo para gozarlos [Health, love, money and the time to enjoy them]
>
> – Traditional Spanish toast

For three decades, economics has been guarding a dangerous and uncomfortable secret, a dragon curled up round the very well of capitalism.

The dragon in question was born in 1974 and its midwife was an economist named Richard Easterlin. For a long time, it had been assumed that money made you happier. Entire theories of economics were built on it. The entire subject seemed threatened with a kind of pointlessness if the assumption wasn't broadly true. And Easterlin found a paradox. *Within* countries, it was clearly true that richer people tended to be happier, poorer people tended to be rather less happy. That was a statistical generalization, of course. There are unhappy millionaires and ecstatic paupers. There are also plenty of other crucial influences on people's happiness: their marital status, their job satisfaction, their optimism, their friendships, their health. All the same, the within-country data suggested more or less what you'd expect it to say, namely that even if money can't buy you love, it'll buy you a spring in your step and a smile on your face. So far, the data said just what everyone expected.

When Easterlin came to look at differences *between* countries, however, he found that once a country generated enough income to meet the basic needs of its population, then income didn't seem to make any noticeable difference to people's happiness. That would imply that once a country had reached an income level roughly equal to today's Poland, Argentina, or Saudi Arabia, then there was no particular point in seeking any further economic growth. A nation might make itself richer, but it wouldn't make itself any happier.

Although this observation became known as the Easterlin Paradox, there was nothing paradoxical about it. According to Easterlin, income had both absolute and relative value. Once a country had reached a certain level of prosperity (roughly $15,000 per capita, or about where Poland is today), the *absolute* value of income dropped to approximately nothing, while *relative* value went right on mattering. People went on caring about having more money than the couple next door whether national GDP per capita was $15,000 per head, or $30,000, or $60,000. The within-country differences meant that better-off types could still experience the immortal satisfaction of driving a more expensive car than their brother- or sister-in law, the deep joy of securing a larger bonus than their workmates. By definition, however, none of this could conceivably make any difference at a national level. One person's gain was another person's loss.

It wasn't just Easterlin who found evidence in support of this broad hypothesis. The importance of relative incomes was confirmed in survey after survey. A bunch of Harvard students was asked which they would prefer out of the following two options:

- Earning $50,000 a year while other people got an average of $25,000.
- Earning $100,000 a year while other people got an average of $250,000.

Unsurprisingly, a majority of students preferred the first option. They'd prefer to take a 50 per cent cut in their absolute incomes than to find themselves behind in the relative pecking order. You don't have to be a go-getting Harvard student to feel the same thing. Nearly all of us would feel the tug of that relative one-upmanship, even if we ended up choosing the second option not the first.

Easterlin's arguments found support in a number of unexpected locations. One of the anchor concepts of mainstream economics – probably *the* anchor concept – is that of *homo economicus*, the perfectly rational economic agent. As a consumer, she'll secure the best deal for her, computing the happiness a particular item will bring against the cost of acquiring it. As an employee, she'll seek the best possible work at the best possible wage, given her (carefully calibrated) educational investment. As a businesswoman, she'll weigh her expenditures, pricing strategies, and hires based on some perfectly calculated goal of profit maximization. Of course, no economist ever thought that all humans operated like this all the time, but they never needed to in order for the theories to work. All that mattered was that most people and most firms acted like this enough of the time, and that any errors in one direction tended to be cancelled out by errors in another.

The theory was beautifully designed. Its finest achievement, the Arrow-Debreu-McKenzie General Equilibrium model, is perhaps the most architecturally perfect model ever produced by social science, a thing of beauty. Unfortunately, when people came to study how humans actually behaved, the tidy *homo economicus* was nowhere to be seen, and the messy pawprints of real life humans had trampled mud all over those beautifully architectured theories.

The mud started with a couple of psychologists, Amos Tversky and Daniel Kahneman, who looked at what judgements humans actually make. Time and again, they found our judgements to be seriously biased in directions that were predictable and repeatable. Before long, an entire menagerie of terms existed to describe the various ways in which we were rubbish. We were diagnosed with hindsight bias, confirmation bias, self-serving bias, projection bias, and (worst of the lot) fundamental attribution error. Humans seemed so lousy at making decisions that it almost seemed as though we should slink back to our caves and give up any pretence of being a race of poets, engineers, and nuclear scientists.

The challenges of this new research affected countless areas of human thought, but economics was as badly affected as any. Take one simple example. If shoppers are given six different samples of jam to taste, they are quite likely to end up buying a jar or two when they're done. If you give shoppers up to twenty-four different jams to taste, they'll likely end up buying no jam at all. The extra choice has killed their appetites. Equally, if you give students a choice of six essay topics that they can write about for extra course credits, they're more likely to do so than if you give them a choice of thirty. Once again, less seems to be more. Nor do you even need to get up to large numbers of choices to detect the onset of consumer paralysis. Amos Tversky, working on this occasion with Eldar Shafir, presented experimental subjects with a Sony-built appliance in a shop-window being sold for an appetizingly bargain-basement price. Needless to say, subjects were enthusiastic. Then when just one further appliance, also good quality, also being sold at a good discount, was displayed in addition, enthusiasm, and the number of sales, actually fell.

The logic of such experiments seemed to suggest that excessive choice could make us less happy. Brains shaped in the low-choice environment of the African savannah might simply be poorly adapted to benefitting from the ever-increasing choices thrown up by industrial capitalism. Arguments such as these were potentially explosive. If Easterlin was right and if

Tversky's experiments were sound, then what was the point in all our striving after gain? What was the point of economics? What was the point of capitalism? These questions were sharpened by yet another research finding. Since the early 1970s, American income per head has roughly doubled in inflation adjusted terms, yet Americans have become no happier. If even the flagship of capitalism was churning its propellers in vain, then the chasing fleet should start to question the value of the chase.

It was almost as though the Industrial Revolution had done its job in shunting large chunks of mankind from a state of poverty to a state of comfortable material well-being. It still had work to do in moving the rest of humanity to the same position, but in Europe and North America and Japan, capitalism might just as well pack up shop. The people of the rich West would still need to work hard enough to make sure they didn't slip below about $15,000 per head – which they could, for the most part achieve just by working from January till June – but they could perfectly well spend the rest of the year practising their t'ai chi, or painting watercolours. Needless to say, no country ever gave serious consideration to those fine alternatives but, according to Easterlin and to the data, every rich world government should have done just that. Indeed, serious economists, including most notably Richard Layard, have given serious thought to what government policy should be if the Easterlin Paradox captured a basic truth.

But does it? Easterlin was writing in the 1970s, using data drawn from the 1940s through to the 1960s. The 1965 data covered just fourteen countries, of which all but four were close to the average level of happiness. From such a limited data pool, it was simply difficult to draw sensible conclusions. It was clear that the French were a gloomy lot in the 1940s and hadn't become much more cheerful by the 1960s, but more solidly useful results were hard to find.

That's changed. Every country wealthy enough to hire a student with a clipboard is busy surveying its population. Where Easterlin had just fourteen mostly rich nations to poke at, contemporary statisticians have more like 130, spanning the entire spectrum from the extremely rich to the extremely poor. That data (compiled by Betsey Stevenson and Justin Wolfers) is presented in this wonderful graph. The dots mark where different countries stand in terms of happiness and income. The richest country (the rightmost dot on the graph) is the United Arab Emirates. The happiest country (the highest dot) is Denmark. The luckless Togolese are, on this data, the least happy people on earth, the Afghans the poorest.

The graph doesn't merely plot the differences between countries, it also ingeniously presents the data within each country. The little line that slices through each dot is aligned according to the extent to which money and happiness are correlated in each society. In happy little Denmark, that line is almost flat, implying that rich Danes are generally a bit happier than poor Danes, but not all that much. In mournful Bulgaria, however, that line is much steeper, implying that rich Bulgars are significantly more content than their poorer brethren.

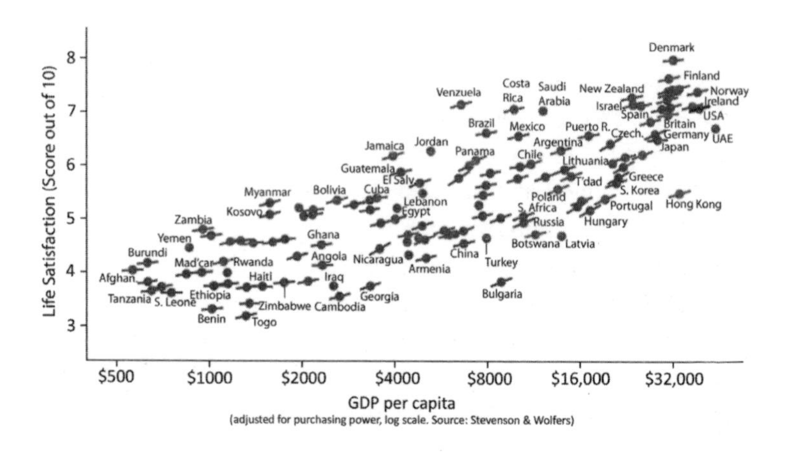

The sheer scale of the data required to put this graph together is gob-smacking. Just think for a moment of the number of students and the number of streets and the number of clipboards and the number of times that people were stopped and asked, in a countless variety of languages, 'Excuse me, could I possibly have a moment of your time ...?' Given that at least 139,000 people around the world did, in fact, stop to answer that question, I'd guess that at least a further 1,390,000 adopted the bland smile and walked on.

More importantly, the graph kills the Easterlin Paradox. There is no paradox. Higher incomes generate happiness. The strength of that relationship is pretty much the same whether you look at it within countries or between countries. Relative income does matter, but absolute income matters too. If you earn more money then, all other things equal, you'll feel a little bit happier than you did before. If you want to get technical about it, then about two-thirds of a nation's happiness can be explained by its income level. Other things matter too, but nothing matters more.

If that's the headline news, there is inevitably a host of footnotes that scurries after. Of these the most important is the nature of the relationship between incomes and happiness. You'll notice that the income scale of the graph is logarithmic – that is, each uniform step along the horizontal axis represents a doubling in income, not any set dollar amount. Afghanistan will achieve as large an increase in happiness for its citizens by improving their incomes from $600 to $1,200 as the United States will by increasing the income of its citizens from $45,000 to $90,000. That finding makes intuitive good sense. The average American household won't be blown away by finding an additional $600 in their kitty each year. The average Afghani household would doubtless feel differently. The capitalist flagship isn't churning its propellers in vain, but this is a sea that stretches further, the greater the distance you've already travelled.

As for the United States itself, the well-publicized finding that its citizens are no happier now than they were thirty years ago conceals one spiky little fact about American incomes. Although the average American income has roughly doubled over the last thirty years, the largest chunk of that gain has accrued to the wealthiest slice of the population. Ordinary Americans haven't noticed much change for three decades – and for reasons that aren't yet understood, American women have become *less* happy in that time, despite the huge advances and achievements of the feminist revolution. The net result is that overall happiness in America has been treading water, even as the economy has steamed ahead.

The US experience is a useful reminder that although money matters, it's never all that matters. Happy Denmark is streets ahead of glum Hong Kong, and wealthy Hong Kong is no more cheerful than poverty-stricken Myanmar. For rich nations, the task of making people happier by making them richer may be a slower and less reliable route to success than working on other things, such as social cohesion, good government, good health, and solid families.*

Over time, though, it's striking what a difference capitalism makes. The strength of the relationship between income and happiness is strong enough that we can use it to stare back into the past. Although polling data on happiness levels is a fairly recent phenomenon, we do have reasonable estimates of income in previous centuries and we can use one to guess the other. In 1900, the average income in Britain was just shy of

---

* For more ambitious governments, there are still other routes to consider. Countries in Latin America and Scandinavia are nearly all happier than their incomes would imply, while ex-communist countries are all less happy. Latvia might therefore benefit from loading itself onto a barge and hauling itself across the Baltic to moor up against happy Finland. Miserable Russia could use its oil and gas wealth to buy a slice of sunny Caribbean real estate. The good folk of Costa Rica are probably too blissful to haggle.

$6,000 per head, and in the US just over $5,000. (All sums here are in 2007 dollars.) That would put those countries somewhere in between modern-day Guatemala and Armenia in terms of happiness – perhaps around 5 out of 10 on the happiness scale. At the start of the nineteenth century, British and American incomes were around $2,200 and $1,550 respectively, or roughly the Zimbabwe-Kosovo levels of happiness. A millennium ago, the average Briton was probably less happy about life than the average Afghan today, which is to say very unhappy indeed.

It's this reflection which provides the strongest possible rebuttal to the idea that capitalism is simply an engine of waste and excess choice and consumer manipulation. It isn't. It's the most powerful engine ever invented for improving the lot of humankind. All those anxieties about excess choice – the twenty-four flavours of jam, the ever-increasing varieties of telephone handset – have an important point to make, but a limited one. Personally, I don't like shopping. I use a mobile handset until it stops working, then I'll buy a cheap replacement, for preference old and second-hand. If it works, I don't care about how many functions it has. Indeed, to be a little more precise, I prefer ones with virtually no functions at all. Give me anything complicated and before you know it, I'll have videoed the inside of my pocket, called the speaking clock in Harare, and set off a mysterious bleeping noise which I can only get rid of by pulling out the battery and swearing at it. I'm a bit better when it comes to jam, but even then I generally grab the first jar that comes to hand. I don't need to be faced with very many choices before I start to find them excessive.

My wife is different. She can't have too much choice. When she buys a phone, she'll make a list of what functions she wants, read countless user-reviews on Amazon, and browse a host of online stores before buying something. Then she sits there with the manual learning how to use every different function – a task which for me would be about as fun as rote-learning a telephone directory. Then, having mastered the gadget, she actually uses it. She doesn't just make phone calls with it, she takes photos, downloads music, sets diary reminders, sends picture texts. And she enjoys all this. She really does. She enjoys it all so much that come the end of the year, she'll sell one gadget on eBay and buy another, just so she can get stuck into a whole new set of technical manuals.

According to the philosophy propounded by anti-globalization protesters and their kin, my wife is a victim who has been duped into wanting stuff she doesn't really want. She suffers from a kind of post-Marxist false consciousness, cleverly avoided by those wise enough to hurl paving slabs through the front windows of McDonald's outlets. According to traditional defenders of the free market, on the other hand, those anti-globalization folk have it all wrong. My wife is an effective maximizer of her own happiness. She *chooses* to devote part of her income to fancy new gadgets. There's no rational basis on which anyone can criticize her way of achieving that goal.

Both sides are missing the point. The gadgets are neither here nor there. My wife is a neurofeedback practitioner – an art that would take another book or two to explain, but which can be thought of as a kind of physiotherapy for damaged brains. She's good at what she does and her skills are in great demand, enabling her to charge a high hourly rate for her services. Often enough, though, the people who need her services the most are the ones who can afford them the least. With most such cases, my wife prefers to reduce her charges or to scrap them completely. The cost of that policy, measured against the amount she could earn by only taking on better-off clients, runs into thousands of pounds a year. Her gadget bill is nowhere close to that. Her real luxury item isn't her shiny bits of electronics or her ever more mountainous shoe collection, but her ability to work with the people who really need her, irrespective of their ability to pay.

That's what income does. It pushes out the boundaries of the possible, making ever wider ranges of choice possible. Some of those choices will be essentially frivolous. Others will be profoundly serious. In poorer societies – the Georgia-Nicaragua-Lebanon sort, for example; or Britain and America in the Victorian era – need and want drive people to maximize their income, not at all costs but as a commanding priority nevertheless. When my wife got ill ten years ago, I was able to leave my lucrative financial job in order to look after her and write novels. From my peak as a banker to my trough as a novelist, my income nose-dived by 93 per cent. (It's perked up again since, though it hasn't regained its former level and most likely never will.) In an affluent society, it was perfectly possible for me to make that choice. In Georgia or Nicaragua or Lebanon or Victorian Britain, it would have been the choice of a madman. I'd have served my wife best by working arduous hours to put bread on the table and finer feelings be damned.

The British utilitarian philosophers of the nineteenth century evolved a formula for happiness which said, approximately, that *Happiness equals the absence of pain plus the presence of pleasure.* That's not a bad formula, but it's too democratic. Pleasures are not all created equal (as J. S. Mill, the most elegant of those philosophers, came to understand). Humans don't just need the joys of shiny gadgets, they need a sense of purpose. That's not some pious platitude, it's a truth which has been road-tested in the life and death conditions of concentration camps, both Soviet and Nazi. Viktor Frankl was a Jewish psychiatrist imprisoned in the camps at Theresienstadt, Auschwitz, and Türkheim. He noticed, in himself and others, that those who stopped believing that their life had any purpose were already on the road to death. He rediscovered his own sense of purpose by helping others to recover theirs. His approach – which he termed logotherapy – wasn't developed to help neurotic New Yorkers or overpampered Londoners. It was there to enable starving prisoners to get through another winter and, as far as was conceivable in those dreadful conditions, it worked.

Frankl's observations and our own common sense suggest that we should adapt that utilitarian formula to read: *happiness equals the absence of pain plus the presence of pleasure plus a sense of meaning*. At lower income levels – let's say, at income levels of $3,000 or less – the absence of pain is likely to dominate. If your family is hungry, you'll care most about feeding them. You'll care about medicine and clean water and machines that can take care of some of the most burdensome tasks around the home or farm.

As income rises – let's say, up to $15,000 or so – the presence of pleasure starts to take centre stage. *Bread Givers*, a novel by Anzia Yezierska, tells the story of a Jewish immigrant family in the New York of the 1910s and 1920s. Per capita in America at that point was about $8,000, though the family Yezierska described is substantially poorer than that. Then, as the mother and her two daughters all get paying jobs, they start to experience a new way of life. Towels replace old rags for drying things. The family starts to acquire dishes and tableware

> so we could all sit down at the table at the same time and eat like people ... We no sooner got used to regular towels than we began to want toothbrushes ... We got the toothbrushes and we began wanting tooth powder to brush our teeth with, instead of ashes. And more and more we wanted more things, and really needed more things, the more we got them.

Notice Yezierska's phrase 'eat like people'. Tableware isn't a necessity. You don't starve without it. But the niceties of a better way of living start to alter a person's experience of existence, converting it from brute struggle to something dignifying and human. When Yezierska's heroine finds out what it's like to eat properly, her previous existence starts to feel different, even to her.

Likewise the sentence, 'And more and more we wanted more things, and really needed more things, the more we got them.' When life was a struggle, it wasn't about toothbrushes or tooth powder. Yet as greater affluence releases those wants, making it possible for the inner being to acknowledge cravings that have long been buried, their force is transformative. At lower income levels, it was unlikely that the family Yezierska describes even thought about tooth powder. Now they don't just want it, they need it and, for the newly humanized family, that need is real.

If *Bread Givers* describes the transition from one income level to another, then Sinclair Lewis's *Babbitt* neatly describes the next step up, the step that moves from pleasure to meaning. Lewis's story is set in the same period as Yezierska's but *Babbitt*'s eponymous hero is a prosperous man, an estate agent, who makes 'nothing in particular, neither butter nor shoes nor poetry', but is 'nimble in the calling of selling houses for more than people could afford to pay'. We don't know exactly what his income is, but what's certain is that no one in the Babbitt household ever brushed their teeth with ashes or got all excited over a toothbrush. Babbitt's consumer wants have long been amply satisfied.

The final scene in the book is the crucial one for our purposes. Babbitt has experienced some kind of mid-life rebellious crisis which finally ebbs, leaving him back where he started. But with a difference. His son – younger, cooler, hard to understand – has spent five of his last six dollars on secretly marrying his girlfriend. He announces that he wants to leave college and work as a mechanic, because he thinks he'd make a pretty good inventor. He reckons he'll get twenty bucks a week, a thousand bucks a year, to start with. In the timid, status- and money-fixated world that Babbitt moves in, his son's plans are somewhere between heresy and lunacy. Yet here's how the older man reacts:

> 'Well—' Babbitt crossed the floor, slowly, ponderously, seeming a little old. 'I've always wanted you to have a college degree ... But I've never – Now, for heaven's sake, don't repeat this to your mother, or she'd remove what little hair I've got left, but practically, I've never done a single thing I've wanted to in my whole life! I don't know's I've accomplished anything except just get along. I figure out I've made about a quarter of an inch out of a possible hundred rods. Well, maybe you'll carry things on further. I don't know. But I do get a kind of sneaking pleasure out of the fact that you knew what you wanted to do and did it. Well, those folks in there will try to bully you, and tame you down. Tell 'em to go to the devil! I'll back you. Take your factory job, if you want to. Don't be scared of the family. No, nor all [the town] of Zenith. Nor of yourself, the way I've been. Go ahead, old man! The world is yours!'

That concluding phrase encapsulates the final, greatest reward of affluence. In a world where money is abundant, we can make choices that aren't driven by money. After we've eliminated pain and found pleasure, we can start to chase after meaning without fear. That doesn't mean that everyone will. It doesn't mean that those who do will make a good job of it. It doesn't mean that we won't simultaneously enjoy fooling around with fast cars or shiny gadgets. And, of course, there's no one level of income sufficient to allow people to follow their dreams. Different strokes for different folks, in this as in everything else.

Babbitt's closing benediction also means that capitalism can breathe a sigh of relief. There *is* a point in it, after all. The Easterlin Paradox was born of inadequate data. Tversky and Kahneman have useful things to say, but nothing that calls into question the overarching usefulness of all our 'getting and spending'. It's probably just as well, since none of us looked like stopping.

SEVENTEEN

Bubbles

> In truth, it was a team effort. We all fucked up. Government. Ratings agencies. Wall Street. Commercial banks. Regulators. Investors. Everybody.
>
> – ALAN SCHWARTZ, the last CEO of Bear Stearns

One warm summer's day in the late 1980s, while I was doing my investment banking apprenticeship at J.P. Morgan, my boss called me over. He told me to drop whatever I was doing and turn my attention instead to an urgent company valuation assignment.

Now valuing companies is hardly an unusual task for an analyst in investment banking. It's what they do, often for eighty hours a week and more. But this was something of an unusual case. For one thing, the results of the valuation were needed in a jaw-droppingly fast forty-eight hours and for that forty-eight hours' work, the bank was to be paid the equally jaw-dropping sum of $1,000,000. The transaction involved was also rather peculiar. The company, the Italian subsidiary of a large American multinational, was being sold *to itself.*

Companies don't normally buy themselves (the actual legal structure was rather more complex than I'm making it sound), but in this case there was a very good reason for the sudden outbreak of financial surrealism, namely the good old-fashioned desire to avoid taxation. At the time Italian tax law was a strange and wonderful pleasure garden, where only those who positively enjoyed paying tax ever felt called upon to do so. Our client – let's call it TitanCorp Italia – had for years been a dutiful corporate citizen, paying its taxes and not complaining about the fact that no one else felt obliged to do the same.

Eventually, however, TitanCorp felt that enough was enough. With J.P. Morgan's help, it put together a deal which, under the rules then in force, would take it from being one of Italy's largest taxpayers to one that paid hardly any tax at all. In Britain or America, that kind of behaviour from a major foreign corporation would attract rather negative headlines, to put it mildly, but Italy had its own sweet attitudes to these things. In any case, for the deal to hold together, the client needed a bullet-proof valuation from a top investment bank and hence my minor role in this saga.

From my point of view, this was all good news. As a junior analyst, it never hurt to get assigned to lucrative deals. This one was certainly lucrative and it wasn't going to involve weeks of travel. Furthermore, I'd be working with someone called Maria, a hopelessly glamorous banker from our Rome office. OK, my late night dinner date with Maria was going to be over a wasteland of cold pizza and company spreadsheets, but I wasn't proud. I'd take whatever was going.

So we set to work. Company valuation is both easy and complicated, but the easy bit is this. Just like holiday homes, or second-hand cars, or paintings by Van Gogh, or pretty much anything else, a company is only worth what someone is prepared to pay for it. Since investors mostly care about profits, then company valuations are most easily viewed as being some multiple of profit. As most major companies in this particular industry were quoted on the world's stock markets, then all we needed to do was dig out company stock prices, compare them with the relevant company's profits, and we would have a valuation multiple which we could then apply to our client, TitanCorp Italia.

Mostly, this was pretty easy work. Pick a whole bunch of American companies. Find their stock prices. Locate their financial stats. Crunch some numbers. Do the same with some British companies. Do the same again with some European companies. Easy. The profit multiples that emerged all made a rough kind of sense. Where a particular profit multiple was much lower than expected, we could normally explain it: maybe the company was running into some problems which meant that its future profits were going to be in decline. Where a company's profit multiple was unusually high, maybe there were huge things expected from that company in the future. But those profit multiples generally lay inside a reasonably tight band, between fifteen and twenty-five times after-tax profits. Maria and I knew what we were doing. The financial data proved easy enough to locate. Forty-eight hours? A million dollars? Easy.

Then we hit Japan. We did the same as before – find some stock prices, dig out the appropriate financial stats, churn out our ratios – but this time our spreadsheets went haywire. Instead of averaging around twenty times company profits, Japanese companies seemed to be valued at multiples of more like *sixty*. This made no sense at all. Profits are profits are profits are profits. Why would a sane investor value one unit of Japanese profit at three or four times the rate of a unit of American or Italian profit? As a matter of fact, it was even crazier than that. The companies we were looking at were mostly very multinational. So though a particular firm might happen to be headquartered in Japan, its business was spread all over the globe, just the way TitanCorp's parent business was. In effect, there didn't seem to be anything uniquely Japanese about these Japanese companies – except for their exceptional profit multiples. If TitanCorp wanted to triple the value of its business overnight, it looked like all it had to do was shift its headquarters to Osaka and change its name to Titanishi.

The anomaly looked lethal. Our company valuation might well end up at the centre of any dispute with the Italian tax authorities (assuming that they cared enough to be disputatious, of course), so it had to be sounder than sound, yet no matter what we tried we couldn't find a way to explain the Japanese exception. We looked at exchange rates and interest rates. We explored differences in company accounting procedures. We called colleagues in our Tokyo office and sought their advice. And we couldn't solve it. When the forty-eight hours were up, we produced our valuation, but we just ditched the Japanese numbers. Our final valuation, in effect, pretended that there were no Japanese companies in TitanCorp's industry – which, in this particular industry, was a little like pretending that there are no Sicilians engaged in organized crime.

In any case, the valuation was accepted. The deal went ahead. Maria went back to Rome and to doing whatever it is that impossibly glamorous Italian bankers spend their time doing. TitanCorp Italia bought itself and, under weird Italian tax law, its tax liabilities vanished almost out of sight. Everyone was happy, except (just possibly) for the Italian tax authorities – and except for me. That Japanese exception continued to nag away at me. It was almost as though the Tokyo stock market was operating in defiance of financial gravity. The damn thing shouldn't just fall, it should collapse.

And it did.

Not long after Maria and I sat up half the night trying to puzzle out those Japanese stock prices, the Nikkei stock market index hit its all time high of almost 39,000. It wasn't just stock prices, it was real estate too. A common claim at the time was that the land under the Imperial Palace in Tokyo was worth more than the entire state of California. Even then, the claim was probably rubbish (and how would you measure it anyway?), but what was significant is that people could make it with a straight face. For the best chunks of Tokyo real estate, you could expect to fork out over $100,000 per square *foot*. The office I'm writing in now is in a little cubbyhole off the living room. It's about seven foot by seven foot. I can't quite sit in my chair and touch both side walls with my hands, but I'm not far off – and yet in the right part of Tokyo, in that winter of 1989, the land under this office would have sold for better than $5,000,000.

But gravity always gets you in the end. The Nikkei started to fall. Deprived of their huge paper profits, people felt poorer. Because they felt poorer, they also felt less inclined to bid $5 million for a ridiculous little cubbyhole that can only comfortably house one medium-sized author and a few piles of books. So real estate prices started to fall too. Before long, a vicious circle of the most pernicious sort had set in. Everything was falling because everything was falling. Banks went bankrupt in all but name. They didn't dare sell their dodgy assets, because that would have meant going public about just what a mess they were in. They couldn't lend money to new ventures, because such capital as they had was spent covering up their existing bad loans. The government tried various stimulus packages, but always too little, too late. So the Japanese economy limped on, a ghost economy, neither properly dead nor properly alive. At the time of writing, almost twenty years after Maria and I spent two long nights trying to understand Japan, the Nikkei index stands at just one fifth of its 1989 peak.

The bubble metaphor for sequences of this kind is a good one. The expansion, the fragility, the pricking, the implosion – the metaphor gets all those elements spot on. But soap bubbles are rather intangible things. They don't knock things over, destroy ornaments, plough through walls, or raze factories to the ground. Bubbles of the financial kind, however, do all these things and more. When the Japanese boom turned to bust, it showed its true nature. The translucent soap bubble now swung like a wrecking ball through the balance sheets of banks. It ripped the heart out of manufacturing firms whose success had relied on inflated credit and inflated demand. It tore chunks out of inefficient service companies, whose deficiencies had been covered up through the years of boom. For ten long years – the 'lost decade' – Japan's economy hardly grew. In 1991, the Japanese economy produced goods and services worth 465 trillion yen. A dozen years later, the economy had limped to just 490 trillion, an annual growth rate of just 0.4 per cent.

If those figures sound too coldly statistical for you, then try this. It's January 1992. You earn £30,000 a year and life is good. Then your boss calls you into his office and asks you if you fancy signing up to a new kind of pay deal, where your growth in earnings is linked to the economy. You can choose to link your pay to the clunky old British economy or the world-beating Japanese one. It's an easy call. You've just finished reading Michael Crichton's *Rising Sun*, which dramatized the economic threat from the emerging superpower. So you take the deal and link your pay to Japan. Your workmates play it safe and link their pay to Britain. You rip the mickey out of them. You talk about Sony and Toyota and Dai-Ichi and Mitsubishi; you hand out *Rising Suns* to everyone you know and you try your very hardest to enjoy *narezushi* with *wasabi* sauce. For a while you feel good – then a little uncertain – then downright miserable. A dozen years later, it's Christmas 2003, and you're earning £31,600. Your workmates are earning a thumping £56,900 and the British economy is still growing faster and the Japanese one is still in the recovery ward.

This illustration overdoes things just a little. The British growth rates include some modest inflation, while the Japanese ones struggle with negative inflation, or deflation. But like puppy fat on a toddler, a little inflation is healthy for an economy. The crucial point is absolutely accurate: the Japanese bubble caused more than a decade's worth of real, tangible, factory-wrecking distress that still isn't entirely over today. And whenever factories get wrecked, then lives do too. In 1990, Japan boasted the most egalitarian society of any rich nation. Its national debt was low. Job security was excellent. Street crime was unheard of. Homelessness did not exist. That's all gone now. Japan suffers from homelessness and street crime, inequality and job insecurity. At getting on for twice national income, Japan's national debt now makes Italy look like a bastion of prudent finance. The wrecking ball has moved on, but the human debris remains. (Though, by the way, that debris does *not* generally include the splattered bodies of finance types leaping from tall buildings. In fact, suicide rates tend to fall in times of crisis because suicidal types are perversely comforted by the fact that everyone else is having a horrible time as well. To each cloud its silver lining.)

In the wake of the credit crunch and our own recent experience of bubbly boom and bubbly bust, it doesn't take a genius to notice that the Japanese experience was hardly exceptional, but almost no one has a genuine sense of how very common such bubbles are. In the boom times of nineteenth-century Britain, for example, there was a crisis in 1810, then again in 1816, and then at roughly ten-year intervals in 1825, 1836, 1847, 1857, and 1866. After the 1866 crash, British bankers obviously learned some kind of lesson because the 1873 crashes came in Germany and America, while the 1882 one pitched up in France. Needless to say, just as British bankers were trimming their cigars and congratulating themselves on having grown out of all that adolescent foolishness, the next major crash arrived bang on time in London in 1890, almost causing the destruction of Barings bank.*

---

* Nick Leeson would later come to celebrate the centenary of Barings' rescue by making unauthorized speculative trades on the Singapore exchange. By 1995, those trades had racked up losses of more than £800 million, thereby killing the bank for good. Next time, maybe just a greetings card?

But it's not just Britain and not just the nineteenth century where bubbles have merrily come and gone. Charles Kindleberger's wonderful book *Manias, Panics and Crashes* documents the fever of speculation in every epoch and every place. His top ten catastrophes range from seventeenth-century Holland to almost every developed country in the modern era.

When?	Where?	What?
1636	Holland	Tulip bulbs
1720	Britain	South Sea company stock
1720	France	Mississippi company stock
1927–9	USA	Stock market
1970s	USA (mostly)	Bank loans to South and Central America
1985–9	Japan	Real estate and stock markets
1985–9	Scandinavia	Real estate and stock markets
1990–3	Mexico	Foreign investment/peso assets
1992–7	Thailand, Malaysia, etc.	Real estate and stock markets
1995–2000	USA (mostly)	Dot.com and other over the counter stocks

My personal favourite of these episodes has to be the Dutch tulip mania. Although modern scholars have cast some doubt on how extensive the bubble actually was, you can't help but love any financial crisis in which a single tulip bulb was said to have been exchanged for a collection of goods comprising two lasts of wheat, four lasts of rye, four fat oxen, eight fat swine, twelve fat sheep, two hogsheads of wine, four tuns of beer, two tons of butter, one thousand pounds of cheese, a bed, a suit of clothes, and a silver drinking cup. Yet strange as all this sounds, it's both strange and modern. Most of the speculation took place on an early form of futures market. In an attempt to quell excesses, the authorities stamped down on short selling. The media of the time loved all these shenanigans and exaggerated them wildly. Derivatives, short-selling bans, and media excess – does that sound familiar?

Maybe that's the point. Kindleberger doesn't mention bubbles in Bolivia or crashes in Cambodia, but the chances are that they're there all right, you only have to look. Indeed, we don't even seem to have learned from experience, as the evidence suggests that bubbles have become more common, not less, over the last thirty years or so. The most recent edition of *Manias* came out before the recent credit crunch, but the 2008/9 financial crisis would cruise into anyone's top ten and most people's number one spot. A US senator, Everett Dirksen, was supposed to have said about the federal budget, 'A billion here, a billion there, pretty soon it adds up to real money.' Multiply that comment by a thousand, and you have a fair summary of the shenanigans of 2008/9, estimated to have brought about several trillion dollars' worth of loss. Bubbles, like death and taxes, are always with us.

All this raises a question. In fact, if you've lost your job or your home because a bunch of Wall Street bankers made a mint from repackaging Ninja* mortgages and flogging them to hideously overpaid hedge fund managers, then you've probably got more than one question you'd like to have answered. One perfectly sound position is to blame human nature. Folly and greed, greed and folly. Or, in the words of the early financial commentator, Ecclesiastes, 'Vanity of vanities, saith the Preacher, vanity of vanities; all is vanity. What profit hath a man of all his labour which he taketh under the sun? One generation passeth away, and another generation cometh: but the earth abideth for ever.' On the Ecclesiastes view, there's nothing to be done about bubbles, other than till the soil and worship the Lord.

---

* That's loans to people with No INcome, Jobs or Assets. And how could *that* possibly go wrong?

On the other hand, Ecclesiastes doesn't offer much by way of analytical insight, and an equally common view of things is to assume that someone, somewhere has been playing the crook. Often enough that assumption is right. When the People's Republic of Albania discarded its own quirky version of communism and began the long march to capitalism, there was a cadre of people (often enough ex-military) who thought it'd be nice to shorten the march. The trick was a nice and easy one. If you opened a bank account with one of those charming former secret policemen, they'd offer you a nice fat interest rate on your money, possibly as much as 30 per cent a month, or the equivalent of more than 2,000 per cent a year. No sooner had such a bank opened shop than it was technically insolvent, its assets instantly overtaken by its galloping liabilities. But insolvency isn't always quick to show its face. The first people to put their money into the bank were soon boasting of their excellent financial good sense. More money poured in. The new money allowed the banks to make the first few interest payments due on the accounts opened by the very first depositors. And the more the news spread, the more it spread. Money continued to pour in. Interest continued to be paid. The bankers were lauded for their entrepreneurial zeal. Medals were struck.

Then, inevitably, the inrushing tide of money proved incapable of matching the outrushing swell of interest payments due. The first interest payments started to be missed. Doubt set in. New money dried up and existing depositors began to withdraw cash, thereby prompting a sudden charge for the exit, a phenomenon termed *Torschlusspanik*, literally 'door-shut-panic', by those ever pithy Germans.

Before long, the whole economy, a veritable pyramid of pyramid schemes, fell hopelessly, calamitously bankrupt. At its peak, the dodgy banks had deposits equal to about half of the Albanian GDP. About two-thirds of Albanian adults were involved in the schemes. Indeed, some Albanians had gone the whole hog: selling their homes, to raise the cash, to deposit in banks, to gain the interest, to pay their rent, and make a thumping profit to boot. When the banks imploded, there was a sudden, catastrophic rebalancing of wealth and debt. Most of the banks involved were knowingly corrupt. Many were involved in smuggling goods into Yugoslavia, contrary to UN sanctions. They may have been money-laundering too. By any definition, most of those involved were out and out crooks.

The aftermath produced all the usual devastation and more. The government fell. Many in the army and police force deserted. More than a million weapons were stolen from state armouries. Tax offices were burned. There was widespread rioting, which left more than 2,000 people dead. Large swathes of the country were left ungovernable. There was extensive emigration. Few of those one million weapons have ever been recovered and they're presumably still being passed around the (never terribly stable) Balkans today.

All this is both saddening and faintly comic. To any half-clued up Westerner, the warning signs were shrieking so loud that one feels only a Tiranese housewife or an Illyrian peasant with no experience of capitalist commerce could possibly be dumb enough to be taken in: 'Thirty per cent a month? That's not enough! I demand that you double my money in two months flat or you won't be getting a cent off me.' Astonishingly enough, people did say more or less that, and banks did, in, fact respond by offering to double depositors' capital in two months flat – a degree of customer responsiveness that my own bank has yet to emulate.

But we shouldn't laugh too loud. The US energy firm, Enron, was essentially just a pyramid scheme, only much more horribly complex. So, in a way, was WorldCom, another major scandal of that era. So, more recently, was Bernie Madoff's extraordinary fraud, and he managed to hoodwink investors who were – or at least claimed to be – exceptionally sophisticated. You could even argue that Lehman Brothers and Bear Stearns and AIG were all pyramid schemes too.

Indeed, all such pyramid schemes are simply versions of so-called 'Ponzi finance', named after one fine Italian-American entrepreneur, Charles Ponzi. Ponzi was a waiter, a gambler, a bank clerk, a vegetable trader, a people-smuggler, a forger, and a jailbird. Your granny would have called him a ne'er-do-well and your granny would have had him nailed. Most of his life was spent dodging from hare-brained scheme to hare-brained scheme, but his moment of glory arrived in 1920 when he came up with an intricate scheme whose modus operandi was exactly the same as those which would be operating in Albania some seventy years later. Ponzi offered his depositors huge returns, raked in money, and was feted as a hero. Told by his adoring fans that he was the greatest Italian of them all, he replied modestly, 'No, no, Columbus and Marconi, they come first.' Strikingly, Ponzi himself probably never really understood the essential bankruptcy of his entire venture. Like many fraudsters of his type, he seemed able to convince himself that the whole thing was going to turn out well in the end. (He had an idea that he'd buy a US warship for $300 million and turn it into a floating shopping mall, an idea about as sensible then as it would be today.)

Inevitably, the whole house of cards came tumbling down. Ponzi was in and out of jail for a while, before being deported back to Italy, as he'd never taken US citizenship. His wife, Rose, stayed in Boston and divorced him – but, touchingly, the pair continued to exchange love letters till the end of their days. Ponzi died, dirt-poor and forgotten, in a Brazilian charity hospital in 1949.

While Albanian peasants and 1920s Bostonians fell sucker to schemes that we'd know to avoid, we go right ahead and fall sucker to more complex ones. Thievery and speculation so gross that it's only a cigarette paper's thickness away from thievery is a recurring feature of most bubbles, and the central feature of many.

Plenty of bubbles, however, have nothing to do with fraud. The recent credit crunch may have had its elements of fraud or ill dealing, but these elements were peripheral to the main issues; they certainly didn't lie at the heart of things. Humans, however, are only human, and if we can't blame criminals, then the urge to blame someone else is almost unconquerably strong. If criminals aren't to blame, then surely we can find someone else to blame: speculators, money-men, profiteers.

This accusation gets a little closer to the mark – which is to say, it gets closer to fingering us. The monster rise in house prices which proceeded the the current financial crisis was brought about by ordinary folk buying houses. Some of us bought houses because we needed a place to live. Others were nudged into buying (or buying bigger, flashier, more expensive) because of an expectation of profit. Still others bought properties in order to let them out, in the expectation that the rents would cover the mortgage.

It's just not clear how irresponsible much of this activity was. Years ago, my wife and I bought a house as an investment property. We worked hard to make our new investment shipshape. We borrowed some money to do it all, but we put in plenty of our own. We created a lovely house and let it to a series of tenants who have mostly been very happy to live there. What we did back in the 1990s, plenty of people did in the Noughties. Is all this an example of speculation or investment? Is there, indeed, any difference between the two things, except that investment is praiseworthy (entrepreneurial, hard-working, risk-taking, economy-boosting) and speculation is evil (profiteering, exploitative, parasitic, economy-draining)? 'Speculator' is, as often as not, just an insulting term for that most loathsome of humans: the person who's invested more wisely than we.

If you want to get closer to the root cause of any bubble, then it's always more productive to go to the environmental factors which helped it grow. Loose money is always an issue. During the 'phrenzy of speculation' that arose in 1857, a London accountant reported that some financial companies possessing just £10,000 of capital were responsible for loans and other liabilities totalling £900,000. If you think that's something that couldn't possibly happen now, you need to go back to Ecclesiastes. When LTCM, a major hedge fund with a couple of Nobel laureates on its board, went bust at the end of the 1990s boom, it had borrowings of $125 billion teetering on top of capital of just $5 billion. Nothing new under the sun, indeed.

Faced with facts like these, any reasonable person's instinct is simple: force financial institutions to carry a proper amount of capital and lock up anyone who misbehaves. Quite right too. Unfortunately, finance is a complicated business and it's not at all obvious when capital is insufficient. For example, I have a bank's balance sheet in front of me. It has €1,817 billion of liabilities on top of capital of just €56 billion. That's more indebted than LTCM when it went bust. It's an elephant balanced on a pin-head. Yet the balance sheet in question belongs to a French bank, BNP Paribas, which is the largest bank in continental Europe, and one of the best and most creditworthy to boot. As I write, in the midst of market meltdown, it boasts a long-term credit rating of AA+, just a single notch down from the AAA ratings of the world's leading central banks. Loose money and inadequate capital matter all right, but they're easiest to spot with hindsight.

It's the same thing with lending and investment. Speculation that looks crazy five years and $3 trillion worth of losses later looks disturbingly plausible at the time. During the dot.com boom, as the Dow Jones index headed up through the 10,000 barrier, a number of books were published to cash in on the boom. One had the provocative title *Dow 36,000: The New*

Strategy for Profiting from the Coming Rise in the Stock Market, and it argued that the Dow could perfectly well rise to the giddy heights of 36,000. Sound crazy? The authors had some pretty fancy arguments to do with the elimination of the equity risk premium and the impact of technological changes on the US economy. Maybe they had a point. If the share of profits in the US economy grew just a little … and if long-term interest rates dropped a notch … and if they were right about those risk premiums … then who knows what might not be achieved? In any case, the good Mr Glassman and Mr Hassett, who co-wrote this book, were swiftly outclassed in their optimism by the admirable Mr Elias, who brought the world *Dow 40,000: Strategies for Profiting from the Greatest Bull Market in History*. It's rather lovely to note that both books emphasized the word 'strategy' in their titles. You'd rather think that if the entire stock market was going to quadruple, then all the strategy you needed would be (1) shove all your money into the stock market, (2) wait, then (3) ker-ching! When the Dow hits the magic level, take your money out and run chortling off to the bank.

Strategists or no, Messrs Glassman, Hassett, and Elias looked like panicky doom-mongers as compared with the peerless Mr Kadlec, who brought the world *Dow 100,000: Fact or Fiction*. In his short but beautifully concise work, Kadlec explained how the world was entering an era of unprecedented stability, prosperity, and non-inflationary growth. He explained how investors could profit from the coming tenfold increase in share prices. And readers loved it. In 1999, the year of publication, Kadlec's work notched up eleven reader reviews on Amazon, all but two of which gave it the maximum five star rating. The book retailed at $25.00.

Sadly, the world has failed to live up to Mr Kadlec's high view of it. At the time of writing, almost ten years later, the Dow Jones was at 8,300, about 20 per cent down on where it was when his book came out. A recent reader review on Amazon gives it a single star, commenting, 'The correct title for Kadlec's supplyside nonsense [should be] "Dow 100,000: Fiction".' The book currently sells for as little as $0.01.

Hindsight turns such predictions into the stuff of comedy, but foresight is a tougher game. The folk who lent cash to all those Ninja home-owners in the United States were mostly neither idiots nor crooks. Subprime borrowers were charged subprime rates in an effort to compensate for the risks involved. Everyone knew there'd be losses, but figured that the losses would be low enough to be covered by the interest rate premiums. The prediction turned out to be hopelessly wrong, but not for want of people thinking about it. Credit committees scrutinized lending standards. Ratings agencies crawled all over the financials. Investors pored over paperwork. Risk managers went on brain-storming 'offsites', trying to find any chinks in their own institution's armoury.

And they screwed up. They were guilty of group-think, of failing to understand how everything connected with everything else, of failing to see how falling prices would squeeze liquidity which would cause prices to fall further thereby triggering outcomes that could never have happened in an ordinary-looking world. Those professionals were paid loads of money to get it right, and they got it royally, magnificently, thumpingly wrong. But suppose you were to ask me, hand on heart, to declare whether I've ever made an equivalent error of judgement in my own professional life, then I've got to tell you the answer is 'yes'. My own misjudgements haven't yet brought the entire capitalist world to its knees, but then no one's ever given me the opportunity to try.

So what's to be learned from all of this? The first lesson, the main one, the Golden Law of all things bubbly, is that bubbles happen. Whenever you have a financial system sophisticated enough to supply credit at reasonable rates to ordinary borrowers, you'll get periods of euphoria followed by periods of bust.

Fraud will sometimes play a part, but the leading part is almost always taken by simple human credulity, yours and mine. It's hard for us to think differently from the herd. Even those people on the risk management committees of banks whose job it was to play the court jester, to shout out what no one wanted to hear, even those people found themselves unable to conceive of the one Armageddon scenario that actually played out.

It's a phenomenon I was aware of as a banker, given the chance to peer in at other people's businesses and industries from the outside. Time after time, we bankers would tend to come up with financial forecasts that struck company insiders as ludicrously pessimistic. We'd point to the company's profit history, which would most likely be studded with its moments of calamity and disaster, only to be told, 'Ah! But that was *then*. That couldn't happen *now* because ...' And they'd be right. Those particular disasters mightn't recur, but something else would. We knew it would, we just couldn't say what or when. As a matter of fact, if you want a Silver Law of all things bubbly, then it's this: whenever enough people are telling you that this time things will be different, you should start to get worried. When supposedly conservative bankers join the chorus, then you should sell everything you possess and live under a stone for the next couple of years.

Closely allied to human credulity is human panic and recrimination – *Torschlusspanik*, indeed. The issue here is partly one of the herd instinct again, given extra force because fear is a stronger (and faster) motivator than greed. Unfortunately, however, that panic invariably creates real problems of its own which grossly compound the original problem. The 2008/9 crisis is the most perfect possible illustration of the issue. In mid-2008, a major ratings agency, Fitch, estimated that the total losses in the subprime mortgage market would be $400 billion or, to be on the safe side, perhaps as much as $550 billion.

Now, those aren't small amounts of money, but in the context of the global financial system they weren't that enormous either. The way Fitch did the sums was this. About half of those $400 billion of losses was held by banks, the rest by financial institutions of different kinds. So the banks' aggregate losses looked to be somewhere between $200 billion (Fitch's best guess) and $275 billion (its most conservative one).

When Fitch published these estimates, the banks as a group had already written off $165 billion in losses, so that left a possible $35 billion of further losses or (if we take the more conservative number) as much as $110 billion. Either way, most of the damage was already out in the open. The banks were already fessing up, taking their hits, *but doing perfectly fine.* The whole point of Fitch's research was to say exactly that. To quote: 'As a significant proportion of the losses have been disclosed, further ratings action arising [from subprime] exposures is likely to be minimal.' That was mid-2008 and a few months later, the world would melt.

Fitch was wrong but it wasn't being crazy. The total subprime market was worth about $1.4 trillion, and Fitch was coolly forecasting a loss of between 30 per cent and 40 per cent of that colossal amount. That's hardly insane optimism – and yet in the middle of 2008, the world banking system was motoring on just fine. If God himself had flung open the roof of heaven to announce that those losses would be not 30 per cent or 40 per cent, but more like 50 or 60 per cent – well, bank shares would have dropped, but the system would still have been able to cope.

In theory.

In theory, but clearly not in practice.

So what happened? *Torschlusspanik* happened. Everyone thought roughly what Fitch thought. There were some bad losses, although nothing uncontrollable ... but just to be on the safe side, lenders got a little more cautious in their lending. They didn't just stop lending to the jobless, asset-less John and

Jane Doe. They slowed their lending to other banks, not so much because they had any imminent worry about those banks, but because it was wise to be prudent. And, of course, the more lending was reduced, the more important it became for any prudent financial institution to conserve its capital. That meant lending was further constrained, thereby aggravating the problem for the system as a whole. This wasn't yet panic, but it was a creeping, infectious nervousness. It was as though everyone knew that the ship had a problem – that it was almost certainly going to be fine – but that it would be prudent to stand a little closer to the lifeboats. Alas, since everyone started to shift a little closer to the lifeboats, the ship's centre of gravity began to shift and the decks began to list.

That was phase one. Phase two was when the problem took on a momentum of its own. Lehman Brothers had been heavily involved in subprime mortgages and was regretting it. But it had done everything by the book. In August 2007 – that is, almost a year *before* Fitch had begun to estimate losses in the hundreds of billions of dollars – it had taken action. It had closed down its subprime lending unit, fired staff, taken the hit. It had done what a bank in its position was meant to do. True, it was still stuck with a huge plateful of securities it no longer wanted – but again, it took the hits. Its accounts still showed the bank to be solvent. But here was the problem: everyone knew that Lehman had a problem. Lehman was the guy standing furthest from those lifeboats. If people were going to restrict their lending to anyone, then it was going to be them.

So banks and other institutions became increasingly reluctant to lend to Lehman.

So it had to pay more for its money.

So its profits dropped.

So its financial position grew worse.

And in order to raise money, it started to sell assets.

And the assets it wanted most badly to sell were the dodgy ones that had got it into trouble in the first place.

And as everyone knew that Lehman was a forced seller of those assets, the prices fell.

And so banks and other institutions became increasingly reluctant to lend to Lehman.

The vicious circle was complete. Cue phase three, the first splash of freezing water across the decks. On 15 September, Lehman filed for bankruptcy. Man overboard. The first casualty.

One casualty meant that the possibility of others simply couldn't be overlooked. Merrill Lynch was the next weakest investment bank. Just like that its funding dried up, because no sane person would lend to it when Lehman's corpse was bobbing in the water. You can't be a bank without access to funding, so Merrill leaped into the arms of Bank of America, its life saved at the cost of its independence (and, as it happened, BoA's balance sheet). But if Merrill was sold and Lehman was dead, then what about Morgan Stanley? What about Goldman? What about AIG? What about the money markets? What about Washington Mutual and Citigroup? What about RBS and HBOS and UBS? What about Fannie Mae and Freddie Mac? What about the German banks? What about the Icelandic banks, *fyrir himinn sök*?*

There was no longer any room for doubt. A disaster on a major scale was unfolding and there was no longer any question of creeping to the lifeboats: it was a question of finding your lifeboat and jumping in. The water around began to darken with corpses. Fear was rampant. Just days after Merrill's collapse, it became clear that the crisis was, by a distance, the most profound financial upheaval in world history. Indeed, since the end of the Second World War only the fall of the Berlin Wall was comparable in global significance.

---

* Financial disaster always creates good jokes. My favourite one goes, Q: What's the capital of Iceland? A: about £2.

Although, predictably, the media soon filled with stories of banker-stupidity and banker-greed, the truth was a little more shaded. At some of the darkest moments, those involved often behaved like true gents. In an emergency swap dealing session held just prior to Lehman's default, most traders honoured the trades they'd made, even though a technicality meant they didn't need to. The solvent banks often did what they could to pick up the pieces of the shattered ones. They were hoping to make a profit of course, but were acting as good corporate citizens too. For all the unseemly aspects of the catastrophe, decent behaviour was still more the rule than not.

Phase four. *Torschlusspanik* proper. You're a bank. A storm is raging and your lifeboat is small. What do you do? Answer: you first need to secure your liquidity position. That means you need to make sure that you have funding available, no matter what craziness is going on in the world beyond. So you cut your lending, instantly and aggressively. No point in lending money that you'd much rather have under your own mattress. And you sell assets. Not tables and chairs, but financial assets, the ones that your balance sheet is full of. In particular, you want to get rid of the sort of assets which other people are going to regard as dodgy. No point in making your balance sheet look bad, when the banks with bad balance sheets are the ones most likely to drown.

So all of a sudden everyone is selling the assets that everyone else believes to be dodgy. And are they dodgy? You bet they are, because everyone is selling them and no one is buying them, so the price has only one way to go. This in turn means that you have to sell more assets than you'd expected when you started to sell the stuff, and that in turn means that an ever spiralling circle of assets start to get caught in the frenzy.

And it was here, at this critical point in world history, with the fate of the global economy hanging in the balance, when you chose to get involved.

You'd been watching the news, reading the paper, gradually understanding the spreading scale of the catastrophe. You saw the world teetering on the edge of disaster and, in your wisdom, you chose to kick it. Phases one to four of the calamity may have been just television news for us, boring or fascinating depending on taste. Phase five wasn't TV news, it was serious. If you had shares, you sold them. If you didn't, you certainly didn't buy any. If you'd been about to buy a house, you dropped your offer or walked away. All those lovely things that made up your former existence – new cars, giant TVs, ridiculously cute but hopelessly expensive shoes – all the stuff of ordinary life suddenly seemed like flim-flam and for once in your over-pampered life you put away the wallet or the purse, at precisely the moment that the world most needed you to do the opposite.

I did the same.

All of a sudden companies which had nothing to do with subprime mortgages – nothing even to do with housing – started to feel the blast of recession. Manufacturers of ridiculously cute but hopelessly expensive shoes felt the pain. So did makers of cars and giant TV sets. So did all sorts of other companies, who did the prudent thing and laid people off, who did the prudent thing and cut their spending. Bankers who had made perfectly sensible loans to makers of shoes and cars and TV sets all of a sudden worried about the viability of those companies and those loans. It was *Torschlusspanik* of the most total sort, and you and I both made it happen.

This was a big disaster, no question, yet its ultimate dynamics relied on just two core ingredients, the same pair of rogues that has underlain every such crisis. The first villain is possibility. Any financial system complex enough to have a free market in borrowing can create disaster. Only systems so sluggish that they'll choke off growth and innovation at birth can be sure of avoiding it. The second villain is we humans. We tend to see things as others do, optimistically and in unison. We can try to build safeguards against our humanity – safeguards that are very necessary, of course, but almost doomed to failure nevertheless. To argue that our most recent crisis was 'about' excessively complex derivatives or was 'about' toxic home-loans is to miss the point. The Dutch tulip bubble wasn't 'about' flowers; it was about humans.

As for cleanup – well, the Japanese experience of boom and bust teaches that the cleanup process can be excruciatingly long and slow. What's more, governments have to be involved. In the up-phase of any cycle, the prophets of euphoria will be talking glowingly of the power of the markets. They'll explain to you how markets are always rational, how new innovations are altering old truths, how the very best that government can do is shrink into a corner and not interfere any more than it absolutely has to.

Just as there are no atheists in a foxhole, however, there are no free market ideologues in the wake of a bust. Only governments have pockets deep enough and motives broad enough to get the whole show back on the road. Action which is quick, broad-ranging, and decisive has the best chance of success. This time around, governments have been impressively sweeping in their policy responses. That's not to say that they've got every last thing right, but generals don't need to. They've got to get the big things broadly right and keep plugging away until the war is won. Thus far, the generals are doing OK. If you contrast that with Japan, where some important structural problems have still not been addressed some twenty years after the bust, then maybe our generals are doing even better than merely OK. The recession will still be a horrible one, but it could have been a whole lot worse.

The final thought in any chapter on bubbles has to be with the human consequences of all that fun and folly. Sometimes those consequences are to be found in jail. The good folks from Enron mostly ended in jail. Ditto those Albanian bankers. Ditto the good Mr Ponzi. Ditto Mike Milken and Ivan Boesky, the dark tsars of 1980s junk bond fame. More often though, the bubble-makers aren't criminal, they're simply ordinary people doing ordinary things who, for a few happy months or years, got seduced into believing that the world was rosier and friendlier than it really is. If history is anything to judge by, then those ordinary folk go about their lives a little poorer and a little wiser – and their new-found wisdom has a shelf life of somewhere around ten years.

For a few poor souls, however, the bubble's bursting never really fades. For the Albanians who emigrated. For the homeless of Tokyo, whose blue plastic tents crowd the parks and line the riverside walks. For those who lose their jobs, their homes, their families, or their savings as a result of economic catastrophe. If any permanent memorial is ever built to commemorate these unlucky souls, there's only one epitaph which would really suit: 'It was good while it lasted.'

PART FIVE

Theories

EIGHTEEN

Economists

Deborah Solomon: There are at least 15,000 professional economists in this country, and you're saying only two or three of them foresaw the mortgage crisis?
JKG: Ten or 12 would be closer than two or three.

– Interview with J. K. GALBRAITH in the *New York Times Magazine*

One of the weirdest publishing phenomena of recent years is the emergence of that least likely of all possible bestsellers, the economics bestseller. *Freakonomics* (tagline: 'A rogue economist explores the hidden side of everything') launched a tidal wave of books bashing away at broadly similar themes. Bookshops saw economists adopt a range of ever so slightly varying disguises: *The Armchair Economist*, *The Undercover Economist*, *The Economic Naturalist*, *The Romantic Economist*, and – because economists need to shower too – *Naked Economics*. We haven't yet seen *The Bedroom Economist*, but it's probably circulating in proof form right now.

The thrust of most of these books is that economics has answers, it sees the truth, it has tools for uncovering the reality of the everyday. The only barely concealed implication for the consumer is that if you read these tomes and absorb their lessons you'll be better equipped to go out and grab life by the throat, get that wage rise, create that business venture, turbocharge your savings, and avoid being ripped off at the supermarket and car salesroom. Indeed, if and when *The Bedroom Economist* comes out, you'll learn how to trade in your existing partner and get yourself a real top-end of the range model. An upgrade is an upgrade after all.

Nor is it just regular economics that's been proudly strutting its stuff. Game theory used to be a geeky mathematical curiosity with questionable real world implications. It is no longer. In *The Art of Strategy*, the authors promise to reveal 'A game theorist's guide to success in business and life' – and then go on to 'prove' the value of their craft in applications ranging from investment to sports and TV game shows. All of a sudden economics is claiming to be the science that can unlock the mysteries and complexities of life itself.

Behind these bold assertions, lies a story about economics which runs something like this:

THE COMPLETE INTELLECTUAL HISTORY OF ECONOMICS

— A shortened version —

Economics was born in 1776 and spent a century or so growing up. Everyone felt very proud of her but nobody thought she was a science.

Then, in the late nineteenth century, Alfred Marshall brought equations into the subject for the first time. These equations made Economics feel terribly grown up, and so she peered over at what all those other scientists were doing with their rock-hammers and their particle accelerators and the like, and she duly noticed that the research papers being produced in those subjects were *highly* mathematical. So she decided that she wanted to be a proper science too, hoping that all those other Real Sciences – Physics, Geology, Astronomy, and the rest – would take her seriously and invite her along to all the right parties. Now Economics realized that she wasn't going to be given a particle accelerator to play with and she couldn't think of any interesting use for a rock-hammer, but she reckoned that if she worked hard enough she could become very mathematical too.

So she did. The building block for all that mathematics was the Rational Optimizing Individual and the Rational Optimizing Firm. Material self-interest was all that mattered. More money was always better than less. Firms were constantly in search of profit, individuals constantly in search of advantage. A few other simplifying assumptions were made, but a beautiful and wondrous mathematics started to emerge. Economics got very excited. She got a new haircut and sorted through her wardrobe to find the very brownest, frumpiest, most scientific-looking frock she could find. Surely the invites would start to come through now?

Alas, the time was the 1930s, the world lay slumped in the midst of the Great Depression – and Economics' beautiful and wondrous mathematics predicted with great confidence that the Great Depression could not exist. Economics felt a bit embarrassed and watched on enviously as Physics discovered quantum theory and Astronomy located Pluto.

Then along came John Maynard Keynes. Keynes was very clever, very well connected and he had a General Theory. The phrase 'General Theory' sounded a lot like 'General Relativity' and what's more when the theory was put into practice (via the admittedly extreme expedient of the Second World War) it seemed to work very well indeed. Economists became important people who got to hang out with Prime ministers and presidents. That wasn't quite the same thing as being considered a Real Science, but it made the waiting a whole lot nicer.

There was, however, a problem; one that was only spoken about in muttered tones among economists themselves, but nevertheless one that bothered them rather a lot. No one understood quite what the General Theory was all about. It was certainly clever, but it wasn't very neat and it wasn't – whisper it softly – very mathematical. So some other clever chaps took Keynes's theory and tidied it up. They made it the sort of thing you could describe with equations. If one of the Real Sciences happened to drop by and ask Economics what she was working on, then she could say something offhand like, 'Oh, nothing much, just this little IS-LM model, a few simple equations really, but amusing enough in their way.'

This was a neat dodge – very scientific – but also slightly disconcerting. Keynes's unmathematical book had seethed with a revolutionary energy. The mathematical form into which that book was later squeezed didn't seethe, wasn't energetic, and the revolution seemed reducible to a couple of important but rather simple ideas. Never mind. It wasn't Keynes's feelings that mattered; it was becoming a Real Science. And eventually, in the glorious year of 1969, Economics achieved her dream: she got her very own Nobel Prize. For sure, it wasn't a prize endowed by Alfred Nobel, and its full name was the rather less impressive 'Sveriges Riksbank Prize in Economic Sciences in Memory of Alfred Nobel' – but nearly everyone called it a Nobel Prize just so they didn't have to get their tongues round the word *Sveriges*. Even if Economics still couldn't get to dance with the most grown-up sciences like Physics and Chemistry, she felt perfectly able to look down her nose at Geology and Oceanography and Materials Science. After all, *they* didn't have a Nobel Prize of any description and who had ever seen a prime minister hanging out with an oceanographer? The good times had begun to roll.

Economics went on doing her thing. The mathematics got more and more complicated. Economists, indeed, developed statistical tools that were way in advance of those developed for other fields. Some economists from the University of Chicago pointed out that the tidied-up, mathematicalized version of Keynesianism implied that people were irrational, and since any

> such irrationality meant that they were leaving money on the table and not maximizing their own advantage, such a thing couldn't possibly be. The models were changed and, it was noticed, Economics in the 1990s and the 2000s looked very much like she had in the 1920s, only a lot, lot cleverer. And the very best thing of all was this: the beautiful and wondrous mathematics of this new golden age predicted with great confidence that another Great Depression could not possibly come to pass ...

This, roughly speaking, was the state of play when the 2008 credit crisis reminded everyone that another Great Depression wasn't just possible, it was looking horribly likely – and virtually no economist had either spotted it coming or possessed rigorous intellectual tools that would help policymakers navigate the storm.

Perhaps, however, there were one or two clues even before 2008 that economists hardly possessed the capacity to see the 'hidden side of everything'. After all, it should be easy enough to test that claim by deploying the most elementary concept in economics: supply and demand. If economists have the key to 'success in business and life', then their services will be considered highly desirable. Businesses will start to bid up the price of the existing economic talent. Young professionals will regard economics as an excellent outlet for their talent and supply will expand accordingly.

That's the theory. The reality is that economists aren't particularly relevant in business. There are vastly fewer economists active in business than there are accountants, lawyers, management consultants, IT technicians, or HR managers. That in itself isn't a problem for the theory. Perhaps the supply of economists is limited by some natural obstacle. Perhaps, for example, only the top 0.01 per cent of the population has the intellectual capacity to master the game theorist's understanding of 'success in business and life'. In that case, the pressure of huge demand crashing on the rocky shores of limited supply should cause economists' pay packets to go through the roof. The top economists would become intellectual superstar celebrity millionaires – an all-in-one combination of Donald Trump, Stephen Hawking and Oprah Winfrey.

Needless to say, nothing could be further from the truth. In all the interviews I conducted for this book, the only people who mentioned economics to me were professional economists themselves. No entrepreneur I spoke to evinced the tiniest interest in the subject. Very few of them would, I believe, have read even a single economics textbook before they took the step that set them decisively on the road to millionaire-dom. Indeed, during my ten years of investment banking, during which time I worked on or witnessed deals worth many tens of billions of dollars, and in contexts where you'd think that understanding the 'hidden side of everything' would really help, I almost never encountered an economist. When I was a junior analyst, I remember being sent off to J.P. Morgan's in-house economist to ferret out a particular bit of data we needed for some financial modelling, but as far as I can recall that was it. And finance, please note, is the area where demand for economists is at its peak. Because financial markets respond to news in part according to what the commentariat says about that news, and because the commentariat is largely made up of people with some background in economics, then you need an economist to predict accurately what other economists are saying. Which isn't quite the 'hidden side of everything', to put it mildly.

Indeed, the dark secret at the heart of economics is this. Far from possessing the hidden key to life, the universe, and everything, economists actually have a tough time understanding economies. Take, for example, a rather straightforward question: 'Why does unemployment exist?' There are all sorts of much more complicated questions we could ask about unemployment, but for now we'll work with the most basic question of all. If economics doesn't offer a decisive answer to such an elementary question, we'll have to doubt its ability to tell us anything useful at all.

The common-sense answer runs as follows. If firms encounter some sort of adverse shock (let's say a spike in the oil price), their goods will get a little more expensive to produce, so consumers will buy a little less, so firms will need to trim their production, so they'll lay some people off. Bingo! You have unemployment.

That's not an explanation which is likely to satisfy an economist, however. To an economist, labour is a commodity that obeys the laws of supply and demand like anything else. They'll be happy with the common-sense explanation as far as it goes, but they'll want to trace the logic all the way to its conclusion. Once some workers have been laid off, those workers will be out looking for work. Unfortunately, the number of workers now exceeds the number of vacancies available. So workers, keen to secure those vacancies, will offer to work for less than they had done before. They'll bid the price of labour down. As wages decline, firms will encounter new profit opportunities from hiring workers, so the number of vacancies will rise, until everyone who wants a job can have one.

Now this theory doesn't quite predict that unemployment can't exist. For one thing, there's always going to be a certain amount of 'frictional' unemployment. If you're fired in Perth or Aberdeen, it may not help you much if there are firms hiring in Portsmouth and Abertillery, so it may just take you time to find a job. Or perhaps you'll need to re-equip yourself with a new set of skills. Neither economics nor common sense has a problem with this sort of real-life issue.

But that's not quite the end of the matter. Let's say a particular worker was earning £400 a week when he was fired. But he loves fishing. He values his leisure time at approximately £350 per week. In the old order of things, before that spike in oil prices, he was happy enough to work, 'gaining' £50 a week as compared with his next best option. In the new order, however, he'd have to bid his wage down to £380 to get a job. On first glance, he's still better off taking the job at £380 than spending his weeks fishing – except that a foolishly benevolent state offers £49 a week by way of unemployment benefit. He'll take the £49, add that to the £350 worth of enjoyment he gets from fishing, and he's just £1 worse off than he was before, and a full £19 better off than he would be working at the wage levels which now prevail.

There are two implications which follow from this logic. First of all, unemployment benefits simply get in the way of market forces. The lower those benefits are, the less the natural processes of the market will be impeded. The jobless won't even be particularly worse off, because the absence of benefits will just nudge them into taking up all those desirable private sector jobs that will sprout up the second they moderate their wage demands.

Secondly, there's no such thing as involuntary unemployment. Putting aside those (relatively minor) issues of frictional unemployment, anyone who is without a job is jobless *because they want to be.*

These two thoughts together form a brew that's sweet nectar to the conservative mind. The recession of the early 1980s saw rioting in a number of urban centres in Britain. Left-wing hearts were touched by the sight of desperate people raging against an unfeeling universe. Right-wing hearts saw only criminality and laziness. Margaret Thatcher's favourite ministerial shock-trooper, Norman Tebbit, famously commented, 'I grew up in the '30s with an unemployed father. He didn't riot. He got on his bike and looked for work, and he kept looking till he found it.' Tebbit's implication that joblessness is chosen may have riled left-wingers at the time, but it sat very well with mainstream economic theory. Indeed, it *was* mainstream economic theory.

Unfortunately for that theory, its predictions simply didn't seem to describe the reality that was staring everyone else in the face. It didn't seem, even remotely, to describe the catastrophic life-changes which often follow redundancy. The notion that 'leisure time' had a positive value and that the unemployed were silently chuckling to themselves in their new-found heaven of daytime TV and economy-brand baked beans seemed simply ludicrous.

The theory didn't do much better in coldly statistical terms either. Margaret Thatcher came into government in 1979, when unemployment stood at around 1.3 million. By the time of the next election, and despite constant downward massaging of the figures, the unemployment count was well over 3 million. Yet wages, far from falling, *rose*. All those hordes of job-seekers didn't depress wages. They didn't even appear to get in the way of wage increases. The theory wasn't merely awry, it seemed to be pointing in the exact wrong direction.

Although some malfunctioning of the core theory could be explained by various other bits of theory, that first Thatcher government lived and breathed according to free market economic orthodoxy. No British government has ever matched it for relentless and energetic pursuit of those orthodox goals. Nor has any American, German, French, or Italian one. The first Thatcher administration did all a government could reasonably or unreasonably do to ensure that the labour market worked as mainstream economics predicted ... and the labour market did no such thing. If theories are to be judged by results, then this one flunked and flunked badly. Time for a new theory.

So, thanks to work by a pair of American economists, Joseph Stiglitz and Carl Shapiro, a new theory was duly born. It arose from a perfectly valid insight. If you buy an apple or an iPod or a cocker spaniel or a space rocket, the thing is what it is. It may be good or bad, a sweet deal or a rip-off, but the item in question doesn't instantly start to morph into something else. The labour market isn't like that. If a firm hires a new employee, then that employee may buy into the firm's corporate goals and work her butt off for the team – or she may decide that she doesn't particularly like the firm and will slack off whenever she can. Firms get more value from workers than shirkers, so they do what they can to make sure they inspire allegiance. That requires firms to pay sweeteners over and above the wage rate that would effectively clear the market. And that in turn means that you can keep your economic theory as pure and clean as ever – everybody is rationally optimizing all the things they're meant to be optimizing – but wages will be set at a level which requires some people to be involuntarily unemployed.

Just 200 years into the development of economics, it seemed like there was a nice clean way to explain unemployment. Relief all round.

Alas, when you start to get clever, it's hard to know when to stop. A whole other set of economists started to pick away at Stiglitz and Shapiro's model. Seniority pay is the rule in most enterprises. Anyone fired for shirking is going to have to start without seniority pay elsewhere. A whole lot more clever mathematics was done and, given a different but perfectly sensible set of assumptions to Stiglitz and Shapiro's, it turned out that firms *didn't* need to pay more than the clearing wage after all. All of a sudden, unemployment became impossible to explain once again. And that's where we stand today. Mainstream, market-oriented economics – the sort where everyone is a rational maximizer of their own advantage; the sort that all those Rogue-Economist-Rips-the-Mask-off-Reality books are on about – that type of economics can't decisively explain why unemployment exists.

It doesn't stop there.

Take pay. Let's think about a very ordinary job – a secretary, for example. Secretaries have some important skills and they require a certain amount of training to do their jobs well. Nevertheless, those skills are more common than, let's say, the skills involved in being a top opera soprano, a bomb disposal expert, or a brain surgeon. So, applying the elements of supply and demand, we'd expect there to be a fair number of secretaries, generally earning less than top opera sopranos, bomb disposal experts and brain surgeons. This is, in fact, the case, so the theory works so far.

But the theory also predicts that no firm is going to waste money by hiring secretaries at a wage in excess of what they need to pay. A secretary of a particular level of skill and experience should expect to earn the same whether she works for a top investment bank or a road haulage company. (Of course, if the road haulage company decides to save money by hiring only rubbish secretaries, then that's a different matter. But rubbish secretaries create costs and cause problems, so there's no particular reason to suppose that hiring poor staff is a profitable strategy for any firm.) The same should be true not just of secretaries but of every occupation where skills are transferable across a range of industries. That's what the laws of supply and demand say. That is the prediction made by mainstream economic theory.

And it's wrong. It's not even close. In one influential study, published in 1951, an economist looked at what one particular occupational group was paid for their labour. He looked at drivers and – to make sure that there weren't other factors biasing the study – he looked at wage rates in just one city, Boston. What he found was very interesting. In the wholesale laundry business and in the scrap iron business, drivers were paid \$1.20 per hour. Piano movers were paid \$1.30 per hour. Those in the linen supply industry were paid \$1.38. These were the guys at the bottom end of the pay spectrum. At the other end of the scale were drivers employed by the magazine, newspaper, and oil industries. These people, the aristocrats of Bostonian driving talent, earned between $2.00 and $2.25, or getting on for double what their down-at-heel brethren in the wholesale laundry business were getting. These were, please note, people of the same average skill level, doing the same job, in the same city, at the same time – yet wage rates varied by almost 100 per cent.

The same with secretaries. Put aside for a moment everything you've learned from those economics bestsellers and ask yourself which of the following you believe:

- A competent secretary at Goldman Sachs earns more (indeed, a lot more) than a similarly capable secretary at a nearby road haulage firm.

Or

- A competent secretary at Goldman Sachs earns the same money as her sister in road haulage.

If you believe the first of those propositions and disbelieve the second, then you're right; of course you are. Everything you've learned about the world tells you where the boodle is. A secretary at Goldman Sachs is extravagantly remunerated by the standards of their peers elsewhere, simply because *everyone* at Goldman Sachs is extravagantly remunerated. If secretaries were the only ones who didn't get to splash around in Goldman's Magical Money Fountain, they'd feel angry and resentful. You wouldn't assuage that resentment by talking to them of pay rates in road haulage, because fairness is about infinitely more than supply and demand.

Economics has almost nothing to say about fairness. It's embarrassed by the idea. Those things beloved of economics –

supply and demand, the notion of a clearing price, the constant quest to maximize profits – all those things say that a guy delivering laundry and a guy delivering magazines cannot and will not be paid differently. That's what the laws say and the laws are wrong.

The problems extend almost everywhere you look. Can traditional economics explain why financial markets are as volatile as they are? No. It predicts much less volatility.

How about the boom-bust cycle in real estate? Can economics help us with that? The answer is no again.

Can traditional economics explain why savings habits are so arbitrary? No, it can't. As a matter of fact, traditional economics teaches that savings habits are anything but arbitrary.

Or take prices. If you compare the cost of goods on sale in a variety of outlets in the same city, you'll find that the maximum and minimum prices to be found for the exact same goods are likely to vary by 150 per cent or more. Traditional economics just can't explain that level of variation – or at least not without so many qualifications and uncertainties that the whole exercise just dissolves into silliness.

Or take executive pay. Chief executives in America today earn about 400 times what an average worker is paid. At the height of the dot.com boom, that figure briefly topped 500. In Germany – hardly an unsuccessful economy – that same ratio is somewhere closer to twenty. The answer can't be that European economies suffer from rampant socialism, because just thirty or forty years ago US CEOs were paid salary multiples broadly similar to those applied in Germany today. This too is a puzzle for which conventional economics has no plausible explanation.

And so on.

Naturally I haven't chosen these examples at random. I've chosen instances that most glaringly highlight the deficiencies of economics as it's currently understood. I've also concentrated more on macroeconomics (which deals with the behaviour of entire economies) than on microeconomics (which deals with the behaviour of individual markets), because the latter subject is in better shape than the former. I've also concentrated on the labour market, because humans are crankier, more cussed commodities than apples, iPods, or cocker spaniels.

Nevertheless, because the subject as a whole is riven with problems, those problems crop up almost wherever you care to look. Take, for example, Robert Frank's number one bestselling *Economic Naturalist* (subtitle: 'Why Economics Explains Almost Everything'). This book is written as a series of questions and answers, the notion being that economic reasoning will unpick all those little mysteries of life. The most interesting aspect to the book is how often, far from explaining everything, economics can't even answer the questions that Robert Frank throws at it.

For example, one of Frank's questions is: why do taxi drivers stop working early on rainy days? His answer: more people want cabs on wet days, so drivers can reach their target income level for the day more quickly, so they knock off work early. The trouble is that, as Frank is candid enough to admit, this behaviour is 'precisely the opposite of what their economic incentives might seem to favor' – because it would make more sense to take time off on slow days than on lucrative ones. So economics actually gets the answer to this question wrong; so wrong, in fact, that it's heading off in the opposite direction. As soon as you start to look at Frank's book and others in this way, you start to see how much sleight of hand is needed to sustain the ludicrous 'economics explains everything' myth.

If it were only me saying these things, you would be within your rights to disbelieve me, but I am not alone. Professor David Blanchflower, an economist who sits on the Bank of England's crucial Monetary Policy Committee, has this to say, for example: 'As a monetary policymaker I have found the cutting edge of current macroeconomic research totally inadequate.'

Paul Krugman, a Nobel Prize winner, puts it rather more bluntly, saying in his 2009 Lionel Robbins lecture at the LSE that: 'It's very hard to avoid the impression that ... most of what we've done in macroeconomics for the past thirty or so years has turned out to be spectacularly useless at best, and positively harmful in some cases.'

Nobel Prize winner George Akerlof and his equally eminent colleague Robert Shiller have this to say:

> Traditional economics teaches the benefits of free markets ... [and that] free market capitalism will be essentially perfect and stable ... but [Adam Smith's] theory fails to describe why there is so much variation in the economy. It does not explain why the economy takes roller-coaster rides. And the takeaway message from Adam Smith – that there is little, or no, need for government intervention – is also unwarranted.

Willem Buiter, chief economist of Citigroup, says the same thing even more bluntly. In a blog article entitled 'The Unfortunate Uselessness of Most "State of the Art" Academic Monetary Economics', he refers to most of the macroeconomics of the last forty years as being 'self-referential, inward-looking distractions'. Another senior monetary policymaker speaks of mainstream economic theory as something that 'excludes everything I am interested in'. Even the newer, cooler, sexier bits of economics don't fare any better. Recanting game theorist Tony Curzon Price has this to say about the discipline he once embraced: 'By some great piece of PR, game theory makes a claim to being the study of strategy. But that is a pretence ... Game theory has a terrible secret: its strongest prediction is that when games are repeated, almost anything is possible. It can make no actual predictions.'

The same isn't quite true of economics, but it's much more true than most economists are happy to admit in public.

The great and terrible problem at the heart of the discipline has to do with the picture of the human being on which it rests, and that picture in turn has long been distorted by the subject's prioritization of mathematics over reality. The figure at the heart of conventional economic theory – The Rational Optimizing Human – isn't a bad first approximation to the way we behave when it comes to matters of money, but real sciences need to get a lot closer than decent first approximations. The trouble is that the Rational Optimizing Human is much easier to model mathematically than inconsistent, illogical, and downright ornery individuals like you and me – the sort who love our Dove soap, who need smells artificially added to our coffee, whose happiness is as likely to be created by offering free help to patients as it is by buying mounds of new electronic gadgets, whose feelings about pay are determined as much by a sense of fairness as by the icy logic of supply and demand, and whose crudely herd-like behaviour causes booms and busts on calamitous scales.

Keynes side-stepped this problem by not bothering too much with the mathematics. His *General Theory* fizzed with energy, because it depicted humans as they were, not as mathematicians would have liked them to be. Since Keynes's time, and as psychologists have started to pin down various patterns in our orneriness, it's true that economists have started to tweak their models away from the pure *homo economicus* of the 1920s. That's better than nothing, for sure, but it's still a backwards way of proceeding; a way that prioritizes mathematical treatment over a complete and plausible picture of the human actor.

The tweaks have also had virtually no impact in the crucial realm of macroeconomics. Indeed, because of the overwhelming belief in the efficiency of financial markets, most macroeconomic models – astonishingly – don't bother to model any financial sector at all. Insolvencies don't exist. Markets don't freeze. Investors don't panic. Humans don't act as we know humans do. Indeed, the central economic model used by the Bank of England does not recognize the existence of any banks at all. It's a bank that doesn't believe in banks. That's not a great way to navigate a financial crisis.

The right way to proceed would be to ask: what are humans? What drives them? How do they feel and behave and think about money and material wealth? Once we have the answers to those questions, it would make sense to start seeing whether mathematics can be brought to bear, but if we start wheeling out the heavy maths before we have a sensible picture of a human then the results are almost certain to fall disastrously short of the truth. Indeed, as we've seen, the results are almost certain to predict that Great Depressions cannot possibly happen, just as banks are falling like ninepins and the unemployment queues are reaching crisis proportions.

Now I'm not about to start offering to refashion economics, but in the course of writing this book I've met a lot of interesting people and talked to them about why they have done what they've done. What has motivated them to do it? What gives them a buzz? What have they observed about the successes and failures of the economic systems that have nourished or destroyed them?

It's time now to put aside the economics and turn instead to human beings.

NINETEEN

Motivations

> If your only goal is to become rich, you will never achieve it.
>
> – JOHN D. ROCKEFELLER

Back in the chapter entitled 'Morons' we raised the question of happiness and we saw that there's good evidence to suggest that increased income does make countries happier over time. The evidence presented in that chapter might seem to suggest that human economic motivations are rather simple: we work hard to make money to be happy. We can call this the Abba Hypothesis:

> Money, money, money
> Must be funny
> In the rich man's world.

Things aren't quite so simple, however. The Abba Hypothesis looks compelling when we stand back and look at the entire globe, from poverty-stricken Afghanistan to super-affluent Luxembourg. If the data permitted, we would very likely see something similar emerging if we looked at the progress of individual nations over the centuries. Britons and Americans are almost certainly a good bit chirpier now than they were 200 or 300 years ago. These, however, are essentially geological effects: the relentless cumulation of small forces acting over a long time.

As soon as we shift from geological scales to more human ones, those same small forces look rather insignificant. It's not that income is irrelevant to happiness; it's just that it's not a very powerful determinant of it. For example, let's suppose you have a very congenial, very satisfying job. If you had to rate your job satisfaction on a scale of 1 to 10, then you'd pick an 8. You earn $65,000 – Canadian dollars, that is, because this example is taken from a study carried out in Canada. You're reasonably contented with life. Your life is full of all those things that happy Canadians like to do.

Then an alternative job is offered to you. It comes with a pay rise, but various aspects of the job in question are less satisfying than the one you already have. You calculate that the new position would give you a job satisfaction of 7 out of 10; hardly a crisis, but a definite step down. The question is how much extra money would you need to compensate you for that one-notch reduction in job satisfaction? How much money, in other words, would take you back to the exact same level of *overall* life satisfaction you had before?

Most people thinking about this question take care not to be excessively materialist in their answer. A pay rise of C$5,000 seems rather too little. For C$15,000 a year, then of course we'd take that other job. Would we do it for C$10,000? Well, maybe, maybe not.

The first point to notice here is that, even in our conscious calculations about these matters, income doesn't figure all that highly. We're demanding a 20 per cent hike in pay to compensate us for a one-point fall in job satisfaction. Even if, in reality, we ended up taking that other job for a pay rise of somewhere between C$5,000 and C$10,000, then income is still only barely keeping pace with job satisfaction when it comes to our inner calculations on these things.

The second point, however, is more striking still. Whether we moved for C$5,000, C$10,000, or C$15,000, we'd be making a colossal error. When researchers actually talk to people about how happy they are, what they earn, how much they enjoy their jobs, and then crunch through all the data they've collected, they discover that job satisfaction is much *more* important and income much *less* important than most people realize. The statistics tell you that you would need a roughly C$30,000 pay increase to give you the same kind of life satisfaction that you had before. And when you think about it, that makes a kind of sense. You spend a huge chunk of your waking life at work, where the pleasures and annoyances of your job form a constant backdrop to everything you are and do. Conversely many of the pleasures of ordinary life just don't have anything to do with money: a Saturday morning lie-in, winter skating, buttered toast, cuddling your kids, walking in the woods, kissing, sunshine.

This particular job-swap example is taken from a Canadian study using Canadian survey data, but countless similar studies have been conducted right across the Western world, using different survey data, different methodologies, and different sets of questions. The message of these studies overwhelmingly confirms the relative feebleness of income as a lever for increasing our happiness. According to one economist who's looked at these things, a 33 per cent drop in family income will, on average, cause a fall of 0.2 points on a happiness scale running from 1 to 10. By contrast, being separated rather than married causes a fall of 0.8 points. To be unemployed causes a fall of 0.6 points. Being employed but without a sense of job security knocks you back 0.3 points. If your subjective assessment of your health declines by 1 point on a 5 point scale, then happiness declines on average by 0.6 points. Political freedoms are worth 0.5 points. Believing in God is worth 0.3 to 0.4 points.

These facts should give us pause. They suggest that the Abba Hypothesis is only really valid if we're thinking about mankind's slow evolution from poverty to affluence. As soon as our focus shifts to individuals, then the best advice on happiness would be to get married, make friends, be sociable, look after your health, and pursue a job that you enjoy in an environment that you trust. Every single one of these factors is a more powerful determinant of happiness than income. The Abba Hypothesis seems a good bit less true than the Beatles' Three Laws of Happiness:

1. I don't care too much for money;
2. Money can't buy me love; and
3. Love is all you need.

There's a puzzle in all this. Nearly all of us put a huge amount of effort into making money. The quest for money dominates our working life and our working life just plain dominates our life. Most European readers of this book will expect to dedicate forty-six or forty-seven weeks a year, from leaving education to retirement, to the job of making money, making an exception only for the care of their children. Most American readers will expect to work even more. If we cared seriously about our happiness, however, we'd do no such thing. We'd make sure we were financially comfortable, of course, but we'd have a realistic view of what comfort means – a decent central heating system, yes; fifty-two-inch TV sets, no. Instead, we'd invest our time and care into all the other things that make up a good life. We'd build and maintain a variety of lasting friendships. We'd prioritize socializing. We'd take care of our health. We'd search out jobs that we were passionate about. We'd seek out environments and people that encouraged freedom and trust. We wouldn't even think about giving up an 8 out of 10 wonderful job for a 7 out of 10 one that paid a measly C$15,000 more.

Paradoxical as it seems, the evidence suggests that we humans do not seek to maximize our own happiness – or, more precisely, whether we seek to maximize it or not, we do a pretty rubbish job of achieving it. We work too hard, we care too much about money, and we cut too many corners on things that matter more.

Perhaps this shouldn't surprise us. Evolution does not care whether monkeys are happy or sad; it cares whether they survive and reproduce. Behaviour that looks inexplicable from the perspective of maximizing happiness may not look so weird from an evolutionary perspective. And if it's evolutionary perspectives you're after, then you can't do any better than consult the classified ad section of *The Tribune*, one of India's leading English language newspapers. It's not any old classified ads that interest us in this context; it's specifically the Brides Wanted section, which runs (in the Chandigarh edition at any rate) to almost four closely set broadsheet pages. Here are some examples, lightly edited for privacy and intelligibility:

> Parents looking for suitable match for Saraswat Brahmin boy innocent legally divorced, handsome fair, 31 / 5' 9", working with India's biggest telecom player at senior position with excellent salary, own house, belongs to respectable family … Sober, homely, educated, beautiful girl with Indian values and modern outlook preferred. Widow and divorcee please excuse.

> Fair smart beautiful tall girl for smart handsome Punjabi Brahmin boy, 22 March 1982 / 6' 1". M.Com, MBA, Sales Manager in Bajaj Allianz.

> Ahluwalia Hindu parents seeking match for their Canada-born son, age 32, height 5' 8", fair and wheatish colour, do not drink and smoke and never married. Doing family own business, just started same business in India. Girl should be family oriented, well educated, fair and beautiful, height should be 5' 3" or more. Please send the girl's biodata.

> Match for legally divorced Brahmin boy 5' 5", 45 yrs (looks 35), 15000/- [approx US$300 monthly salary], government job. Only issueless divorcee/employed girl preferred. Caste no bar.

> Suitable match for physically handicapped fair handsome Hindu boy, 25, 5' 2", MA Eng, B.Ed., Govt job. Small family. Caste/dowry no bar.

These ads are more blatant than the equivalent entries in a Western lonely hearts column or online dating site, but most of their underlying concerns would be recognizable in any culture and any age. Men need to be tall and rich; women need to be beautiful and modest. Intelligence is a plus for both sexes. So is 'good family'. So is a favourable horoscope: that's why 'biodata' is often requested and given.

Not all virtues rank equally, however. The first ad in the group above sets out a very demanding wish list for prospective brides. Women must be sober, homely (that is, willing to be homemakers), educated, and beautiful, with the right set of values and without any previous marriage. The penultimate ad drops almost all these requirements, confining itself to a simple preference that prospective brides should have a job and, if divorced, be childless. The rather touching final ad makes no demands and states no preferences. Indeed, it does the opposite, telling women not to worry if they come from a lowly social background or have no money to bring to the marriage.

Most of what partners are looking for has an obvious genetic translation. Facial symmetry, height, clear skin, and good health are powerful indicators of good genes. Because brains are very energy-intensive and complex organs, then intelligence is also an excellent signal of good genes. When the Ahluwalia Hindu parents of the third ad stated their desire to find a girl who was 'well educated, fair and beautiful, [with a] height … [of] 5' 3" or more', they were in effect saying they wanted a girl with good genes, good genes, good genes, and good genes, and with enough health and nutrition in childhood to have permitted those genes to have expressed themselves to the full.

So much for what the men wanted, but what were they offering in return? Height is clearly a factor. Virtually every ad among the 800 or so that I have in front of me gives a precise measurement of the man's height. Where no measurement is given, the ad normally just says 'tall'. Most of the time, men are also described as handsome or beautiful. Occasionally they are described as fair, golden, or (I love this) wheatish. Education is also widely mentioned. These things – height, good looks, education/intelligence – are all clearly advertising good genes, in just the same way as good genes are being sought from potential brides.

Yet take another look at what those Ahluwalia Hindu parents were offering in exchange for the 'good genes, good genes, good genes, and good genes' they were expecting from their future daughter-in-law. Their son was Canada-born, he was 32, he was of no more than average height (for an Indian), he avoided a couple of minor drugs, he hadn't been married, and he was delightfully wheatish. Of those only the last may have anything to do with good genes.* On the face of it, those pushy parents were demanding a great deal of genetic loveliness from their daughter-in-law without having much to offer in return.

Except, that is, money. Being Canada-born means possession of a Western income. Ownership of businesses in two countries implies a very high level of both affluence and security. The entire ad was really a way to say, 'We've got the money, you bring the genes.'

---

* There's a theory that pale skin is quicker to reveal infection than dark skin, so having clear-and-pale skin is a stronger signal of health than clear-and-dark skin. But it's only a theory and may well not be true. Personally I suspect that Bollywood has more to do with it than botulism.

The first two ads say largely the same thing. Because nearly all the men are described as being handsome, you can decide for yourself just how handsome this first pair is likely to be in reality. The 'smart handsome Punjabi Brahmin boy' of the second ad is certainly tall, but Mr 'Innocent Legally Divorced' of the first ad is nothing special. Except that both individuals can flash the cash. A senior position with India's leading telecoms firm? With his own house? And a respectable (that is, financially prosperous) family to boot? That's a fairly irresistible proposition. Or what about an MBA graduate with an excellent managerial job at India's leading non-life insurance firm? If I were an educated, fair, and modest Indian girl, I'd be picking out my best sari, jingling my bangles, and polishing up that horoscope.

In the West, there's more gender equality and a less overt emphasis on the size of a potential partner's bank account, but these concerns are universal ones nonetheless. From an evolutionary standpoint, it would be bewildering if they weren't. Genes matter, of course, but the survival of offspring into reproductive maturity matters every bit as much. In the rich world of today, nearly all children, rich or poor, will survive to that age, but that's been a recent enough development that our genetic make-up couldn't possibly have started to reflect it.

These ruminations lead us to the happily poptastic conclusion that the Abba Hypothesis and the Beatles' Three Laws can *both* be true, as long as we understand them correctly. Abba's emphasis on the importance of money is correct, if you understand the Swedish quartet to be talking about mate competition, offspring survival, and the deeply laid impulses bequeathed to us by our genes. The Fab Four are broadly right, as long as we put evolution out of our heads and consider what makes us happy. The two things don't pull in opposite directions exactly, but they don't reliably pull the same way either. Things that would be sensible to do for our happiness sometimes just strike our genes as too wrong to be endured, and so we end up with some half-cocked compromise between the two. That's why Canadians with highly satisfying jobs are excessively prone to giving them up in exchange for a too-small pay rise. It's why nearly all of us are excessively prone to the same kind of error.

There are, however, certain groups of people who are more immune from this mistake than the rest. Creative types are the most notable example. The editorial company which I run has a team of about eighty novelists, poets, screenwriters, and other authors. Many of them have won or been shortlisted for literary awards, including some of the best known and most respected. Yet not one of the team makes a reliable living wage from their writing. But writers don't write because they're not smart enough to be investment bankers. They write because they're passionate about it. If you talk to a writer (or a painter or a musician or an actor) and ask them why they do what they do, they'll almost certainly answer you with a kind of shrug. Writers *have to* write. It's in them to do so. If they were forced to stop, they'd lose a little part of themselves and wouldn't quite feel right until they had a pen in their hands once again. In a sense, for any true born creative, the choice of career doesn't really exist, just as you couldn't really say that a fish *chooses* to swim. I say this with some confidence, because I feel just the same way myself.

All this I knew before embarking on the interviews for this book. What I hadn't expected, however, what came as the single biggest surprise of my research, was this. *Entrepreneurs don't care about money either*. Really not. That's not what fires up those entrepreneurial V8s and gets them roaring away from the starting line. Entrepreneurs are creatives of action. They set themselves a very difficult challenge: to create a viable business in a world teeming with well-resourced competitors. Achieving that aim, nurturing their creation, watching it grow – that is what gives an entrepreneur their satisfaction. Ask an entrepreneur why they do what they do and, more likely than not, you'll find yourself facing that same writerly shrug. Entrepreneurs create because they have to. They're fish that are born to swim.

This basic urge to create is buttressed by a number of supporting motivations. Entrepreneurs, for example, are natural competitors, for whom business – a world defined by competition – is their only logical habitat. What's more, when these natural born competitors take a look at the world around them, they can't help but notice that 'success' has widely been come to be seen as a synonym for 'wealth', so their competitive instincts naturally lock on to wealth as the ultimate proving ground. If humans happened to despise money but venerated explorers instead, then plenty of entrepreneurs would be ditching the business suits in favour of dogsleds and snowshoes.

Since entrepreneurs do choose to compete in the business world then naturally enough they can't do what they do and not care whether their business makes money or not. That would be like being a gardener and not caring whether your plants lived or died. In the same way, entrepreneurs are passionately focused on the profitability and all round financial health of their creations. The inevitable consequence of that absorption, when it suceeds, is that it will make its possessor rich and possibly very rich indeed. Since money is a nice thing to have, then the entrepreneur is hardly going to be appalled or upset when it comes their way, but the money is like some magical side-effect; a side-effect which makes the whole exercise more delightful in every way, but a side-effect nonetheless.

There are, therefore, at least three major motivations which drive entrepreneurs. Number one is the sheer creative joy of action, of building something from nothing, of setting themselves a vastly difficult challenge and then meeting it. Number two is the pleasure of competition – and in particular competition for money, which simple observation suggests is the thing that many humans care most about. Number three is the pleasure of money itself, the inevitable byproduct of entrepreneurial success.

Of these three motivations the last one is, in my view, the weakest. When I talked to entrepreneurs, I asked most of them the following question. 'Imagine that, in your early twenties, you had been presented with two options. Option one: you could work your butt off for ten years, quite likely sacrificing relationships and friendships along the way, and you might – just might – end up with a business worth £30 million. Alternatively, option two, you could be given a lottery ticket worth £30 million pounds, on condition that for the next ten years you had to lead a life of leisure: sitting by the beach, getting a tan, going waterskiing, reading books, travelling a bit, flirting. Which option would you have picked?'

No one evinced the tiniest bit of hesitation in answering. There was only one possible answer: option one. Option two would have driven them crazy. No risk, no action, no sense of adventure, no achievement, nothing created, the world left unchanged. I doubt if any serious entrepreneur in history would have chosen option two.

Entrepreneurs themselves understand this perfectly. One man spoke to me about his intention of selling his business. I was surprised since his business still had plenty of growth in it. He was young. For sure, he'd already made easily enough to retire on, but I couldn't see that he'd be remotely happy as a 40-year-old retiree. I quizzed him about this, and then he saw that I'd misunderstood him. He didn't want to sell his business because he wanted to move to Florida and work on his golf game. He intended to sell it, so he had capital to invest in all the other enterprises he was bursting to get started. It wasn't the money, he explained. 'The cheque would make me happy for about half an hour ... then I'd want to get busy.'

This kind of comment was repeated ad infinitum in my other interviews. One businessman I spoke to, David

Giampaolo, had made his money in health clubs before moving sideways into the private equity business. When I asked him if he did what he did for the money, he raised his hands to the ceiling. 'I've *got* money,' he told me, as if I was an imbecile. When I asked him how felt on making his first significant chunk of cash, he told me that his thoughts ran, 'I've got it [the financial reward]. That felt good for a nanosecond, now what do I do?'

I was told about a thousand times, 'I've got to keep busy.' The word 'busy' as used by entrepreneurs doesn't mean 'occupied', it means creating something. When I suggested to Sir Martyn Rose that the amount of money a person made was an accurate metric of their success in business, he rebuked me. 'It's making your ideas *happen* that counts.'

Or when I spoke to Bill Browder, the hedge fund manager, about his attitudes to money, he said, 'You don't spend most of your time looking at a bank statement, you spend your time doing what you do.' When I asked him how his life had been changed by his material success, he simply shrugged. 'I have the same lifestyle now I had ten years ago.' That wasn't quite a 'no', please notice. No one hates finding themselves rich and some other entrepreneurs I spoke to had gone in for the whole fine-art-and-Bentleys shtick. But it was an accurate answer nonetheless. The thrill of action, risk, and creation – those things are essentials. The money – well, it's a nice-to-have.

What's more, it's not just entrepreneurs who hold these attitudes. I'd guess that pretty much *any* businessperson who does an excellent job does it for reasons that go far beyond money. One of the most interesting interviews I had in this context was with Jeremy Wood, a senior director of Nationwide, a building society which is wholly owned by its customers.

In the early and mid-1990s, there had been a craze for demutualizing building societies and turning them into shareholder owned institutions. There were various intellectual arguments behind the craze, but one argument was perhaps more potent than the rest. Building societies had been rather strait-laced, rather sober, rather worthy institutions. They were not the sort of outfits to shove bundles of money into the pockets of top executives until their seams bulged and the stitching ripped. Banks, on the other hand, especially dynamic young financial institutions piloted by go-ahead management teams, wouldn't really know what to do to themselves unless they sought to drown top management beneath a shower of stock options and cash bonuses, so that's just what they did. The question which faced Nationwide was: why not demutualize too?

I put just that question to Jeremy Wood and he told me, rather blandly, that the company 'had something special' and didn't want to put that specialness at risk. On Planet Economics that answer made no sense. Wood and his colleagues could have demutualized if they'd chosen to; they'd have made themselves rich if they'd done so. For *homo economicus*, there wouldn't even have been a choice. They'd have demutualized every time.

But Wood and his colleagues had other values. He told me that when the crucial decisions were made, Nationwide was a 'fantastic place to work, it really was'. It had given him 'some of the best times of my life'. He felt what he and his colleagues were building was something 'really worthwhile'. He said he still keeps in touch with his customers from those times today. Those things mattered more to him than having his shirt pockets explode with the amount of stock options thrust into them. They mattered more to his colleagues. Central to this outlook was a notion that the Nationwide was doing something intrinsically valuable, that it was itself a creation of value. That sense didn't spring from some abstract set of arguments about (say) the importance of access to property finance, or anything like that. Rather, it came from a sense that Nationwide was doing a difficult thing well, that it treated its employees right, that it embodied values of substance, that it was a well-run business whose excellence showed itself in everything from the smiles of branch staff to the detail of its annual accounts.

The punchline of the tale arrived belatedly in 2008. All those go-getting banks for whom money had been the be-all and the end-all – the Northern Rocks, the RBSs – discovered, to their cost and ours, that money turned out to be the end-all. A company, any company, that is founded only on the desire to make money is a company that is just a few financial quarters away from catastrophe. The passion that Wood and his colleagues had for their business is only a Rizla paper's thickness away from the passion that entrepreneurs feel for their creations. The same is true of every good business, everywhere, always.

Indeed, one of the deepest conclusions of this book, and one of the most surprising to me, is that *all* good businesses are driven by passion. If a business's senior management starts to be driven by money alone, then they may string together a few decent years of financial results, but you can bet heavily against that business being a long term success. Some years ago – well before the 2008/9 crisis – a senior executive at Volkswagen said to me, 'The trouble with Ford is that they only care about making money. Here at Volkswagen, we only care about making cars.' At the time, I thought to myself that, if that was the case, I'd sooner buy shares in Ford than in Volkswagen. Why would I want my share capital to subsidize the car obsession of a bunch of German engineers?

Fortunately for me, however, that thought never translated into a punt on the stock market. At the time of writing, Chrysler is in court-protected bankruptcy, hoping to be rescued by Fiat. General Motors, once *the* symbol of American capitalism, went bankrupt too and will be rescued only by bucketloads of federal cash. Ford, as it happens, has done least abysmally of the three, but is still in a horrible mess. Volkswagen has suffered an uncomfortable six months by its standards but is still worth

€70 or €80 billion, or enough to buy Ford, General Motors, and Chrysler four times over – and still have a few billions left over for dismantling Detroit and reopening it as a theme park.

The same point can be made more narrowly and more precisely in relation to the 2008/9 financial meltdown. It's a point that puts the whole heated discussion about bonuses and incentives rather into context. Banks whose chief executives had their pay packages most *closely* tied to the fortunes of their firm did *worst* in the crisis. Banks whose chief executives were most insulated from the ups and downs of their company's stock price performed best.

Economics as it is now generally understood simply cannot explain this finding. Indeed, it predicts the opposite. Reality, according to economics, must simply have got it wrong.

And yet, as soon as we set economics to one side, the finding is not so hard to understand. Chief executives who are told at all costs to boost the share price, will seek to do so – at all costs. Costs including, in some cases, the destruction of their firms and the near annihilation of government balance sheets. On the other hand, a chief executive with some greater stability in his pay is being sent a different message. A message which, decoded, might run roughly like this: 'Yes, we want you to create profits for the firm. If you do well for us, we will reward you. But don't go crazy. This is an old, great, established company. It wasn't built in a day, and yet it could be destroyed in one. You are privileged to inherit this great position and we expect you to treat it with respect.'

This is a message which talks, and talks meaningfully, about performance and reward, of course. But it speaks of other things too: history, privilege, duty. Indeed, I think that the best banks – the best *firms*, never mind which industry – retain some sense that honour matters. It doesn't simply matter for commercial reasons. (It wouldn't be honour if it did.) It matters for reasons beyond economics, beyond money. We've encountered paradox a couple of times already in this book, but if you want the deepest and most important, then here it is. The people who will be most successful at making money in the long term will be those for whom making money is a side-effect of passion. That passion will always concern itself with money, of course. If your passion is to create a wonderful business, then you also need to make sure that it is a thriving, profitable one. But the passion will come first, the money will come second.*

And since we're making friends with paradox, here's one more for the collection. The more you care about making money, the less satisfaction you'll get from it. That's not my long-suppressed crypto-Marxism speaking, that's a research finding which has been demonstrated again and again in the literature on happiness. The fools and rogues who plunged the world economy into turmoil may have got rich but they probably never got happy. So much for *homo economicus*. He got what he deserved.

As for economics, it needs to learn something too. If economists were ever to venture past the doors of their universities, they'd discover a world in which *homo economicus* doesn't exist. They'd discover a world where passion matters, where fairness matters, where individuals become insanely optimistic because their next door neighbour is insanely optimistic too. This would be a good thing.

If I'm being completely honest, however, I'd have to say that although there are glaring deficiencies in mainstream economics as it stands today, it's not economists that most need to shape up, but politicians. It's not economic theories that most need to change, but ideologies. It's to those areas we turn now.

---

* It even came first for Willie Sutton, the prolific bank robber quoted at the start of the chapter on bankers. It wasn't the money he cared about. It was the robbing.

TWENTY

Ideologies

> Everything was so clean, it was like a movie. The roads, the pavements, the people – nothing in my life had ever looked like this ... The landscape looked like geometry class, or physics, where everything was in straight lines and had to be perfect and precise. These buildings were cubes and triangles, and they gave me that same neutral, almost frightening feeling.
>
> – AYAAN HIRSI ALI, *Infidel*

Our world is miraculous. We live inside a miracle whose most remarkable feature is how profoundly we have come to take it for granted.

Not everyone has the luxury of miracle and not everyone takes it for granted. The quotation above describes the moment when Ayaan Hirsi Ali, a Somali Muslim woman, with a powerful father and of high clan status, first set foot in the West, just outside Düsseldorf airport in Germany. Ali was theoretically on her way to Canada, in order to join up with her 'husband' who lived there. I've dressed the word 'husband' in inverted commas, because this was an arranged marriage, which Ali had been forced to enter against her will, to a man she had barely met and didn't like. Encountering the extraordinary world of the West, a world she'd been taught to believe was decadent and corrupt, she found the courage to break away from her family, her clan, her country, and ultimately her religion. She went from

Germany to Holland and there sought asylum. At the receiving centre for refugees in Zwolle, she encountered her first Western policeman, who told her she needed to go somewhere else, and gave her a bus card, a train ticket, and some instructions for the journey. He complimented her on her English. She was baffled. 'Police to me were oppressors, demanders of bribes. They were never *helpful*. I asked him, "Why are you helping me?" and he smiled and said, "Those are the rules." I asked, "And is every policeman this kind?" and he replied, "I sure hope so."'

This was a still more amazing moment for Ali than the vision outside Düsseldorf airport. The governments that she knew about – she'd spent time in Somalia, Kenya, Ethiopia, and Saudi Arabia – were out to oppress and exploit their citizens. In Holland, a policeman was not only kind, but was being kind to a *foreigner*. 'How on earth did [these people] treat their own clans,' she wondered. When she waited for a bus that was due to arrive at 2.37 p.m. and, lo and behold, the bus arrived at 2.37 exactly, she was blown away. 'Did these people also control the rules of time?'

Now, it's true that Ali happened to arrive in the order of Düsseldorf, not the chaos of Heathrow. She encountered a Dutch policeman, not one from a less accommodating nation. Her first glance fell, perhaps, on the best of the West, not the worst. Yet to focus on the Teutonic taste for the *ordentlich* is utterly to miss Ali's point. *All* Western nations are miraculous. In these lands of miracle, you simply don't find piles of rubbish rotting on city streets, kids playing beside open sewers, policemen on the take, bus drivers who'll rape you, people living in tin shacks, civil wars, food unfit to eat, kids dying of diarrhoea, politicians seeking to outdo others in corruption, dangerous infrastructure, non-existent health care – or countless other things which have been prevalent during almost all of human history and which are still prevalent in too much of the world today. When we in the West moan – because our morning train ran ten minutes late, or because elected politicians fiddled their expenses to the tune of a few thousand pounds – we tend to forget how even our moans prove Ali's point. Ten minutes late! A few thousand pounds! What wouldn't Somalis give for such problems? What wouldn't almost any non-Westerner give?

It's significant, perhaps, that her comments are directed particularly towards those things where the hand of government is most visible: airports, urban planning, policemen, buses. Developing countries are seldom without their rich people, the big villas, and the black four-by-fours. Wealth alone might have impressed Ali, but it wouldn't have been entirely novel. What was extraordinary for her was the ordered benevolence of the societies she encountered. Later on, she was impressed by their freedom, tolerance, and rationality too; their warm encouragement of the individual.

These governmental and social virtues are intimately linked to the raw capitalist energies that give them breath. There's money, for starters. Rich countries can afford to pay for things that poor countries can only dream of. Shiny airports are the least of it. Kindness to refugees, officials too well paid to dream of corruption, policemen who give you stuff – these things are easily afforded by the frighteningly capable wealth-generating machines of Holland and Germany, Britain and America. Poorer countries have to claw their way to such munificence, and it'll be a long, hard claw for many.

Yet money's only part of it. Take trust, a quality which we in the West are often said to have lost. In tribal cultures, an interaction between individuals of different tribes, different clans is a highly dangerous affair. Extended studies of the Yanomamö people of Amazonia suggest that 44 per cent of adult males have participated in killing someone, about 30 per cent of adult males meet their death by violence, and almost 70 per cent of older adults have lost a close relative to homicide. The permanent rolling massacre of these people is in large part because the

Yanomamö have evolved one phase beyond that of stateless hunter-gatherer. They are horticulturalists, who grow plantains and peach palms. Those resources are valuable and competition for them inflames the slaughter. Yet in the West, where our resources are vastly more abundant than a handful of peach palms, violent death is, by historical standards, exceptionally rare. In Europe, homicide is about fifty times less common than it was eight centuries back. Although we notice (and are outraged by) the times when our trust is misplaced or has to be suspended, we take for granted countless interactions based on a quite extraordinary degree of trust.

My editorial consultancy business, for example, frequently receives cheques in the post. We bank those cheques the same way. Specifically, we put them in an envelope, drop the envelope into the little post box that's set into the wall of my house, and that's it. A few minutes before 3.45 in the afternoon, a postman's van will turn up and park in the little farm track that leads to the field behind my house. At 3.45 exactly but not a minute before, the postman will open the post box and remove any mail. He (and it is usually a he) won't open the post box any sooner, because he has to scan the box electronically when he's done and the scanner will report any attempt to move off early.

The van will then leave with the mail, which will be dumped into a huge sorting system, there to pass through many pairs of anonymous hands. I don't know how that sorting system works, and I don't need to know. All I care is that it works and, sure enough, I can be certain that the envelope containing the cheques for my business will end up in the mailroom of some bank, where many further people unknown to me will sort out those slips of paper and credit my account with some electronic money. If I chose to go to a real life bricks-and-mortar bank and get my hands on that money in crinkly, printed banknotes, then some entirely other person would give it to me. I could even take some of those banknotes into a shop and persuade yet another stranger to give me lovely, useful, costly things in exchange for a few pictures of a youthful-looking queen and a quaint-sounding promise from the Chief Cashier of the Bank of England.*

All this is extraordinary. Hundreds of thousands of pounds have flowed through that little post box outside my house. The envelopes we use to mail the cheques aren't even disguised. They're preprinted by the bank and boast the bank's name in bright red capitals across the front. Yet we've never had a cheque stolen. Never once has an envelope gone astray. Never once has the bank failed to credit my account. Never once has the bank refused to turn weird electronic money into the real, folding stuff. Never once has a shop refused to take my pictures of a youthful-looking queen in exchange for goods. Far from fearing constantly for my life, as I would if I were a Yanomamö peach palm proprietor, my interactions with every human element of this system are a pleasure and a delight.

These miracles of trust are partly miracles of mistrust. The Royal Mail requires its staff to scan letterboxes because it's aware that they have a tendency to grab the mail and leave before they should. Any thefts from the system are investigated intensively. Banks, too, have all sorts of ways to guard against fraud and theft. And so on. Because each element of the system is careful to avoid incurring any losses, the resultant system is astonishingly flexible, resilient, and trustworthy. The miraculous outcome is that I'm far happier entrusting huge amounts of money to perfect strangers than I would be about lending it

---

* Specifically, 'I promise to pay the bearer on demand the sum of twenty pounds', or whatever. That promise used to be backed by gold and was the crucial innovation which turned the notes from a private contract between the bank and one specific depositor into a publicly useful means of exchange. Britain left the gold standard permanently in 1931, so if you try to cash your £20 note in at the Bank of England today you'll just get a £20 note back again.

to my next door neighbour. Capitalism is a trust-creator, because it's so effective as a cheat-avoider.

The same applies to freedom. Friedrich von Hayek famously argued in *The Road to Serfdom* that planned economies (among which he included the corporatist Nazi Germany) were inevitably hostile to political freedom. Since a small coterie of central planners could hardly hope to replicate the dazzling speed and accuracy of market-based resource allocation, errors would inevitably occur. Such errors would call forth a coercive response, as the system aimed to cover its tracks by compelling humans to fit the system, rather than vice versa. He also argued that voters in planned economies would seek a 'strong man' to get things done, rather than a liberal leader, keen to undo the system itself.

I'm not certain, myself, that von Hayek quite nailed the issue, but he certainly had a point. Poor countries today are highly likely to be relatively unfree. Rich countries – especially rich countries without oil – are highly likely to be free. There are at least two complementary reasons for this. The first has to do with the wonderfully sensitive systems that capitalism has devised to nurture its inner selfishness. There's not a lot of point being an entrepreneur, if you fear the government is going to steal everything you've created, so capitalism and private property rights are intimately connected. Britain was the world's first true capitalist nation in large part because it was precocious in guarding the property rights of the individual against the greedy fingers of the king, queen, or noble. Guarding property rights may sound tedious, but it means the rule of law. It means an effective court system. It means redress of wrongs and efficient enforcement mechanisms. All that doesn't quite amount to freedom, but it takes you a long way in the right direction.

The second reason is that political progress mostly shambles forward in an untidy, rolling wave. You don't get political movements made up only of would-be Buffets, Gateses, Mittals, and Bransons. You don't get reform slogans demanding 'Efficient Property Rights Enforcement Now!', nor protest marches consisting only of Blackberry-toting yuppies. What in fact happens is that people demand a better life; they agitate for and seize freedoms as they can; things get better. By the time progress has ticked every box on the capitalist property-rights wish-list, it'll quite likely have ticked plenty of other boxes too, including many more important ones.

China is a particularly aberrant example of economic success in part because the untidy, rolling wave model of reform doesn't suit it at all. A generation or so ago a few gerontocrats in Mao suits decided that it would be a good idea to permit capitalist-style economic freedoms. So they did. Broader political freedoms – free speech, free assembly, the free practice of religion, democracy – aren't very much more advanced now than they were twenty or thirty years ago. That's not, thank goodness, a particularly common recipe for success.

Or take creativity. I've argued that the entrepreneurial instinct is a wonderful example of creativity in action. It is, indeed, the ultimate expression of the creativity *of* action. But capitalism also creates a million opportunities for the rest of us to find a niche that fulfils us. The particular genius of rocket engineer Alan Bond couldn't have expressed itself had it not been for the technological excellence of Rolls Royce, British Aerospace, and, later on, the company that he founded and (in significant part) funded. Likewise for auto engineers, cryogeneticists, and aviation nuts. Likewise for almost anything that's high-technology and high expense.

In the same way, the fashion industry doesn't merely offer an outlet for the creativity of clothes designers. It offers a wonderful habitat for models and photographers, textile designers and milliners, magazine editors and fashion journalists, shop designers and retail gurus. Something similar is true of the entertainment industry, the news industry, the software industry, the oil industry – indeed, pretty much any industry you care to think of. Capitalism drives towards specialization, and specialization means that individuals can express themselves through their work, not merely find a way to put food on the table. Even in areas where governments or charities play a larger part than private firms – blue-sky scientific research, human rights activism, teaching, social work – capitalism's wealth and standards of excellence push for outcomes that are far better in the West than they are in any other society under the sun.

Once Ayaan Hirsi Ali had managed to orient herself in Dutch society, she found it was her ability to express her passions and her personality which mattered more than anything to do with the punctuality of Dutch buses or the geometrical precision of the Düsseldorf landscape. The market economy has on the whole had a pretty bad press when it comes to creativity: just think of Blake's dark Satanic mills, of Dickens's *Hard Times*, of Sinclair Lewis's *Babbitt*. But the market doesn't care about its PR; it just does what it does and in the process throws open a world of creative self-expression unimaginable to foregoing generations, unimaginable to the average Somali peasant.

Indeed, you can take pretty much any other social positive that you like – tolerance, fairness, democracy, inclusiveness, opportunity, environmental responsibility – and you'll most likely find that it and capitalism go pretty much hand in hand. Not in an ironclad There Are No Exceptions sort of way, but in a rough and ready, rule of thumb, good enough to be going along with sort of way, nevertheless. As people get richer, they can demand more and society can afford more. It gets a little easier to be nice and do good. The Harvard professor, Benjamin Friedman, has argued impressively that phases of social progress in history tend to occur at times when societies are getting richer, doing well. When times are tougher, people get meaner.

Trust, freedom, creativity, democracy, tolerance – all this, and capitalism makes you richer too! It gives you ride-on lawnmowers, and mobile phones, and ridiculously cute shoes, and smoked foie gras with paupiette of squab. It gives you the wherewithal to make the life choices that you want, the serious ones as well as the frivolous. It's a geological process that slowly and steadily makes humans happier than once they were. In case you haven't yet twigged, I *like* capitalism. I think it's great.

I also like wine and sex and rock-climbing. I think they're great too. But that doesn't mean that my enthusiasm for these things is without measure. It's the same thing with capitalism. It's obviously a good wheeze and long may it continue, but that doesn't mean that more is always better. If government intervention is seen as the opposite of capitalism, then the United States is some socialist hellhole as compared with the glories of über-capitalist Somalia, with its minuscule state, freebooting warlords, and anarchic misrule. Free enterprise just doesn't get much freer than it does in the crazy world of Somali piracy. Nor are these wonderful freedoms only to be found in Somalia. On the contrary, as *New York Times* columnist Thomas Friedman puts it, 'come to Africa – it's a freshman Republican's paradise. Yes sir, nobody in Liberia pays taxes. There's no gun control in Angola. There's no welfare as we know it in Burundi and no big government to interfere in the market in Rwanda.' It's a wonder that Ayaan Hirsi Ali found anything in Germany to be impressed by.

Indeed, for all that some Americans love to disparage Europeans for their supposed socialism, and for all that some Europeans love to disparage Americans for their red-in-tooth-and-claw capitalism, the truth is that the differences between the two cultures are vanishingly small compared with their similarities. In 2007 (that is, before recession wrecked government finances across the globe), the US government spent around 37 cents in every dollar of American GDP. In Germany and Britain, government spent 43 or 44 cents or pennies in every euro or pound. There's a difference here, but it's hardly vast.

Indeed, these figures may even exaggerate that difference. For one thing, government spending data can understate the extent of a government's involvement in the economy. The US government uses tax exemptions to subsidize health care, for example, but in a way that never passes through the government accounts. Less prudently, it also chose to subsidize the mortgage market via an implicit and uncosted guarantee of Fannie Mae and Freddie Mac, which must have seemed like a nifty dodge until both institutions exploded and the jaw-dropping cost of the guarantee became apparent for the first time.

Perhaps more intriguingly, Americans put in a lot more hours at the office or factory than do Europeans while, logically enough, demanding to pay lower average taxes. It's as though everyone – American or European – is happy to work a 46-week year and be taxed like a German or a Frenchman. Then the Americans choose to work another three or four weeks, free of tax, while the Europeans prefer to spend those extra weeks on the beach or ski slope. There is a cultural difference here to be sure, but whether it's what Rush Limbaugh, US radio talk-show host and political commentator, makes of it is open to question. Indeed, the overwhelmingly obvious conclusion to draw from looking at Western economies through Ayaan Hirsi Ali's eyes is that capitalism and governments are two halves of a whole; society clasped in their clamshell embrace. One just doesn't work without the other.

Economists, almost all of them, think the same thing. Although the great classical theories of economics – notably the Arrow-Debreu-McKenzie General Equilibrium model mentioned in the chapter on happiness – are all, in their ways, hymns to the power and perfection of markets, the great classical theories of economics are bunk. They are beautiful creations, but simply don't describe reality. If you had to summarize the thrust of economics research since 1970, then it's been the gradual dismantling of those theories – or rather, their elaboration in ways which voids them of their easy, soundbite-style conclusions.

We've already looked at two major qualifications to the classical theories. One is the way that firms themselves become centrally planned creations, engaging with the market at their peripheries, but not their interiors. We saw how the agent–principal problem introduces a huge amount of weakness into the chains of control that link owners and managers. These two issues alone, however, and giant as they are, barely scrape the surface.

For instance, though we haven't directly broached the concept of externalities – costs or benefits not picked up by the parties to a transaction – it has often hovered close by, nevertheless. When, for example, we looked at advertising, we couldn't help but think about the effects of advertising on others. If you advertise junk food to children, you are quite likely stimulating obesity and health problems in the young. Those problems have a direct economic cost – someone has to pick up the tab for all the extra health care – and they have a crucial, non-monetary cost as well: kids having a worse quality of life than they'd otherwise enjoy. If those costs aren't picked up by junk food advertisers (and they most certainly aren't), then the market can't possibly deliver optimal outcomes because the market hasn't been given the data needed to compute them. Given the sheer complexity of human life, it's actually quite hard to think of major issues in which externalities of one sort or another aren't significant. Indeed, the biggest challenge of our twenty-first century looks set to be the emission of carbon dioxide, an externality which has so far been free to the polluter but at vast cost to the planet.

Or take another example of market failure: asymmetric information. Classical economics assumes that both parties to a transaction know everything they need to know about the deal in question. Yet in countless markets this just isn't the case. The buyer of a used car never knows quite what he's buying. The seller of a health insurance policy never knows the true health risks of the person she's just signed up. In the labour market, an employer never knows quite how hard or well his or her new employee is performing.

And so on. Taxes create market failures. Oligopolies create market failures. Dominant firms create market failures. Transaction costs create market failures. The absence of certain property rights creates market failures. The absence of certain markets creates market failures elsewhere. Outside a number of broad and deep financial markets, it's genuinely hard to think of a single industry untouched by some problem of this type. I personally can't think of one and I doubt if anyone else can either. Even in the financial markets, there's no proof of the existence of *homo economicus* – and the existence of huge boom and bust cycles suggests strongly that he's nowhere to be seen when most it counts.

The Nobel Prize-winning economist, Joseph Stiglitz, summarized these issues in an interview, saying:

> The theories that I (and others) helped develop explained why unfettered markets often not only do not lead to social justice, but do not even produce efficient outcomes. Interestingly, there has been no intellectual challenge to the refutation of Adam Smith's invisible hand. Individuals and firms, in the pursuit of their self-interest, are not necessarily, or in general, led as if by an invisible hand, to economic efficiency.

Stiglitz's summary is deliberately blunt. He enjoys baiting and offending those he terms 'free markets fundamentalists' and the above paragraph is a giant raspberry blown in the general direction of the University of Chicago.

Yet he's also right. Unfettered markets do not lead to social justice. They do not produce efficient outcomes. There is no reputable theory which argues otherwise. When Britons or Americans or Germans say that they favour the free market, what they mean is that they favour a system very much like the one they enjoy today. They do not want to move to Somalia.

Ayaan Hirsi Ali encountered a world of miracle, because she encountered a world where government and market worked together to produce a society that performed wonderfully well: a true clamshell society. She now lives in the United States, where the balance between market and state is struck a little differently, but it's a clamshell society too, just with a slightly different arrangement of shell. Rather than get too hung up on how different clams should arrange their shells, I personally adopt the rather uncontroversial view that democratic societies are probably quite good at sorting these things out for themselves. Americans probably quite like the way things are in America. Swedes presumably like the way things get done in Sweden.

The question really is how come any other ideology can possibly have traction. If modern rich-world governments all do much the same sort of thing in much the same sort of way, if economists all agree that free markets are good as long as they're not particularly free, if Western populations all broadly support government by clamshell, then how come anyone ever argues otherwise?

The answer has to do with history. When Ronald Reagan entered the White House in January 1981, non-defence federal spending had been rising continuously for decades as a proportion of national income. Inflation was rampant. Unemployment was uncomfortably high. Unions were strong. Oil prices were on the march. America had a set of problems which the Carter White House had been plainly unable to fix. In his inauguration speech, Reagan said, 'In this present crisis, government is not the solution to our problem, government is the problem.'

He was right. Things had been getting out of hand. Federal spending didn't, in fact, decline in the Reagan years, but that 1981 speech marked the moment when it stopped growing. More to the point, perhaps, legislators began to remember that regulations carry a cost. So do complications of the tax code. So do filings and licences and approvals and all the rest of it. I'm not suggesting that Reagan got everything right. That same inauguration speech, for example, railed against the budget deficit which would go on to grow wildly out of check until Bill Clinton tamed it. Nevertheless, in 1981, the United States needed an administration that would rebalance the relationship between government and business and, thanks to Reagan, it got one.

Britain experienced much the same thing: high inflation, high unemployment, strong unions, excessive personal taxes. An outgoing government that had waded out into the deep sea of impotence and couldn't see the way back to shore. In May 1979, Margaret Thatcher became prime minister.

Now let me be honest here. I loathed Margaret Thatcher. She had a voice that could curdle milk, a stare that could freeze blood, a way of speaking to people that called to mind some dystopian future, where robots ruled and humans were put to work in uranium mines.

She was also catastrophically wrong about some gigantic issues. She was, for example, an out-and-out monetarist, believing that there was a direct connection between inflation and the growth of the money supply. Now there certainly is some kind of link here, but virtually no one today believes that the link is either simple or predictable. What was more, in the early 1980s, Britain's own position was complicated by huge oil finds in the North Sea (which had the effect of pushing the exchange rate up) and various structural changes in the financial sector (which had the effect of pushing the money supply up, for reasons that had nothing much to do with inflation). A thoughtful, responsible policymaker would have said, 'There's a lot going on here, let's proceed cautiously.' Thatcher didn't know the word for 'caution', so the monetarist medicine was applied at five times the lethal dose. The exchange rate shot up. British manufacturing rolled over onto its back and died. Unemployment reached colossal levels. The money supply still grew wildly – because of everything that was going on in the financial sector – and Thatcher didn't even notice how fantastically wrong she had been.

You can, therefore, mark me down as less than completely enamoured of Margaret Thatcher, and yet even I am obliged to admit that Britain did need a touch of something like Thatcherism. Unions were pegged back. Companies were privatized and (where necessary) regulated. The level of personal taxation no longer caused people to feel that they were being bled by some particularly grasping medieval king. British business started to recover its confidence and vim. The sea of impotence drained away, leaving a shell-shocked but vigorous country.

Two countries, two leaders, two revolutions – but one philosophy: a smaller state, lower taxes, more freedom for the market, less regulation. Implementing the change didn't just mean tweaking budgets and passing laws, it meant altering the way people thought, bringing them to see that the old stagflationary assumptions of the 1970s needed to change.

In America, that meant the genial, self-deprecating wit of Ronald Reagan: 'The nine most terrifying words in the English language are, "I'm from the government and I'm here to help."' According to Reagan, 'The government's view of the economy could be summed up in a few short phrases: If it moves, tax it. If it keeps moving, regulate it. And if it stops moving, subsidize it.'

What's more, he walked his talk – or, to be precise, he snoozed it. An activist president would need to be always busy, always meddling. Reagan wanted to be available, for sure, but not *too* available, commenting, 'I have left orders to be awakened at any time in case of national emergency, even if I'm in a cabinet meeting.' He avoided coffee for the same reason, finding that it 'keeps me awake in the afternoon'.

In the uranium mines of Britain, meantime, there wasn't much room for snoozing, wit, or self-deprecation. (Thatcher once introduced a Bible quotation by saying, 'As God once said, and I think rightly ...') Nevertheless in her milk-curdling, statistics-spouting way, she too did what Reagan did: shifted attitudes, altered assumptions, changed mindsets. Margaret Thatcher's greatest achievement was arguably Tony Blair: a political leader from the other side of the political spectrum who privatized companies, praised the market, and kept personal taxation low. A true blue Thatcherite, dressed in Labour red.

Revolutionary slogans, however, are shaped for revolutionary times. They're there to shock people into thinking differently, not to offer nuanced policy advice. Once the revolution is over, once its lessons have been absorbed, those slogans become dangerous, breeding contagion like carrion rotting in the water supply, mutating and multiplying. What makes them dangerous is their tempting simplicity of logic. Reagan, let's remember, did not reduce federal spending, nor did he radically simplify the tax code. He brought change, but the change was measured.

In the 1990s, the ideologues of the free market started to simplify the message, altering and corrupting it. Newt Gingrich, the most important Republican politician of the 1990s, had this to say: 'Look, the one thing we do know is that bureaucracy is not compassionate, that bureaucracy has not worked, that bureaucracy has not delivered.' In case you missed the point, he also said: 'True compassion is measured by our own good works, not by how many tax dollars we spend to support a failed federal bureaucracy.'

These failed and uncompassionate bureaucracies, presumably, would be the exact same ones that have made available clean water, safe food, universal education, the police and law enforcement, the armed forces, welfare support, roads and airports, health care for the poor and elderly, and vastly more besides. Gingrich, ever the theorist, traced these thoughts to their logical conclusion. If federal bureaucracy was bad then private capital was good, howsoever directed. The notion that there could even be a question about how that capital was put to use was not merely heresy, but (worse still) socialist heresy: 'The idea that a congressman would be tainted by accepting money from private industry or private sources is essentially a socialist argument.'

Gingrich may have been guilty of deliberately oversimplifying the issues, but at least he had a brain capable of rational thought and a tongue capable of getting from one end of a sentence to the other without tripping over the very first comma. The most important Republican politician of the Noughties lacked those elementary virtues. In the person of George W. Bush, Reaganism had become an almost entirely corrupted creed. It's hard, actually, to tease out what Bush thought. He largely avoided unscripted encounters with the press, but when it became impossible to dodge them, the mumbling incoherence of his words often eluded rational construction. The reader or listener becomes like an archaeologist trying to reconstruct a forgotten language from a few inscriptions and some broken pottery. Nevertheless, if you're happy to play Indiana Jones, we'll do precisely that.

In 2002, the 43rd President of the United States had this to say about the economic situation: 'And so therefore, in the face of this recession, which turned out to be a recession, which turned out to be a recession, the tax cut came at the right time in American economic history.'

That presumably was the same sentiment which inspired him to say: 'When your economy is kind of ooching along, it's important to let people have more of their own money.'

He had total command of the laws of supply and demand, revealing to a startled public that: 'The feed stock for gasoline is oil. So when you hear "my gasoline prices are going up" you got to understand the main reason why is because oil prices are going up.'

And when, the free market failed to deliver as expected, his recipes were refreshingly simple:

> Then we had some corporate scandals, scandals which affected our confidence. The capital system requires honesty and openness. But we dealt with it straightforward. We said, if you're going to lie or cheat or steal, if you don't tell the truth to your shareholders and your employees, there will be serious consequences.

For Bush things were simple. Low taxes are good. Government spending is bad. Markets work. If they don't work, that's because of bad people who need to be punished.

These attitudes were the ones that steered the administration through the worst financial crisis in world history. Alas, they weren't enough. The financial crisis – a problem that originated entirely in the private sector – grew progressively worse. When Lehman went bust, and the scale of the disaster became apparent, a Republican administration was forced to ask a Democrat Congress for $750 billion in bail-out money, or more than ten times the budget deficit in 1980, the year that Reagan was elected. 'Those of you who have followed my career know that I'm a free market person,' said Bush.

> And, listen, I understand America's frustrations – better than you can possibly know. I went home out there to west Texas where I was raised. Some old guy said, you know, hey, man, what are you doing? And I said, I'm recognizing reality, that this is a serious economic situation that requires strong government action.

That last sentence, please note, was the opposite of what Ronald Reagan said in his 1981 inauguration speech. Reagan had said, 'In this present crisis ... government is the problem.' Twenty-eight years later another Republican president was telling the nation that in *this* present crisis, government was the only solution. It was a 180 degree turn. The last Reaganite president brought his administration to a close by abandoning the defining concept of Reaganism. As Bush sadly commented, 'It turns out that there's a lot of interlinks throughout the financial system.' Indeed there are.

Now I don't mean to pick on US Republicans specifically. The point here is that *all* British and American politicians, and to a lesser extent politicians of further afield too, were in thrall to the success of Reagan and Thatcher. Clinton and Blair were as much in thrall as the hapless Bush ever was. Nor do I mean that Reaganism was misconceived. It wasn't. No one in their right minds would want to roll back the clock to the pre-Reagan America or the pre-Thatcher Britain.

But things went too far. In an era when economists were doing more and more to explore the frailties of markets, politicians were coming more and and more to believe in their sacredness. Why were regulators so feeble in the face of crazed lending in the mortgage sector? Because it was a market. Why were they so toothless in checking unwise expansion in the banking industry? Because it was a market. Why was there so little questioning of rampaging pay increases for CEOs? Because it was a market. The list of policy failures, of supine acceptance of the way things were, can be extended almost indefinitely: the insane expansion of household debt; the non-regulation of hedge funds; the feeble track record of most fund managers; the dangerous spread of leveraged buyouts; the increase in derivatives use by firms who didn't know one end of a derivative from the other; the morphing of old, solid, dependable financial institutions into wannabe whizkids, and so on.

Economics had been built on a false conception of the human being. Through an accident of history, politics too ended up following suit. Neither politicians nor economists could get to grips with the disasters of 2008/9 because neither of them had ever understood what really makes an entrepreneur tick, or what truly gives longevity to a business.

This book was given birth as Wall Street collapsed, as banks failed, as markets tumbled, as phrases from Karl Marx entered my head and wouldn't leave. It would take a lot more than a banking crisis to make Somalia preferable to the clamshells of Europe and North America, and yet that crisis continues to matter. You can't lose $4 trillion and pretend that nothing's happened. Just patting your trouser pockets and feeling down behind the sofa cushions isn't going to be enough. Something happened all right, an event of globe-spanning, history-making, epoch-shifting significance. When I set out to research and write a book about the world of money, I knew I had to confront this disaster head-on. I needed to meet entrepreneurs, talk to inventors, interview bankers, comprehend India and the emerging markets – and all to understand this: the world that melted and the new one now struggling to be born. This book began with a financial crisis and it must end there too.

PART SIX

Genius, Risk and the Secret of Capitalism

TWENTY-ONE

Genius, Risk and the Secret of Capitalism

In conducting interviews for this book, I collected many dozen hours of tape recordings; interviews with millionaires and bankers sitting alongside conversations with Indian shiftworkers and financial whistleblowers. I've transcribed many of those conversations, listened to all of them more than once, some of them repeatedly. I have on tape the words of people who have, between them, accomplished an extraordinary amount, seen the world and shaped it. And in all those countless hours of tape, one moment stands out.

It took place during the Christmas holidays in 2008. My wife and I were hosting two old friends of ours and their three children, over from New York. The father, Ethan, used to work at J.P. Morgan, which had developed a uniquely powerful methodology for managing risk in financial institutions. Ethan saw that the technology would be attractive to firms beyond J.P Morgan. and persuaded the bank to spin it off as a separate company, with himself as CEO. The new firm did well. Its private backers launched it onto the stock market. It bulked up through growth and organic acquisition. It's been a thoroughgoing success, an example of exactly the kind of creativity and daring which this book has been all about. As CEO of what is surely the world's most sophisticated risk-management consultancy, Ethan has had an extraordinary vantage point from which to view the carnage on Wall Street: a lighthouse keeper overlooking this once-in-a-century storm.

And his commentary was devastating. I'm hardly financially illiterate and hardly averse to expressing myself forcefully, yet it hadn't occurred to me to go as far as he did that night. We were talking about the great casualties of that autumn – Lehman and RBS, AIG and HBOS, the end of investment banking as we knew it – and Ethan said, 'American capitalism has failed.' Just that: American capitalism has failed. He didn't mean this in some metaphorical way. His sentence wasn't shorthand for a longer one that might have run something like '... has failed to deliver consistent improvements in the living standard of the middle classes'.

No, he meant what he said: American capitalism failed. The government saved it. Not just with words and promises, but with cash. If the US government – and the governments of Britain, France, Germany, and the rest – hadn't found extraordinary quantities of cash to keep things going, then an inconceivably large quantity of ordure would have struck the global air conditioning system. If Ethan's summary still strikes you as dramatic, then allow yourself to do this thought experiment, in which you imagine what would have happened if governments had not stepped in. Imagine that the banks had not been saved. Imagine that we're back on 15 September 2008, that the governments of the world are by-the-book Reaganites, that Mr Market is to be left to sort things out.

Lehman has just gone bust. Its balance sheet has liabilities of $600 billion or so, which have promptly added to the volume of toxic assets swooshing around the system, currently estimated at two trillion or so, depending on who you ask. Matters have just got 30 per cent worse.

AIG too is tottering. Speculators are attacking its shares. The government is studiously looking in another direction and whistling Louis Armstrong's 'Gone Fishin''. AIG too files for bankruptcy.

Its liabilities amount to about $1 trillion. They too are now deeply toxic and they too are starting to swoosh dangerously. Matters are now getting on for twice as bad as they were on 14 September.

But AIG's collapse means that other institutions are buckling too. Merrill Lynch is too weak to resist. It files for bankruptcy. So do (in no particular order) Fannie Mae, Freddie Mac, Citigroup, and Washington Mutual in the United States; RBS and HBOS in the UK; UBS, Dexia, and Hypo Real Estate in Europe. Merrill's liabilities aren't far away from the $1 trillion mark. Citigroup and RBS have debts more like $2 trillion each. If you just tot up the first and biggest names on Death Row 2008, you quickly arrive at a toxic debt load of $10 trillion or so, *on top of* the problem debts which originated the crisis.

A problem that threatened to sweep away the weakest is now threatening to sweep away the strongest. No risk management system in the world was designed to manage this risk. This was the event that could not happen.

In this thought experiment, the consequences of each new collapse are unthinkable. The banking system, which seemed all tickety-boo just a year or so back, now looks like a row of neutron bombs. When one goes bang, it releases a blast of toxic liabilities ten or twenty times greater than its own share capital. Each blast creates more bad debt, more fear, more failures, more bomb blasts.

In the face of such a sequence, virtually no bank would have been immune. The only institutions left standing would be ones that were too remote from the global financial system to be much touched by it. This would, in effect, be a post-apocalypse world, inhabited by a few remote tribes sharing a common story about the day the sky was set on fire. In such a world, the cash machines would literally have run dry. Countless businesses would have folded. Indeed, in a world without banks then money itself is on the point of losing all meaning. What is a pound or a dollar or a euro worth, if there's no bank to store it, no way to transmit it, no known future in which to exchange it?

The last Great Depression ended in world war. This one didn't, and didn't get close, partly because governments did what they had to do, and did it fast, courageously, and on a colossal scale. Capitalism failed. The government saved it. However nasty the subsequent recession has proved to be, it was still only a recession.

Hearing Ethan's words on tape now brings that moment over my Christmas dining table back to life. His three kids are normally delightfully behaved, but that night they were fractious from jetlag and their squabbles from the sitting room next door formed background music to our conversation. I can hear my wife shifting crockery. I hear myself pouring wine and offering coffee. And then those words, the sombre, unexaggerated truth: 'American capitalism has failed.' They raise a prickle on my arm even now; an eerie echo of the quotation from Karl Marx and Friedrich Engels at the beginning of this book. And these are words, please note, from an out-and-out capitalist, an entrepreneur and a Wall Streeter, from someone whose entire career has exemplified all that Marx most loathed.

What lesson do we learn from all this? Just to be clear, the lesson not to be learned is that there's any better system than Western capitalism. Fast cars occasionally crash. That doesn't mean horses would be better. But we can learn something about the ideology that we might call Bastardized Reaganism – that is, Reaganism with all the subtlety taken out; the ideology of Gordon 'greed is good' Gekko; of the worst parts of the Bush-Cheney era; of conservative talk-show hosts keener to make a point than to resolve a problem.

In this Bastardized Reaganism, greed *is* good. The philosophy, roughly speaking, amounts to this:

1. The greedier you are, the more you want money, so the more you do to acquire that money, and because economics says that the pursuit of private interest works seamlessly to foster the public good, the net result of all that greed is that you make yourself happier and the country happier too. Win-win.
2. Government, on the other hand, can only get in the way of the market. It puts obstacles in the way of private ambition. And the more you impede energetic and talented people from being energetic and talented in their own cause, the more you impede them from creating enterprises which give jobs and salaries to the needy. Big government is a road-block to success, not just for the top echelon of society, but for everyone else too. Lose-lose.
3. The moral of these stories: you need to cut government down; you need to deregulate markets; you need to foster a culture of success, which is the exact same thing as a culture of self-enrichment, because there's no difference between the two. Rich people are rich because they've brought success not just to themselves, but to society too. Money, indeed, is a mark of social virtue.

Every single element of this is wrong. Every single part. That doesn't mean that the opposite must be true, because it isn't. The opposite is completely wrong as well. If one era ended with Bush and a new one dawned with Obama, then that era needs an entirely new philosophy to succeed, a philosophy of shade and subtlety, not soundbite and simplicity. I don't presume to suggest what that philosophy should be, but I do know what needs to lie at its heart, namely: passion and creativity; a love of action; a delight in innovation and problem-solving; a zeal for doing something difficult and doing it wonderfully well; and a recognition that economies are inhabited by humans and not by robots.

One final vignette to close the book. One self-made multi-millionaire told me with contempt about some hedge fund types who had come to him, wanting him to invest in their nascent fund. They asked for fees of 2 per cent each and every year *and* 20 per cent of profits in a good year *and* they demanded that he commit his funds to the company for a minimum two-year period. He asked about that last requirement, and the would-be hedgies told him that they needed the two-year lock-in so they could be sure of covering their office costs, including their own salaries.

The multimillionaire's contempt for this pitch was boundless. The hedgies were speaking to someone who got his own break by investing everything he owned plus everything he could borrow in the company that made his fortune. He didn't have anyone covering his salary and his office costs. Indeed, at the time, he didn't have much of a salary to cover. If the company had failed, he'd have lost every last penny. He'd have been left sleeping in his car, except that he wouldn't have had a car to sleep in. That's what risk is. That's what self-belief means. That's why entrepreneurs deserve the money they make.

These hedge fund 'entrepreneurs', on the other hand, reckoned that their services – untried and unproven – should be worth 2 per cent a year, or roughly double what a conventional fund manager would charge. They wanted to take profits in a good year but to escape losses in a bad one. And they didn't even have the *cojones* to put anything of their own at stake as they got their company off the ground.

That wasn't capitalism of a sort that anyone should admire. It was bankrupt in spirit and the sign of a financial system that would quite soon become bankrupt in the wallet as well. The rotting timbers that splintered so spectacularly in 2008 were the failed props of a failed philosophy. When the destroying ocean roared in, it washed away that philosophy – and, let's hope, did so permanently. We'll see.

As for the kind of capitalism which this book has mostly been about – the creative sort, renewing and energetic, ethical and impassioned – well, that's never gone away and never will. It isn't hard to distinguish the versions which are worth preserving and those that aren't. All you have to do is to look at the act of wealth creation itself. Look at its motivations, its principles, its passions. And above all look at its origins. Real enterprise begins where it always has done. It begins with character. Character, and a moment of risk.

ACKNOWLEDGEMENTS

My thanks to all those who agreed to give me interviews: both those named in the text and the many others whose names are not given. This book largely arises out of those interviews, so I am deeply grateful for the time and attention given to me by those who had plenty else to be getting on with. My thanks also to Robin Harvie and all the team at 4th Estate, and to Bill Hamilton for his calm, dependable good sense. This book has been a pleasure from start to finish, not least because of their always helpful input.

FURTHER READING

My previous book – *This Little Britain*, a book about British history – covered so much ground, all so well covered by scholarship, that when it came to constructing a bibliography for it, I simply ducked the challenge, worried that any bibliography might end up longer than the book. This time around, I have almost the opposite embarrassment. This book, after all, isn't a book on economics. Nor is it a history of wealth creation. Nor a how-to guide on getting rich. Nor a contribution to any of the softer social sciences (sociology, anthropology, social psychology or the rest). When asked to define the book, I still – to the frustration of almost everyone who knows me – persist in defining it as a travel guide to the Land of Money. And travel guides don't come with bibliographies, they come with hotel receipts.

What follows then is a somewhat random assemblage of the hotel receipts accumulated on my journeys. If I had to pick out any guiding lights, then I'd warmly recommend Akerlof and Shiller's *Animal Spirits* (Princeton University Press, 2009). It's a book by two eminent economists which tries to bring some of our haphazard, illogical humanity back into economics. Indeed, if I have a worry about the book and the research programme implicit behind it, then it's that Akerlof and Shiller are too likely to be too keen to get our illogical natures firmly tied up in mathematics. I'd prefer to see the illogic given priority, with the mathematics left to catch up as best it can. It's a wonderful book, however, and well worth a read. The same could be said of Joseph Stiglitz's *Freefall* (Allen Lane, 2010).

Of the large crop of more conventional economics-for-the-layman books, then my firm preference is for John Kay's wonderfully sane *The Truth About Markets* (Penguin, 2004 for the newest edition). I also recommend John McMillan's *Reinventing the Bazaar* (Norton 2002) for a good and accessible overview of the market and the many varieties of market failure. For a historical overview of trade, then you can't do any better than William Bernstein's *A Splendid Exchange* (Atlantic Books, 2008). Niall Ferguson's *Ascent of Money* (Allen Lane, 2008) covers different territory, but covers it well. Martin Wolf's *Why Globalization Works* (Yale University Press, 2004) was also an illuminating text for me. Further key references follow in the notes.

NOTES

Page xi *All that is solid*: Karl Marx, Friedrich Engels, *The Communist Manifesto*, available online and for example Longman, 2005.

Page xiv *In 1674, the average Briton*: Data drawn from Angus Maddison, *The World Economy: A millennial perspective*, OECD, 2001. A remarkable collection of data and a landmark in economic history.

Page 4 *William Knox D'Arcy*: There's no good single source for information about this remarkable story, but the best place to start (and a terrific place to stay) is Daniel Yergin's epic *The Prize: The Epic Quest for Oil, Money and Power* (Simon & Schuster, 2009). There's excellent biographical information on Knox D'Arcy available online at *turtlebunbury.com*. It's also worth checking out information on the Mount Morgan mine itself by going to *rootsweb.ancestry.com* and searching for Mt Morgan.

Page 9 *I'm being a bit vague*: Those with an interest in understanding how historical prices can best be converted into present day ones should visit measuringworth.com, the best of a number of similar websites.

Page 11 *Enter the Ariaal*: Eisenberg D. T., Campbell B., Gray P. B., Sorenson M. D. 'Dopamine receptor genetic polymorphisms and body composition in undernourished pastoralists: an exploration of nutrition indices among nomadic and recently settled Ariaal men of northern Kenya'. *BMC Evol. Biol.* 2008. There are intelligible discussions of this paper available from *The Economist* and *New Scientist*.

Page 12 *cheek swabs from billionaires*: See for example the discussion on the Guy's and St Thomas's website ('Are entrepreneurs born or made?' at guysandstthomas.nhs.uk).

Page 13 *A very intriguing study*: Discussion available at jbs.cam.ac.uk, 'Entrepreneurs – born or made?', 12 November 2008.

Page 13 *Bold, please note, is not the same*: See Noam Wasserman, *Founder-CEO Succession and the Paradox of Entrepreneurial Success*, Organization Science, 2003.

Page 16 *One of the oddest results*: Summary available from cass.city.ac.uk, 'Entrepreneurs five times more likely to suffer from dyslexia', 22 November 2004. Full paper available online.

Page 19 *Paul Getty had a problem*: Paul Getty, *How to Be Rich*, Jove Publications, 1996.

Page 21 *A collection of rice paddies*: Strangely, there's no good source on Mittal's career. The best offering by far (Tim Bouquet and Byron Ousey, *Cold Steel*, Little Brown, 2008) focuses on the Mittal takeover of Arcelor, by which point Mittal Steel was already a global powerhouse.

Page 30 *Rockefeller's creation of Standard Oil*: I couldn't quite find an excuse to talk about Rockefeller at length in this book, but I'd warmly recommend Ron Chernow's epic *Titan: The Life of John D Rockefeller* (Little Brown, 1998). Charles Morris's *The Tycoons: How Andrew Carnegie, John D. Rockefeller, Jay Gould, and J.P. Morgan Invented the American Supereconomy* is less assured overall, but still gives a useful introduction to the most remarkable period in American economic history. And since we're digressing here, then please allow me to toss Chernow's *House of Morgan* (Atlantic, 1990) onto your reading list.

Page 36 *A pleasingly classical ring*: See Roland Marchaud, *Advertising the American Dream*, University of California Press,

1985. *20 Ads that Shook the World* (Twitchell, Random House, New Edition 2002) is also well worth a look.

Page 41 *A man that I'll simply call Tom*: His memoir is due to be published by John Blake Publishing, but at the time of writing the release date, title and even the author's name are still all to be determined. I'd recommend it, though.

Page 50 *Their website baldly summarizes*: Further information available via reactionengines.co.uk.

Page 56 *innovative marine safety company*: Further information available via martek-marine.com.

Page 63 *the sale of human tissue*: If you've got the stomach for it, then check out 'The Organ Grinder' by Randall Patterson, 8 Oct 2006, in the *New York Magazine*, also available online.

Page 67 *median household wealth*: See Banks, Blundell and Smith, *Wealth Inequality in the United States and Great Britain*, Institute for Fiscal Studies, 2000.

Page 68 *It is not from the benevolence*: Adam Smith's most famous work is best approached through Kathryn Sutherland's deftly abridged *Wealth of Nations: A Selected Edition*, Smith & Sutherland, Oxford Paperbacks, 2008.

Page 72 *no professional or academic qualifications*: Felix Dennis, *How To Get Rich*, Ebury, New edition 2007. Wonderfully enjoyable.

Page 80 *a strange beast*: You can read what the British Competition Commission had to say about the whole thing on their website (competition-commission.org.uk) and search for 'Stora Kopparbergs and Gillette'.

Page 89 *Banks all run their own version*: *The Economist*'s 'Special Report on Financial Risk' (11 Feb 2010) offers a useful post-apocalypse survey.

Page 96 *the fund did well*: there's a host of research available on Hermitage's track record in Russia, a selection of which is available via the fund's website at hermitagefund.com.

Page 97 *in jail for 'tax evasion'*: And now on trial again for an equally manufactured (and contradictory) charge. You can get more information – and send messages of support – via khodorkovskycenter.com.

Page 102 *twenty-five Exxon Valdez spills a month*: See for example 'Russia's Environmental Crisis', *The Nation*, 18 September 2000.

Page 111 *I interviewed with a number of firms*: If you can't face the interviews, you can try Charles Ellis's *The Partnership: The Making of Goldman Sachs* (Penguin 2009) instead. The book's main weakness is that the timing of its publication caused it to miss the seismic events of the financial crisis and their tumultuous aftermath, though no doubt there's an updated edition in the works now.

Page 116 *Eat, Pray, Love:* Viking Press, 2006, in case you wondered.

Page 120 *American Psycho*: Picador, 1991.

Page 122 *Liar's Poker*: Norton, 1990. The book feels like a period piece now, its players having long since left the stage – but what a period! And what a piece! If you haven't read it yet, then do.

Page 123 *Traders, Guns and Money*: Financial Times/Prentice Hall, 2006. A book that has only got more relevant since publication, and remarkably readable given its subject matter.

Page 124 *John Major and Norman Lamont*: To be precise, the pound was never fixed, it was permitted to float within a narrowly defined trading band.

Page 141 *the bit the government is prepared to admit to*: A good place to start research on the implications of an ageing population is *The Economist*'s 'Special Report on Ageing Populations', 25 June 2009. The report includes a startling graph contrasting the costs of the financial crisis with the probable costs of ageing. Scary stuff.

Page 142 *Enron first*: Elkind and McLean's *The Smartest Guys in the Room* (new edition, Penguin, 2004) provides an entertaining survey.

Page 152 *those early chicken-scented markets*: See Mark Overton, *Agricultural Revolution in England*, Cambridge University Press, 1996.

Page 155 *one historian has gone so far*: Gregory Clark, *Markets and Economic Growth: The Grain Market of Medieval England*, University of California at Davis, working paper (2001) most easily accessed online.

Page 156 *a company called Cargill, Inc*: Further information available through its website at cargill.com. The quotation from Greg Page was taken from the website at time of writing.

Page 160 *A tale, told by an idiot*: You don't need me to tell you that this is from Shakespeare's *Macbeth*.

Page 172 *the solution to this riddle*: Ronald Coase, 'The Nature of the Firm', *Economica*, 1937.

Page 180 *you FedEx-ed it*: There's almost nothing published on DHL's history and the company's website isn't all that helpful (or colourful) either. Fedex has spawned a better literature, of which the pick is Roger Frock's *Changing How the World Does Business*, Berrett-Koehler, 2006.

Page 193 *psychopaths*: Joel Bakan's thoughtful *The Corporation* (Penguin Books Canada, 2004) provided much of the impetus for this chapter. The epigraph from Robert Monks is drawn from Bakan's film of the same title.

Page 196 *kidney sales are legal*: You've got to love *The Economist*, which covers the kidney market (among other things) in an article on organ transplants entitled 'The gap between supply and demand', 9 Oct 2008.

Page 198 *in one notorious case*: Notorious enough to have generated its own literature. For example, Douglas Birsch and John Fielder, *The Ford Pinto Case*, State University of New York Press, 1994.

Page 200 *$10,000,000*: There's a huge and messy literature on this, but see for example, W. Kip Viscusi, 'The Value of Life:

Estimates with Risks by Occupation and Industry', *Economic Inquiry*, 2004.

Page 200 *another, larger cost*: There's a fast growing body of work on trust and reputation. A useful survey can be found online by searching for Luis Cabral's *The Economics of Trust and Reputation: A Primer* – 2005 in the version I used.

Page 208 *I wanted to go out there*: Edward Luce offers a much fuller survey in his *In Spite of the Gods*, Little Brown, 2006.

Page 225 *100,000,000 Guinea Pigs*: Kallet & Schlink, Vanguard Press, 1933.

Page 226 *lipsticks contain lead*: For a calm overview, go to the US Food and Drug Administration's site (fda.gov) and search for 'lipstick and lead'.

Page 227 *A recent mammoth study*: David J. Faulds and Subhash C. Lonial, 'Price-Quality Relationships of Nondurable Consumer Products: A European and United States Perspective', *Journal of Economic and Social Research*, 2001. The number of products cited double-counts similar or identical products released in different countries in the study.

Page 228 *The consumer is not a moron*: See David Ogilvy's entertaining and insightful *Ogilvy on Advertising*, Crown Publishing, 1983.

Page 230 *the weirdest market research experiments*: Much of the subsequent discussion draws on Martin Lindstrom's *Buyology*, Random House, 2008.

Page 235 *a tax on all consumption*: J. K. Galbraith, *The Affluent Society*, 5th Revised Edition, Penguin, 1999.

Page 236 *Business propaganda*: Ludwig von Mises, *Human Action: A Treatise on Economics*, Yale University Press, 1949. Available in full online.

Page 239 *The dragon in question*: Richard Easterlin, 'Does Economic Growth Improve the Human Lot?' in *Nations and Households in Economic Growth*, eds. P. A. David and M. W. Reder, Academic Press, 1974.

Page 240 *A bunch of Harvard students*: A good introduction to these topics can be found in Michael Shermer, *The Mind of the Market*, Henry Holt, 2009.

Page 241 *The mud started*: For most people, the discussion on Cognitive Bias on Wikipedia will provide all they need. Gilovich, Griffin, and Kahneman's *Heuristics and Biases* (Cambridge University Press, 2002) offers a much more complete survey. See also a good discussion in the *New Yorker*, 'Select All: Can you have too many choices?' by Christopher Caldwell.

Page 243 *serious economists*: Richard Layard, *Happiness*, Penguin, 2005.

Page 244 *That data is presented*: Betsey Stevenson and Justin Wolfers, *Economic Growth and Subjective Well-Being*, IZA Discussion Paper, 2008.

Page 246 *American women*: See Betsey Stevenson & Justin Wolfers, 'The Paradox of Declining Female Happiness,' American Economic Journal, 2009.

Page 246 *The average income in Britain*: Data based on Angus Maddison, *The World Economy: A millennial perspective*, OECD, 2001, updated by the author to 2007 prices using a GDP deflator sourced from the OECD.

Page 249 *Viktor Frankl*: *Man's Search for Meaning*, Hodder & Stoughton, Revised edition 1987.

Page 250 *A sense of meaning*: Since writing this sentence, I've come across an almost precisely identical formulation in Rita Carter's *Mapping the Mind*, Weidenfeld & Nicolson, 1998. Modern brain science, in other words, now endorses the argument of this section.

Page 250 *Bread Givers:* Anna Yezierska, Persea Books, 1925.

Page 251 Sinclair Lewis's *Babbitt*: Harcourt Brace, 1922.

Page 260 Michael Crichton's *Rising Sun*: Century, 1992.

Page 261 *A bastion of prudent finance*: Japanese net debt is less high, but still alarming. See, for example, 'Crisis in Slow Motion', *The Economist*, 8 April 2010.

Page 262 *Charles Kindleberger's wonderful book*: Best read in its most updated edition, currently *Manias, Panics and Crashes*, Palgrave Macmillan, 6th Edition, 2009.

Page 262 *A silver drinking cup*: Disappointingly, it's probable that this transaction never took place. The list of goods is more likely to have represented an attempt to illustrate the value of 2,500 florins, the price at which some bulbs did, in fact, change hands.

Page 263 *was supposed to have said*: Alas, he probably didn't. In the words of the Dirksen Center website, 'Based on an exhaustive search of the paper and audio records of The Dirksen Congressional Center, staffers there have found no evidence that Dirksen ever uttered the phrase popularly attributed to him.' Shucks.

Page 264 *The long march to capitalism*: There's a useful overview of the Albanian experience on the IMF website (imf.org). It's 'The Rise and Fall of Albania's Pyramid Schemes' by Christopher Jarvis, *Finance & Development*, 2000.

Page 266 *one fine Italian-American entrepreneur*: You can read more in Donald Dunn's *Ponzi*, Broadway Books, 2004.

Page 268 *Dow 36,000*: Glassman and Hassett, Times Books 1999.

Page 269 *Dow 40,000*: David Elias, McGraw Hill, 1999.

Page 269 *Dow 100,000*: David Kadlec, Prentice Hall, 1999.

Page 271 *a major ratings agency*: See for example, Reuters, 'Banks have disclosed 80 percent of subprime losses', 14 May 2008.

Page 281 *J. K. Galbraith Interview*: 31 October, 2008.

Page 282 *The Art of Strategy*: Dixit and Nalebuff, Norton, 2008.

Page 289 *a new theory was duly born*: Carl Shapiro and Joseph Stiglitz, 'Equilibrium Unemployment as a Worker Discipline Device', *The American Economic Review*, 1984.

Page 291 *in one influential study*: Melvin Lurie, 'Government Regulation and Union Power: A Case Study of the Boston Transit Industry', *Journal of Law and Economics*, 1960.

Page 292 *Economics has almost nothing to say*: Much of the argument of this section is based on Akerlof and Shiller's *Animal Spirits,* Princeton University Press, 2009.

Page 293 *Or take executive pay*: See for example, Jan Greenfield, 'Study finds Inequities in CEO Pay, Worker Pay, Profits', *Working Staff Journal*, 1999.

Page 294 *Robert Frank's* Economic Naturalist: Basic Books, 2007.

Page 294 *As a monetary policymaker*: 'The Future of Monetary Policy', David Blanchflower, Open Lecture, Cardiff University 2009. Available from Bank of England website (bankofengland.co.uk).

Page 295 *It's very hard to avoid the impression*: 'The Return of Depression Economics', Paul Krugman, Lionel Robbins Lecture, LSE, 2009.

Page 295 *Traditional economics teaches*: Akerlof and Shiller, *Animal Spirits,* Princeton University Press, 2009.

Page 295 *Willem Buiter*: See his blogs at blogs.ft.com/maverecon/.

Page 295 *excludes everything I am interested in*: Charles Goodhart, quoted by Buiter, *ibid.*

Page 295 *By some great piece of PR*: Tony Curzon-Price, 'A shallow strategy', *Spectator Business*, 13 January 2009.

Page 296 *Keynes side-stepped*: John Maynard Keynes, *General Theory of Employment, Interest and Money*, Harcourt Brace, 1935.

Page 300 *You earn $65,000*: There's a good discussion of this particular study (by John Helliwell) in 'The Economics of Happiness', *Canadian Business Online*, 9 May 2005. For a fuller analysis by the same scholar, see John Helliwell, 'How's life?', *Economic Modelling*, 2003.

Page 303 *the classified ad section of* The Tribune: These ads are taken from the 31 January 2009 Chandigarh edition of *The Tribune,* and have been very slightly edited.

Page 313 *Banks whose chief executives*: There's a useful discussion of these themes (including references to some of the most interesting papers) in 'Firmly Hooked', *The Economist*, 11 August 2009.

Page 315 *Everything was so clean*: Ayaan Hirsi Ali, *Infidel*, Free Press, 2007.

Page 317 *Yanomamö people*: Statistics from Paul Ehrlich, *Human Natures: Genes, Cultures, and the Human Prospect*, Island Press, 2000.

Page 318 *fifty times less common*: Something I discuss more fully in my *This Little Britain*, Fourth Estate, 2007.

Page 320 *The Road to Serfdom*: Friedrich von Hayek, Routledge & Kegan Paul, 1944.

Page 323 *come to Africa*: An article well worth a look. 'A Manifesto for a Fast World', by Thomas Friedman, *New York Times*, 28 March 1999.

Page 323 *the US government spent around*: OECD data from 2007. Pre-crisis data was chosen in order to avoid distortion by bank rescues and fiscal stimulus packages.

Page 326 *summarized these issues in an interview*: The interview (for which I haven't been able to locate an accurate date) is available at beppegrillo.it, Joseph Stiglitz, 'The pact with the devil'.

Page 329 *the genial, self-deprecating wit*: There are compilations of Reagan's bons mots all over the internet. You can find some worthy collections at pbs.com or reaganlibrary.com. You'll have more fun elsewhere, though.

Page 331 *the 43rd President of the United States*: All these quotes can be tracked back to the White House website, but an easier (and more delightful) source can be found at estnyboer.com/bush/. Well worth a browse.

INDEX